T0305848

Micropolitics in the Multinational Corporation

Over the past decade, politics perspectives in international business have moved into the mainstream repertoire of research, theory development and teaching about the organizational behaviour of multinational corporations (MNCs). Politics perspectives contribute substantially to understanding the behaviour in and of MNCs in their different contexts and environments but so far these burgeoning perspectives have not been systematically and comprehensively reviewed. This book offers the first detailed overview of the theoretical foundations, methodologies and empirical applications of politics perspectives in MNCs. A group of international authors discuss twelve seminal contributions to the study of politics, power and conflict in MNCs, followed by a summary and synthesis of the literature into a comprehensive analytical framework. The book closes with a discussion of future directions in the field. This is a thorough introduction to political behaviour in MNCs written for scholars and graduate students in the fields of organization studies and international business.

FLORIAN A. A. BECKER-RITTERSPACH is Professor of Economic and Organizational Sociology at Hochschule für Technik und Wirtschaft (HTW), Berlin. Next to knowledge transfer and learning, his research focuses on issues of power, politics and conflict in multinationals. His main theoretical interest centres on combining international management approaches with organizational theory.

SUSANNE BLAZEJEWSKI is Professor of Sustainable Organization and Work Design at Alanus University of Arts and Social Science, Bonn. Her research interests focus on micropolitics and conflict in multinational organizations, identity, aesthetics and work design and sustainable organizational development.

CHRISTOPH DÖRRENBÄCHER is Professor of Organizational Design and Behaviour in International Business at the Berlin School of Economics and Law. His current research focus is on management, subsidiary role development, headquarters–subsidiary relationships and careers in multinational corporations. He is the founding director of the Berlin Institute for International Business Studies.

MIKE GEPPERT is Professor of Strategic and International Management at the Friedrich Schiller University, Jena, and Visiting Professor at the Turku School of Economics. His current research focus is on socio-political issues and sense-making within multinational companies, and on cross-national comparisons of management and organization in various industrial sectors, including beer brewing, food retailing and the airline industry.

Micropolitics in the Multinational Corporation

Foundations, Applications and New Directions

Edited by

FLORIAN A. A. BECKER-RITTERSPACH,
SUSANNE BLAZEJEWSKI,
CHRISTOPH DÖRRENBÄCHER
AND MIKE GEPPERT

CAMBRIDGE
UNIVERSITY PRESS

CAMBRIDGE
UNIVERSITY PRESS

University Printing House, Cambridge CB2 8BS, United Kingdom

Cambridge University Press is part of the University of Cambridge.

It furthers the University's mission by disseminating knowledge in the pursuit of education, learning and research at the highest international levels of excellence.

www.cambridge.org
Information on this title: www.cambridge.org/9781107053670

© Cambridge University Press 2016

First published 2016

A catalogue record for this publication is available from the British Library

ISBN 978-1-107-05367-0 Hardback

Contents

Figure

Tables

Contributors

FLORIAN A. A. BECKER-RITTERSPACH is Professor of Economic and Organizational Sociology at the Hochschule für Technik und Wirtschaft (HTW), Berlin, Germany. He received his PhD from the University of Groningen and completed his habilitation in 2014 at the University of Potsdam. Prior to joining the HTW, he worked as a tenured Professor of International Business at the German University in Cairo (GUC) and as a tenured Assistant Professor of International Business and Management at the University of Groningen. He has also held visiting positions at the Social Science Research Center Berlin (WZB), the Copenhagen Business School (CBS) and the Berlin School of Economics and Law (HWR). Next to questions of power, politics and conflict, his research focuses on multinationals in and from emerging markets as well as on knowledge transfer and learning in multinational enterprises. His main theoretical interest centres on combining international management approaches with organizational theory. He has published his work in, among others, *Journal of International Management, Management International Review, Management Learning, Organization Studies* and the *British Journal of Management*. He has continuously acted as convenor and organizer at international research conferences such as the European Group for Organizational Studies (EGOS) or the Society for the Advancement of Socio-Economics (SASE).

SUSANNE BLAZEJEWSKI is Professor of Sustainable Organisation and Work Design at Alanus University of Arts and Social Science, Bonn, Germany. She previously held an Assistant Professorship of Management and Organization at the European University Viadrina in Frankfurt/Oder, Germany. Susanne received her academic education at the University of Saarbrücken, Germany, University College Dublin, Ireland, and the University of Michigan, USA. She holds a double Master's degree in Business Administration and Comparative Literature from Saarbrücken University, Germany and a PhD in Cultural Studies from the European University Viadrina, Frankfurt/Oder. Her research focuses on issues of identities, politics and conflict in multinational organizations and organizational design for sustainable development and innovation. Her work has been published in *Journal of World Business* and *Competition and Change*, among others. She serves on the editorial board of *Critical Perspectives on International Business* and the *Journal of Eastern European Management Studies* and since 2012 co-ordinates the EGOS Standing Working Group on 'MNCs as social actors' together with Mike Geppert and Florian Becker-Ritterspach.

CHRISTOPH DÖRRENBÄCHER is Professor of Organizational Design and Behaviour in International Business at the Berlin School of Economics and Law (Department of Business and Economics), Berlin, Germany. Previously he worked as a consultant and research fellow at various organizations in Germany and abroad, including the Social Science Research Centre, Berlin and the University of Groningen, the Netherlands. Visiting appointments were with the United Nations Centre on Transnational Corporations (New York), Central European University (Budapest) and Manchester Metropolitan University. He holds a PhD from the Faculty of Social Sciences of the Free University, Berlin. His current research focus is on management, labour relations and headquarters–subsidiary relationships in multinational corporations. He has published widely in renowned international academic journals including *British Journal of Management*, *International Business Review*, *International Journal of Management Reviews*, *Journal of World Business*, *Management International Review* and *Journal of International Management*. He currently serves as a co-editor-in-chief of *Critical Perspectives on International Business* and he is the founding director of the Berlin Institute for International Business Studies.

JENS GAMMELGAARD is Professor with Specific Responsibilities in International Business at Copenhagen Business School, where he also earned his PhD. He serves as Head of Department of International Economics and Management. His main research area is the strategic development of MNC subsidiaries, international negotiation, internationalization processes and international business strategy. He has recently co-edited the book *The Global Brewery Industry* (together with C. Dörrenbächer). He serves as a national representative in the

European International Business Academy Board. He has published in journals such as *British Journal of Management, Journal of World Business, International Business Review* and *Critical Perspectives on International Business.*

MIKE GEPPERT is Professor of Strategic and International Management at the Friedrich Schiller University in Jena, and Visiting Professor at the Turku School of Economics. Other recent visiting appointments were with the University of Technology, Sydney, Stanford University and the University of Regensburg. Mike holds a PhD from the Humboldt University in Berlin. His current research focus is on socio-political issues and sensemaking within multinational companies, and on cross-national comparisons of management and employment relations in various industrial sectors. He has published in highly recognized academic journals including *British Journal of Management, Human Relations, International Journal of Human Resource Management, International Journal of Management Reviews, Journal of International Management, Journal of Management Studies, Management International Review* and *Organization Studies.* Mike currently serves as Vice-chair of EGOS and is co-organizer of the EGOS Standing Working Group on 'Multinational corporations: social agency and institutional change'.

KNUT S. G. LANGE is Senior Lecturer in International Business at Royal Holloway's School of Management. Prior to joining Royal Holloway, he worked at the University of Surrey and as a Research Fellow at Humboldt and Freie Universität in Berlin. In addition, he worked as a Post-doc Researcher at the Max Planck Institute for the Study of Societies in Cologne, and at the University of Groningen at the Department of International Business and Management, where he also did his PhD. His general research interests include the areas of institutional theory, comparative capitalism approaches, innovations, family offices and business models. His research has been published in journals such as *Research Policy, British Journal of Management, Organizational Dynamics, European Management Journal* and *Socio-Economic Review.*

REBECCA PIEKKARI is Professor of International Business at Aalto University, School of Business (formerly known as Helsinki School of Economics). Her research focuses on the challenges of managing multinational corporations. She has contributed to two main research streams, language in international business and the use of qualitative methods, particularly the case study in international business and management research. She has also participated in a discussion about language as a methodological question in management and organization studies. Her work has been published in journals such as *Academy of Management Review*, *Journal of Management Studies* and *Journal of International Business Studies*, as well as in several handbooks in the area.

JOANNE ROBERTS is Professor in Arts and Cultural Management at Winchester School of Art, University of Southampton, UK. She has held posts in the business schools of Newcastle, Durham and Northumbria Universities, UK. Her research interests include the internationalization of knowledge-intensive services, knowledge, innovation and luxury. Joanne has published articles in a wide range of international journals, and she is author or co-editor of five books, most recently *A Very Short, Fairly Interesting and Reasonably Cheap Book about Knowledge Management*. Joanne is also the co-founder and co-editor of the journal *Critical Perspectives on International Business* and an editor of the journal *Prometheus: Critical Studies in Innovation*.

SUSANNE TIETZE is Professor of Management at Keele University, UK. The focus of her current research is on language use and translation in international work contexts; and in particular on the language-based choices made by bilingual or multilingual employees who are located at the interstices of knowledge transfer and exchange. Drawing on traditions of translation studies, her work is informed by sociological, context-sensitive approaches to understand the language choices such agents make in situated, multilingual work contexts. She has led several funded research projects, including one investigating the role of English in international business and management and has published her research in several books. Most recently, she has been co-editor of the *Routledge Companion to Cross-Cultural Management*, a book intended to set new trajectories for language-based, culturally and context sensitive approaches to managing in global, networked organizations.

KAREN WILLIAMS is Associate Professor in International Employment Relations in the School of Management, Swansea University, Wales. Her background is in linguistics (German and French) and international relations. She completed her PhD on conflict resolution in the German and British manufacturing industry at the University of Surrey. Research interests include the transfer of employment relations strategies and practices in multinational companies and the influence of different societal and organizationally based systems of employment on the world of work. She has worked with Mike Geppert and Dirk Matten on an Anglo-German study of change management in the engineering industry, and with an international team on the internationalization strategies of food retail multinational companies in Europe and the effect on working conditions and employment relations. The research has led to publications in *Journal of Management Studies*, *Human Relations* and *International Human Resource Management*, among other key journals, as well as a co-edited book and book chapters.

Foreword

For some years I had a small presence in the research area of multi-national organizations, largely as a result of the good auspices of the editors of this volume, who have found my more general work on power and politics useful in the field. Over the years I have delved into the fields of strategy, globalization and international business. These experiences required a considerable amount of reading on my part. It was somewhat surprising to find that so much of the literature on and around multinationals seemed quite blind to issues of power and politics; the overwhelming approaches were founded in an economics perspective that seemed immune to social, organizational and political relations.

If only this volume had been available to me earlier! It really is an indispensable guide to current thinking from the more sociologically oriented literature, which, as the editors suggest, has seen a recent and sustained flowering. The flowering is acutely represented in this volume. It begins with consideration of fundamental definitions and core concepts, mainly derived from organizational studies and organizational sociology, which will help researchers interested in phenomena related to politics and power in the multinational in framing their literature search. The authors draw on the wider literature in politics, political and sociological theory to inform their scanning of the field in a version of scholarship that seeks to facilitate translation between fields – an important and necessary task, especially where that field might seem to practise intellectual border control as an art form.

The field of international business and management (IB&M) emerged largely from the contributions of economists for whom consideration of power, politics and conflict was not a central disposition. However, the introduction of organization studies prepared perspectives that were far more attuned to conceptions of multinationals as essentially political entities constituted by diverse actors with different power and conflicting interests, that occupied space already populated by others, both organizations and citizens, with specific and sometimes antagonistic interests, sometimes interests affording opportunities for co-optation, hegemony, or positive power alignment.

Three power, politics and conflict streams are identified within IB&M: functionalist, institutionalist and critical approaches, each of which is explored in the chapters in Part II of the volume. This section of the book is particularly useful to the student because it identifies and critically analyses a number of key positioning statements that have made a significant impact on the field in terms of citation and use. We should consider these contributions and their discussion not merely as distinguished foundations, as relics from a recent past, but as frameworks that can project further research in the future.

While the functionalist approaches that are reviewed are not a great distance from the more orthodox foundations of the field, the institutionalist approaches do begin to introduce significant theoretical and conceptual innovation into the field. The frontiers are pushed further by the critical management school's concern with ideologies and societal structures leading to unequal power relations and situations of domination and resistance. Critical management, with its various heterodox roots in Marxist theory, post-structuralism and critical theory, is indeed a great distance from the early foundations of the field. Implicit in many earlier approaches to international business and multinationals was an underlying theme of modernization, of laggard parts of the world being pulled into modernity through the leading edge, in which multinationals played a central role as bringers of enlightenment. Of course, from perspectives influenced by underdevelopment theory, post-colonialism and conflict approaches the modernization theses received short shrift. Theorization from critical management perspectives is more likely to be attuned to issues of domination and hegemony, to conflict and control and to power and resistance, as the selected exemplars suggest.

The focus thus far in the volume has been more macro than micro. It might be assumed that a concern with multinationals, power and politics would have little room for more microanalysis but that assumption would be wrong. A micropolitical agency perspective sees the processes and outcomes produced by individual actors or sets of individual actors who interact politically as producing organization-level effects. There are microfoundations for organizational events, outcomes and processes in multinationals: for instance, takeover battles, mergers and organizational closures often occur as intense interpersonal and emotional struggles between people whose identity, status and career is irrevocably tied to the fate of these struggles.

Methodologically, the field is hugely diverse: econometrics, discourse analysis, network analysis, surveys, ethnographies, modelling – almost any approach can be applied to analysis of multinationals. Some of these approaches will be easier to field than others: if there are databases to work with, for instance. Others require a great deal of tacit work that is not as evident in the finished paper. Multinationals are full of people who are powerful and know they are powerful; often their powerfulness is projected as a form of paranoia about maintaining the boundaries and boundedness of their organization. In contemporary times, where ethics approval is an integral and necessary prerequisite for doing research, these powerful and sometimes paranoid people can be really important gatekeepers and blockers. Gaining access, navigating diverse historical, political, cultural and linguistic contexts requires researchers to focus attention on the practical politics of negotiating and securing and legitimating access and use of research methods. Language can be a major issue: do you speak the language of the host country that you are investigating? Are you familiar with its culture, its history, its etiquette and mores? You have to be a practical politician in negotiating orderly access and it is especially politic to manage the niceties of the interaction settings in which one finds oneself. An essential element of power is communicative competence and research in multinationals will involve many of us, using many ethnographic and interviewing approaches, in communications with highly sophisticated and privileged people for whom our concerns as researchers will at best be unimportant and at worst, viewed as not only inconsequential but also potentially threatening.

The future for multinational research looks exciting from the vantage point of this volume. In the final chapters, the authors delineate new directions for future multinational research. What is recommended is an analysis of discursive sensemaking, politicking, global élites and emerging markets. Each of these, of course, is entangled with the others. The field is ripe – multinationals are the vehicles for contemporary global élite formation and these global élites have distinctive ways of sensemaking, politicking and lobbying (as well as bribing and corrupting), of projecting their identities as celebrity chief executive officers, striding the global stage. Emerging markets make these processes even more interesting: along with Anglo-Saxon, European and other established élites globally, there are new élites: Russian oligarchs, Chinese property developers, Brazilian industrialists, East Asian manufacturers. We know very little about the new, emerging global élites; indeed, we know very little about the established élites other than what they mostly want us to know. There are few fields of endeavour more open to opportunity than research on multinationals.

STEWART CLEGG
June, 2015

1 | Introduction

FLORIAN A. A. BECKER-RITTERSPACH, SUSANNE
BLAZEJEWSKI, CHRISTOPH DÖRRENBÄCHER
AND MIKE GEPPERT

Six o'clock in the morning: Clark Webster, a 42-year-old American manager in Germany, wakes up. Everything is still quiet in the house and, while awakening, Clark goes over what's up for the coming day.[1] As usual, the day will be busy with many meetings, a number of chats here and there and some decisions to be taken. Clark's company, the German arm of a US-based player in the food business, is a traditional producer of frozen vegetables employing some 900 people.

The first meeting is delicate. Clark has scheduled an early work session with his personal assistant to finalize a bid for a company internal tender to produce 500 tons of mixed vegetables for a private brand of a large European discount retailer. While winning the bid would definitely be beneficial for capacity utilization at the plant, the head of marketing will certainly complain, as she is always very concerned about brand identity in the German market. However, what is more worrying for Clark, who has career ambitions in headquarters, is the fact that the Italian subsidiary might win the bid. As he knows from a chat he recently had with a young Italian engineer at a corporate-wide total quality management (TQM) meeting, the factory in Italy has further automatized production, which could drive down their costs, if it works. But does it work? Clark thinks about calling the Italian engineer. But what could be an unsuspicious reason to call? How could he find out whether the automatized processes are operational or what he could offer the engineer as an exchange for information? Momentarily Clark thinks about calling the chief executive officer (CEO) of the Italian subsidiary to discuss what could be reasonable prices to offer in the bid, but he quickly abandons this idea as he hardly knows and even

---

[1] This fictional case is based on a series of thirty interviews with managers and labour representatives at foreign-owned companies in Germany, carried out by one of the authors in 2015. While for didactical reasons the case blends information from several interviews and companies, the description of what roles power, politics and conflict play in multinational corporations (MNCs) fully matches the overall picture provided by the interview partners.

less trusts the Italian subsidiary manager, who is said to have international career ambitions, too.

Without coming to a conclusion Clark's thoughts wander to his next meeting that day: a meeting called for by the head of the local works council. Clark's relationship with this man is ambiguous. While Clark finds him to be a better negotiating partner than other more conflict-oriented worker representatives, he can get very tough when issues get a bit close to the bone. Clark presumes that the head of the local works council wants to talk about the implementation of a corporate-wide efficiency programme called 'Fit', which was piloted in the UK subsidiary the previous month and involved a layoff of sixty people there. While it has already been decided to implement this programme in Germany as well, Clark is reasoning whether he should let the cat out of the bag today or play for time. Weighing the pros and cons in his mind, he comes to the conclusion that it is best to properly inform the works council today, as he is obliged to do so by German law this week anyway. He knows from experience that once the head of the local works council smells a rat he will not stop infuriating the workers and lobby in the headquarters, which would cast doubts over whether Clark is running a tight ship.

Clark hopes that the meeting can be ended without going over time, as there is another important item on the agenda. At two o´clock a weekly call is scheduled with Jacob Brown at US headquarters, who is responsible for Europe, Middle East and Africa (EMEA) business. These calls used to be enjoyable as Jacob is an old friend from university. In fact, it was Jacob who helped Clark to secure his current position, when Clark was in a career deadlock with his previous employer. However, things have changed, particularly since a private equity investor took control of the US firm and its subsidiaries. In earlier times, there was always a down-to-earth discussion on what could be done to develop the German subsidiary considering the peculiarities of the German market as well as its dense legal and regulatory environment. More recently, though, Jacob is just hammering out some 'in the cloud' target margins, asks for quick and deep job cuts and comes up with crude proposals such as one to use cheaper genetically modified corn. Obviously, he does not realise that this is not yet allowed in Germany and would be unlikely to be accepted by customers. But getting the figures right is the only thing Jacob seems to be interested in now. Clark is angry. But would he behave differently? Getting the figures right means a bonanza for Jacob, especially when the figures facilitate a lucrative exit from the private equity firm. And a bonanza is definitely what Clark would also need in order to finance his life dream: a 62-foot catamaran he recently saw at Lake Constance. Cherishing a dream of crossing the Atlantic with this catamaran, Clark is suddenly roused from slumber by the cry of his 2-year-old son awakening. It's time to get up.

This introductory case-study illustrates that interest-based behaviour, political manoeuvring and power-laden conflicts are everyday occurrences in MNCs. Interest-based behaviour is visible throughout the intro case, with all actors presented having well-defined interests that shape their behaviours. These interests are typically selfish since they represent the particular personal situation and the functional role of the beholder, with these interests sometimes going well together but at other times colliding. For instance, both the head of the local works council as well as Clark have an interest in winning the company internal tender to produce a large batch of mixed vegetables. For Clark, winning the tender would enable him to sustain his career ambitions as he would attract attention from headquarters and would be able to demonstrate his qualities. For the head of the local works council winning the bid would help to safeguard jobs thereby securing his position. However, Clark and the head of the works council are very much at odds when it comes to the implementation of the corporate-wide efficiency programme called 'Fit'. While for Clark this too would be another opportunity to show his good performance, it directly violates the local works council's interests in securing jobs. It is here that political manoeuvring starts. While Clark is under pressure from his own aspirations and the expectations of headquarters bluntly communicated by Jacob, he nevertheless is well advised to co-operate with the present head of the local works council, at least to some extent. Trying to rigorously implement the efficiency programme might lead the workforce to work to rule (the opposite of what is needed to win and serve the tender) and in the long term it might support the radical forces in the local works council. Careful manoeuvring seems to be required with Clark in the first instance following a strategy of legitimation vis-à-vis the works council by carefully complying to the provisions of the German labour law on the local works council's information and communications rights. However, given the strong diversity of interests it is foreseeable that a power-laden conflict will evolve. While

Jacob, at US headquarters, spurred by the financial logic of the private equity owner, will not stop calling for further cost reductions and job cuts, the works council will make full use of the opportunities the German institutional environment provides to safeguard labour rights in such instances. Moreover, the local works council might involve outside actors such as local governments and the German media, which can be critical of private equity investors. This, in turn, might have an adverse impact on headquarters' decisions about future investments in the German subsidiary.

While many cases similar to our fictional intro case have been reported in the business press over the years, interest-based behaviour, political manoeuvring and power-laden conflicts have for a long time been ignored in the international business (IB) literature. More recently, however, there has been increasing recognition that both behaviour in as well as of MNCs is very much underwritten if not constituted by power, politics and conflict as well as by the purposeful (inter)action of self-interested actors. Over the last years, this perspective not only became part of the repertoire of IB research (Dörrenbächer and Geppert 2011) and theory (e.g. Forsgren 2008; Collinson and Morgan 2009) but has also become an essential tool for students to understand MNCs. At the same time, this burgeoning perspective we call 'micropolitics' has provided us so far with few if any systematic and comprehensive overviews of the state of the field and its theoretical foundations. Specifically, what is missing is a systematic and comprehensive discussion of key contributions, their different theoretical lenses and the empirical domains or levels of analysis they address. It is this gap that the present book seeks to fill.

The rationale of the book

From early on, politics, power and conflict perspectives had a place in the IB literature. This notwithstanding, their treatment was limited in a number of ways. On the one hand, politics, power and conflict were either only implicitly addressed (e.g. Bartlett and Ghoshal 1989) or they were treated as aberrations that were at worst dysfunctional and at best controllable through appropriate organizational design and processes. On the other hand, only a few theoretical lenses found application, primarily involving contingency, resource dependency and agency perspectives (Doz *et al.* 1981; Roth and Nigh 1992; Pahl and Roth 1993).

Challenging this rather limited understanding of politics, power and conflict in and around MNCs, the last decade has seen a vast shift and widening of perspectives in both theoretical and empirical terms. For example, while contingency, resource dependency and agency perspectives are still part of the theoretical repertoire (Tasoluk *et al.* 2006; Mudambi and Pedersen 2007; Mudambi and Navarra 2004; Gupta and Cao 2005; Bouquet and Birkinshaw 2008), a new wide spectrum of perspectives has been added including: network perspectives (Forsgren *et al.* 2005; Andersson *et al.* 2007), neo- and comparative institutional perspectives (Kostova 1999; Whitley 1999; Kostova and Roth 2002), micropolitical perspectives (Kristensen and Zeitlin 2001, 2005; Dörrenbächer and Geppert 2006; Ferner *et al.* 2006; Blazejewski 2009), game theory (Rössing 2005; Kaufmann and Rössing 2005), social identity and role theory (Vora and Kostova 2007; Vora *et al.* 2007; Schmid and Daniel 2007), critical perspectives such as the postcolonial theory (Frenkel 2008; Mir and Sharpe 2009), labour process theory (Elger and Smith 1998; Elger and Smith 2006; Edwards and Bélanger 2009), the neo-Gramscian approach (Böhm *et al.* 2008) or discursive approaches (Geppert 2003; Vaara and Tienari 2008). Significantly, along with this development, there have been increasing efforts to introduce IB to genuine politics, power and conflict perspectives from social and organizational theory as well as organizational psychology (e.g. Dahl 1957; French and Raven 1960; Burns 1961; Etzioni 1964; Pondy 1967; Hickson *et al.* 1971; Deutsch 1973; Pfeffer and Salancik 1974; Crozier and Friedberg 1981; Mintzberg 1983; Thomas 1992; Astley and Zajac 1990; Rothman and Friedman 2001; Lukes 2005; Clegg *et al.* 2006).

At the empirical end, politics, power and conflict saw also an increasingly differentiated treatment over time. Rather than being conceived as well-orchestrated, controllable and harmoniously integrated entities, MNCs became increasingly conceptualized as 'transnational social spaces' (Morgan and Kristensen 2006), 'contested terrains' (Collinson and Morgan 2009; Edwards and Bélanger 2009) or even 'battlefields' (Kristensen and Zeitlin 2001), full of political struggle, conflict and discourses (Dörrenbächer and Geppert 2011) involving diverse interests and identities (Ybema and Byun 2011; Koveshnikov

2011), giving rise to different types of strategies (Becker-Ritterspach and Dörrenbächer 2011; Williams and Geppert 2011; Maclean and Hollinshead 2011), micropolitics (Morgan and Kristensen 2006) and game-playing (Morgan and Kristensen 2006; Dörrenbächer and Geppert 2009a).

Importantly, not only have the antecedents and consequences of politics, power and conflict in MNCs become the main interest of a substantial number of IB studies in a variety of empirical domains, they have also been looked at on a great variety of analytical levels with vastly different units of analysis and explanatory context. For instance, the consideration of conflict in MNCs ranges from intrapersonal (Vora and Kostova 2007) to interorganizational and international levels (Bélanger and Edwards 2006; Blazejewski and Becker-Ritterspach 2011). The focus of empirical domains stretches from developing a better understanding of intragroup conflicts (e.g. Jehn *et al.* 1999), resource mobilization strategies in intrafirm competition (Becker-Ritterspach and Dörrenbächer 2011), different power games in subsidiary mandate changes (Dörrenbächer and Geppert 2009b; Dörrenbächer and Gammelgaard 2010, 2011), subsidiary lobbying (Bouquet and Birkinshaw 2008) and initiatives (Bouquet and Birkinshaw 2008), local investment decisions (Sorge and Rothe 2011), to knowledge flows (Mudambi and Navarra 2004; Fenton-O'Creevy 2011) and mergers and acquisitions (Vaara and Tienari 2011). The methodologies and underlying epistemologies and methods of research on politics, power and conflict in MNCs have also been highly diverse, ranging from positivistic cross-sectional surveys to critical realist epistemologies in ethnographic case-studies.

Politics perspectives have more recently moved into the mainstream of IB research and theory development. They contribute substantially to the understanding of behaviour in and of MNCs in their different contexts and environments. At the same time, this wealth of perspectives has so far not been systematically and comprehensively reviewed and presented. What is missing is a comprehensive overview that not only maps the seminal contributions on politics, power and conflict in MNCs, but also provides a systematic discussion of the key theories, methodologies and empirical applications in the field. Hence, in this book we wish to take stock of the new developments in the field particularly of the last decade.

Overview of the book

Our book seeks to provide a systematic and comprehensive reference guide in particular to students, post-docs and early career scholars but also lecturers and senior scholars in the fields of international business, international management, international human resources management and organization theory who want to understand key issues and concepts of politics, power and conflict in MNCs. To this end our book is based on four thematic building blocks.

The goal of Part I, 'Foundations of politics, power and conflict in MNCs', is to introduce the reader to the topic and to the major theoretical foundations in the field. In Chapter 2, which follows this Introduction, we focus on 'Theoretical foundations and conceptual definitions' (Blazejewski and Becker-Ritterspach). The chapter delineates the development of theoretical perspectives on power and politics from their roots in organizational studies, sociology and organizational psychology. We shed light on core concepts in the field such as actors, interests and power and seek to demonstrate how different conceptualizations over time and across disciplinary traditions intersect in the current theoretical approaches to power and politics in organizations. Chapter 3, 'The evolution of a politics perspective of the multinational enterprise – past developments and current applications' (Becker-Ritterspach and Blazejewski) provides a comprehensive review of past and current literature on politics, power and conflict in MNCs. The review is ordered along historical developments of the field of international business and theoretical perspectives adopted. This includes a systematic discussion of key concepts and definitions, units and levels of analysis and explanatory context as well as an overview of empirical domains in the MNC that have been looked at from politics, power and conflict perspectives.

Part II, 'Seminal contributions', presents and discusses in depth twelve seminal contributions on politics, power and conflict in MNCs, with the aim to convey a thorough understanding of these papers in terms of their theoretical foundations and empirical explorations. The selection of the papers is based on at least two of the following three criteria: first, they have a major impact on the field; second, they have a solid foundation in genuine politics, power and conflict theory; and third, they contribute to major research schools. In line with these criteria, Chapter 4 discusses contributions of the rationalistic-managerialist school (Becker-Ritterspach and Gammel-gaard), Chapter 5 focuses on contributions from the institutionalist school (Geppert and Williams) and Chapter 6 deals with contributions of the critical management school (Dörrenbächer and Roberts).

Building on the two previous parts, Part III, 'Analytical tools and applications', provides a summary and synthesis of the literature in a comprehensive analytical framework. This is provided in Chapter 7 entitled 'Understanding organizational behaviour in MNCs from a micropolitical perspective: a stratified analytical framework' (Becker-Ritterspach and Blazejewski), which also contains a discussion of methodological challenges in researching power and politics in an international business environment. Chapter 8, 'Doing research on power and politics in MNCs: a methodological perspective' (Piekkari and Tietze), extends this methodological discussion by drawing attention to the political dimension of the research process itself.

Finally, Part IV, 'Reflections and new directions for research' is primarily concerned with identifying and discussing future research directions in the fields. It contains a number of shorter chapters on new directions and is written by various authors and teams of authors. This section includes Chapter 9, 'Advancing research on political issues in and around MNCs: the role of discursive sensemaking' (Geppert and Dörrenbächer); Chapter 10, 'Zooming in on politicking and issue-selling tactics as new research directions for the study of micro-politics in MNCs' (Dörrenbächer and Gammelgaard); Chapter 11, 'Advancing research on micropolitics in MNCs: an élite perspective' (Dörrenbächer and Geppert); and Chapter 12, 'Micropolitics in emerging market multinational corporations (EMNCs) as a field of new research' (Lange and Becker-Ritterspach).

References

Andersson, U., Forsgren, M. and Holm, U. 2007. Balancing subsidiary influence in the federative MNC: a business network view. *Journal of International Business Studies*, 38(5): 802–818.

Astley, W. G. and Zajac, E. J. 1990. Beyond dyadic exchange: functional interdependence and sub-unit power. *Organisation Studies*, 11(4): 481–501.

Bartlett, C. and Ghoshal, S. 1989. *Managing Across Borders: the Transnational Solution*. Cambridge, MA: Harvard Business School Press.

Becker-Ritterspach, F. and Dörrenbächer, C. 2011. An organizational politics perspective on intra-firm competition in multinational corporations. *Management International Review*, 50(4): 533–559.

Bélanger, J. and Edwards, P. 2006. Towards a political economy framework: TNCs as national and international players. In A. Ferner, J. Quintanilla and C. Sànchez-Runde (eds.), *Multinationals, Institutions and the Construction of Transnational Practices*. Basingstoke: Palgrave Macmillan, 24–52.

Blazejewski, S. 2009. Actors' interests and local contexts in intrafirm conflict: the 2004 GM and Opel crisis. *Competition and Change*, 13(3): 229–250.

Blazejewski, S. and Becker-Ritterspach, F. 2011. Conflict in headquarters–subsidiary relations: a critical literature review and new directions. *Political Power in the Multinational Corporation. The Role of Institutions, Interests and Identities*. Cambridge University Press, 139–190.

Böhm, S., Spicer, A. and Felming, P. 2008. Infra-political dimensions of resistance to international business: a neo-Gramscian approach. *Scandinavian Journal of Management*, 24(3): 169–182.

Bouquet, C. and Birkinshaw, J. 2008. Managing power in the multinational corporation: how low-power actors gain influence. *Journal of Management*, 34(3): 477–508.

Burns, T. 1961. Micropolitics: mechanisms of institutional change. *Administrative Science Quarterly*, 6(3): 257–281.

Clegg. S. R., Courpasson, D. and Phillips, N. 2006. *Power and Organizations*. London: Sage.

Collinson, S. and Morgan, G. 2009. *Images of the Multinational Firm*. Chichester: John Wiley and Sons.

Crozier, M. and Friedberg, E. 1981. *Actors and Systems*. Chicago University Press.

Dahl, R. 1963. *Modern Political Analysis*. Englewood Cliffs, NJ: Prentice-Hall.

Deutsch, M. 1973. *The Resolution of Conflict*. London: Yale University Press.

Dörrenbächer, C. and Gammelgaard, J. 2010. Multinational corporations, inter-organizational networks and subsidiary charter removals. *Journal of World Business*, 45(2): 206–216.

2011. Subsidiary power in multinational corporations: the subtle role of micro-political bargaining power. *Critical Perspectives on International Business*, 7(1): 30–47.

Dörrenbächer, C. and Geppert, M. 2006. Micro-politics and conflicts in multinational corporations: Current debates, re-framing, and contributions of this special issue. *Journal of International Management*, 12(3): 251–265.

2009a. A micro-political perspective on subsidiary initiative-taking: evidence from German-owned subsidiaries in France. *European Management Journal*, 27(2): 100–112.

2009b. Micro-political games in the multinational corporation: the case of mandate change. *Management Revue*, 20(4): 373–391.

2011. *Politics and Power in the Multinational Corporation: the role of Institutions, Interests and Identities*. Cambridge University Press.

Doz, Y. L., Bartlett, C. A. and Prahalad, C. K. 1981. Global competitive pressures and host country demands, managing tensions in MNCs. *California Management Review*, 23(3): 63–73.

Edwards, P. K. and Bélanger, J. 2009. The MNC as a contested terrain. In S. Collinson and G. Morgan (eds.), *Images of the Multinational*. Oxford: Wiley, 193–216.

Elger, T. and Smith, C. 1998. Exit, voice and 'mandate': management strategies and labour practices of Japanese firms in Britain. *British Journal of Industrial Relations*, 36(2): 185–207.

2006. Theorizing the role of international subsidiary: transplant, hybrids and branch – plants revisited. In A. Ferner, J. Quintanilla and C. Sànchez-Runde (eds.), *Multinationals, Institutions and the Construction of Transnational Practices*. New York: Palgrave Macmillan, 56–63.

Etzioni, A. 1964. *Modern Organizations*. Englewood Cliffs, NJ: Prentice-Hall.

Fenton-O'Creevy, M., Gooderham, P., Cerdin, J-L. and Ronning, R. 2011. Bridging roles, social skill and embedded knowing in multinational organizations. In C. Dörrenbächer and M. Geppert (eds.), *Politics and Power in the International Corporation: the Role of Institutions, Interests and Identities*. Cambridge University Press, 101–136.

Ferner, A., Quintanilla, J. and Sanchez-Runde, C. 2006. *Multinationals, Institutions and the Construction of Transnational Practices*. Basingstoke: Palgrave.

Forsgren, M. 2008. *Theories of the Multinational: a Multidimensional Creature in the Global Economy*. Cheltenham, UK: Edward Elgar.

Forsgren, M., Holm, U. and Johanson, J. 2005. *Managing the Embedded Multinational: a Business Network View*. Cheltenham, UK: Edward Elgar.

French, J. P. R. and Raven, B. 1960. The bases of social power. In D. Cartwright and A. Zander (eds.), *Group Dynamics*. New York: Harper and Row, 607–623.

Frenkel, M. 2008. The multinational corporation as a third space: rethinking international management discourse on knowledge transfer through Homi Bhabha. *Academy of Management Review*, 33(4): 924–942.

Geppert, M. 2003. Sensemaking and politics in MNCs: a comparative analysis of vocabularies within the global manufacturing discourse in one industrial sector. *Journal of Management Inquiry*, 12(4): 312–329.

Gutpa, A. K. and Cao, Q. 2005. Parent–subsidiary conflict within multinational enterprises. Working Paper presented at *Academy of Management*.

Hickson, D. J., Hinings, C. R., Lee, C. A., Schneck, R. E. and Pennings, J. M. 1971. Strategic contingencies' theory of intraorganizational power. *Administrative Science Quarterly*, 16(2): 216–229.

Jehn, K. A., Northcraft, G. B. and Neale, M. A. 1999. Why differences make a difference: a field study of diversity, conflict, and performance in workgroups. *Administrative Science Quarterly*, 44(4): 741–763.

Kaufmann, L. and Rössing, S. 2005. Managing conflicts of interests between headquarters and their subsidiaries regarding technology transfer to emerging markets – a framework. *Journal of World Business*, 40(3): 235–253.

Kostova, T. 1999. Transnational transfer of strategic organizational practices: a contextual perspective. *Academy of Management Review*, 24(2): 308–324.

Kostova, T. and Roth, K. 2002. Adoption of an organizational practice by subsidiaries of multinational corporations: institutional and relational effects. *Academy of Management Journal*, 45(1): 215–233.

Koveshnikov, A. 2011. National identities in times of organizational globalization: a case study of Russian managers in two Finnish-Russian organizations. In C. Dörrenbächer and M. Geppert (eds.), *Politics and Power in the International Corporation: the Role of Institutions, Interests and Identities*. Cambridge University Press, 346–379.

Kristensen, P. H. and Zeitlin, J. 2001. The making of a global firm: local pathways to multinational enterprise. In G. Morgan, P. H. Kristensen and R. Whitley (eds.), *The Multinational Firm. Organizing Across Institutional and National Divides*. Oxford University Press, 172–195.

2005. *Local Players in Global Games: the Strategic Constitution of a Multinational Corporation*. Oxford University Press.

Lukes, S. (2005). *Power: a Radical View* (2nd edn). New York: Palgrave Macmillan.

Maclean, M. and Hollinshead, G. 2011. Contesting social space in the Balkan region: the social dimensions of a 'red' joint venture. In C. Dörrenbächer and M. Geppert (eds), *Politics and Power in the International Corporation: the Role of Institutions, Interests and Identities*. Cambridge University Press, 380–411.

Mintzberg, H. 1983. *Power in Organizations*. Englewood Cliffs: Prentice Hall.

Mir, R., and Sharpe, D. R. 2009. The multinational firm as an instrument of exploitation and domination. In S. Collinson and G. Morgan (eds.), *Images of the Multinational Firm*. Chichester: Wiley, 247–265.

Morgan, G. and Kristensen, P. H. 2006. The contested space of multinationals: varieties of institutionalism, varieties of capitalism. *Human Relations*, 59(11): 1467–1490.

Mudambi, R. and Navarra, P. 2004. Is knowledge power? Knowledge flows, subsidiary power and rent-seeking within MNCs. *Journal of International Business Studies*, 35(5): 385–406.

Mudambi, R. and Pedersen, T. 2007. Agency theory and resource dependence theory: complementary explanations for subsidiary power in multinational corporations. SMG Working Paper, Copenhagen Business School. Available at: http://openarchive.cbs.dk/bitstream/handle/10398/7472/cbs%20forskningsindberetning%20smg%2075 %202007-005.pdf?sequence=1.

Pahl, J. M. and Roth, K. 1993. Managing the headquarters–foreign subsidiary relationship: the roles of strategy, conflict, and integration. *The International Journal of Conflict Management*, 4(2): 139–165.

Pfeffer, J. and Salancik, G. R. 1974. Organizational decision making as a political process: the case of a university budget. *Administrative Science Quarterly*, 19(2): 135–151.

Pondy, L. R. 1967. Organizational conflict: concepts and models. *Administrative Science Quarterly*, 12(2): 296–320.

Rössing, S. M. 2005. *Technology Transfer to China*. Frankfurt/Main: European Management Publications.

Roth, K. and Nigh, D. 1992. The effectiveness of headquarters–subsidiary relationships: the role of coordination, control, and conflict. *Journal of Business Research*, 25(4): 277–301.

Rothman, J. and Friedman, V. J. 2001. Identity, conflict and organizational learning. In M. Dierkes, A. Berthoin Antal, J. Child and I. Nonaka (eds.), *The Handbook of Organizational Learning and Knowledge*, Oxford University Press, 582–597.

Schmid, S. and Daniel, A. 2007. Are subsidiary roles a matter of perception? A review of the literature and avenues for future research. Working Paper No. 30, *ESCP-EAP European School of Management*.

Sorge, A. and Rothe, K. 2011. Resource dependence and construction, and macro- and micro-politics in transnational enterprises and alliances: the case of jet engine manufacturers in Germany. In C. Dörrenbächer and M. Geppert (eds.), *Politics and Power in the International Corporation:*

the *Role of Institutions, Interests and Identities*. Cambridge University Press, 41–70.

Tasoluk, B., Yaprak, A. and Calantone, R. J. 2006. Conflict and collaboration in headquarter–subsidiary relationships. An agency theory perspective on product rollouts in an emerging market. *International Journal of Conflict Management*, 17(4): 332–351.

Thomas, K. W. 1992. Conflict and conflict management: reflections and update. *Journal of Organizational Behavior*, 13(3): 265–274.

Vaara, E. and Tienari, J. 2008. A discursive perspective on legitimation strategies in multinational corporations. *Academy of Management Review*, 33(4): 985–993.

2011. On the narrative construction of multinational corporations: an antenarrative analysis of legitimation and resistance in a cross-border merger. *Organization Science*, 22(2): 370–390.

Vora, D. and Kostova, T. 2007. A model of dual organizational identification in the context of the multinational enterprise. *Journal of Organizational Behavior*, 28(3): 327–350.

Vora, D., Kostova, T. and Roth, K. 2007. Roles of subsidiary managers in multinational corporations: the effect of dual organizational identification. *Management International Review*, 47(4): 595–620.

Whitley, R., 1999. *Divergent Capitalisms. The Social Structuring and Change of Business Systems*, Oxford University Press.

Williams, K. and Geppert, M. 2011. Bargained globalization: employment relations providing robust 'tool kits' for socio-political strategizing in MNCs in Germany. In C. Dörrenbächer and M. Geppert (eds.), *Politics and Power in the International Corporation: the Role of Institutions, Interests and Identities*. Cambridge University Press, 72–100.

Ybema, S. and Byun, H. 2011. Unequal power relations, identity discourse, and cultural distinction drawing in MNCs. In C. Dörrenbächer and M. Geppert (eds.), *Politics and Power in the International Corporation: the Role of Institutions, Interests and Identities*. Cambridge University Press, 315–345.

Foundations of politics, power and conflict in MNCs

Introduction

Research on politics, power and conflict has been around in the international business field for some time. However, this research remained fragmented or partial and a comprehensive overview of the field has been missing. Part I of this volume offers a systematic review of the development of the field, which has been growing dynamically over the last ten years, and helps to discover the main lines of theoretical development on power and politics in the international business (IB) literature. It also provides a comprehensive introduction to this research field for students and colleagues who are working from other theoretical paradigms – in the hope that they will help enrich and enlarge the multifaceted research on micropolitics in the MNC.

Chapter 2 (re-)connects the research on power, politics and conflict in the MNC to its theoretical foundations in political sciences and organizational studies. This seems necessary since authors writing on power and politics in the international business field more often than not work with terms such as interests, actors, power and conflict without explicitly defining them and without clearly locating them vis-à-vis the sometimes incommensurable conceptualizations developed in theoretically strong traditions such as organization studies. In addition, Chapter 2 clarifies what the authors of this book take as *their* specific perspective on key concepts such as power, interests and actors and thus should enable the reader to retrace the theoretical perspective underlying the entire book.

Chapter 3 provides a comprehensive review of the discussion of power, politics and conflict in the IB field. It does so by closely following the overall development in the IB literature from closed rational to open natural paradigmatic positions over the last fifty years and by disclosing how the different theoretical approaches come to terms with notions or questions on power and politics in the MNC – or how they refrain from addressing such questions. Starting with Hymer's *Theory of the Multinational Firm* and closing with more recent critical approaches to IB, Chapter 3 reveals that (i) questions of power and politics have been a recurrent phenomenon of interest from the early beginnings of MNC research and, at the same time, that (ii) through the introduction of critical perspectives in the IB field such as new institutionalism, micropolitics and critical discourse approaches the investigation of power and politics in the MNC has slowly moved centre stage over the last decade.

2 | Theoretical foundations and conceptual definitions

SUSANNE BLAZEJEWSKI AND FLORIAN A. A.
BECKER-RITTERSPACH

Introduction

This chapter discusses fundamental definitions and core concepts, mainly derived from organizational studies and organizational sociology, which help researchers to theoretically take account of the phenomena related to politics and power in the multinational corporation (MNC). It delineates the historical and theoretical development of the central construct of 'organizational politics' and then reconstructs some of the more important academic debates concerning key concepts such as power, interests, agency and conflict. As we discuss below, we regard these as defining elements of 'politics'. Since power as well as politics can be considered key concepts in the social sciences, a multitude of researchers, theories, approaches and perspectives exists, to which we cannot claim to do any justice in this chapter. At the same time, the politics and power approach as it is employed in organization studies but also in the international business (IB) literature is not a coherent theory but rather a theoretical perspective with multiple faces, many definitional facets and competing constructs. We therefore more modestly focus on concepts actually employed in existing research on power and politics in MNCs and at the same time seek to provide some avenues for a more thorough and more diversified application of theoretical approaches and concepts in the future. As we will see, the discussion on power, politics, interests and actors in organizational studies and sociology is often much more complex and advanced than the eclectic application in the IB and MNC literature might suggest (Kostova *et al.* 2008: 994).

Politics

A first understanding of the term politics is readily at hand when we look at the tripartite vocabulary of polity – policy – politics offered

by the English language. Whereas 'polity' denotes – in the tradition of
Aristotle's politeia-concept (Aristotle 1984) – the institutional dimension of a political system and comprises the fundamental principles
(law, constitution) establishing the political order, e.g. of a state (government bodies, party system), 'policy' describes the substantiative
dimension. Policies are the strategic objectives and plans, political
programmes, concepts and guidelines which (should) keep political
actors on track and provide ideal-type directions for their activities.
In turn, 'politics' denotes a procedural dimension and refers to the
actual behaviour of political actors who seek to pursue or enforce their
respective political interests. Machiavelli's work (Machiavelli 1998) is
predominantly associated with this dimension of politics-as-action and
also clearly marks politics as a process of employing power to further
one's own ends. Polity, policy and politics are not to be considered three
separate spheres of political life. Instead, they constitute a conceptual
triangle in which each part/concept is interdependent with and shaped
through the other two. For instance, policies (e.g. a new strategy) come
about through political activities (e.g. tactics like influencing, persuad-
ing, bribing) in and around interested political bodies (e.g. parties, constituencies, governance bodies). Similarly, the effectiveness of political
action (politics) in safeguarding policy goals – as we discuss in more
detail below – depends on the structural positioning and the legitimacy
of the political actors/bodies (polity) involved.

Regarding politics *in organizations*, Burns (1961) is generally considered to be the first to introduce the term to organizational studies. He focused on 'micropolitics' as political behaviour inside the organization when actors make use of available resources (material and
human) in competitive situations (e.g. to further their career interests).
While the focus on *micro*politics, i.e. political behaviour of individual or group actors *inside* the organization, has developed into the
dominant research focus in the field and is also our key interest here,
organizational politics potentially cover a broader field: political processes also occur around and at the margins of organizations (involving
stakeholder groups, nongovernmental organizations [NGOs], public
voices, unions, competitors etc.). In addition, the term can also refer
to the political activities of the organization, e.g. in supplementing or
replacing functions and institutions usually conducted by state bodies
or in pursuing a strategic political agenda. To ensure terminological
clarity for our further discussion we distinguish between politics *of*

organizations and organizational politics as political behaviour on the micro-level *in and around* organizations.

In the literature we can identify two broad perspectives on organizational politics (Küpper and Felsch 2000). (i) Approaches that view organizational politics as an aspect, a phenomenon in organizational life. Political behaviour such as mobbing, manipulating or influencing may or may not occur in organizations; organizations are less or more politicized. Studies then investigate the degree of politicization in particular organizations or seek to understand and explain the processes and consequences of this particular kind of behaviour. (ii) Approaches which consider politics as a generic concept, a root metaphor in understanding organizations per se. Organizations are then conceptualized as political systems where actors pursuing idiosyncratic interests and the strategic use of power means are constitutive of organizational life. This conceptual or generic perspective on organizational politics was mainly developed by authors based in the behavioural theory of the firm such as March, Cyert, Simon and Olson (Cyert and March 1959; March 1962, 1988; March and Olson 1994; March and Simon 1958) but also proponents from resource dependence theory (Pfeffer 1981, 1992; Salancik and Pfeffer 1974) and organizational sociology (Crozier and Friedberg 1980; Friedberg 1995; Perrow 1972). The image of organizations as political systems was set against the then dominating view in management research of organizations as ordered social systems structured by rationality and functionality and directed towards the achievement of coherent, identifiable objectives. As we will discuss (Chapter 3) this rationalistic view of organization has – at least implicitly – remained prevalent in IB research for an even longer period of time. The generic view of organizational politics in turn acknowledges that 'the organization' as a homogeneous, goal-directed entity is an essentialist chimera and that organizations are constituted by multiple individual and collective actors (groups, coalitions) with idiosyncratic interests pursuing heterogeneous objectives which make sense to them even though they might eventually clash with 'official' goals legitimized by a leading coalition, e.g. top management. Organizational politics as a theoretical concept consistently takes strategic actors, their behaviour and the potential conflicts arising from the heterogeneity of interests pursued in situations of mutual interdependencies as points of departure for understanding and explaining organizational behaviour. Since organizational behaviour can thus only be understood in

reference to the actors' interests and their strategies in safeguarding these interests in interactional situations, all organizational actors
potentially become 'politicians' in this sense.

As Table 2.1 exhibits, authors working in the generic perspective
still define organizational politics in quite different ways. While Pfeffer (1981), for instance, emphasizes the intricate linkage between politics and power (politics as the mobilization of power bases), Crozier
and Friedberg (1980) draw attention to the interdependencies between
local strategic actors pursuing diverging interests in a joint organizational context with overlapping scopes of action and shared rules of the
'game'. Similarly, Bacharach and Lawler (1981) accentuate the organizational context of politics which is both a condition and an outcome
of political behaviour. For March (1962) the structural embeddedness
of political behaviour and the negotiative nature of all strategies, goals
and rules of an organization are constitutive of the firm as a 'political
system'.

Proponents of the aspectual view of politics in organizations tend to
come from the field of organizational psychology or human resource
research (Blickle *et al.* 2008; Drory and Romm 1990; Ferris *et al.* 1989;
Vigoda-Gadot and Drory 2006) but also from management research
(Mintzberg 1983, 1985). Politics here are understood as a particular
type of behaviour (e.g. manipulation, mobbing, coercing) associated
with predominantly negative consequences for some members of the
organization (stress, demotivation, attendance, turnover) – even when
some authors later distanced themselves from a purely negative view of
politics (Ferris *et al.* 2002). Politics thus is seen as a phenomenon organizations must seek to keep at bay, to be contained through rational
and 'better' management. Such a definition of politics as a specific, illegitimate type of behaviour which disrupts organizational life discloses two implicit assumptions: (i) in order to see politics as disruptive,
illegitimate behaviour, we must hold an understanding of organizations
as generally ordered, coherent, legitimate phenomena. (ii) If politics
constitute only one, specific aspect of human behaviour in organizations, the concept cannot serve as a general explanative theory of organizational life at large. Organizations here are not viewed as political
systems as in the generic understanding; politics is just one (potential,
disruptive, unwanted) aspect or appearance in organizations.

This rather narrow view of politics as negative and unwanted
behaviour draws a further critical question: negative for whom? Whose

Table 2.1 *Definitions of organizational politics*

Perspective	Definition
Generic	'Behaviour is defined as political when others are made use of as resources in competitive situations' (Burns 1961: 257).
	'The business organization is properly viewed as a political system... The composition of the firm is not given; it is negotiated. The goals of the firm are not given; they are bargained' (March 1962: 672).
	'Political behaviour is defined as behaviour by individuals, or, in collective terms, by subunits within an organization which makes a claim against the resource-sharing system of the organization' (Pettigrew 1973/2001: 17).
	'Power in action' (Pfeffer 1981: 7).
	'Political behavior in organizations may be defined as those activities that are not required as part of one's organizational role but that influence, or attempt to influence, the distribution of advantages and disadvantages within the organization' (Farrell and Petersen 1982: 405).
	'Basically, collective action is nothing but everyday politics; power is its raw material... In a nutshell: everything is politics, because everything is based on power and domination' (Crozier and Friedberg 1993).
	'Organizational politics are the efforts of individuals or groups in organizations to mobilize support for or opposition to organizational strategies, policies, or practices in which they have a stake or interest... From a political perspective, organizations are arenas in which actors are interdependent, purposive (instrumental or goal-oriented) and take into account the actual or prospective action of others inside and outside of the organization (responsiveness)' (Bacharach and Lawler 1998: 69).
	'Acts of influence to enhance or protect the self-interest of individuals or groups' (Allen *et al.* 1979: 77).
Aspectual	'Individual or group behaviour that is informal, ostensibly parochial, typically divisive, and above all, in the technical sense, illegitimate – sanctioned neither by formal authority, accepted ideology, nor certified expertise' (Mintzberg 1983: 172).

(cont.)

Table 2.1 *(cont.)*

Perspective	Definition
	'Behavior not formally sanctioned by the organization, which produces conflict and disharmony in the work environment by pitting individuals and/or groups against one another, or against the organization' (Ferris *et al.* 1996: 234).
	'Those actions not officially approved by an organization taken to influence others to meet one's personal goals' (Greenberg and Baron 1997).
	'Intra-organizational influence tactics used by organization members to promote self-interests or organizational goals in different ways' (Vigoda 2003: 31).

perspective is taken when we classify behaviour as political? Whose perspective is implicitly privileged? Again, this leads us to the assertion that the aspectual approach to organizational politics is fundamentally based on an image of order and coherence about what is good and bad, what is wanted and unwanted for 'the' organization or its leading coalition. In our view, however, whether a specific type of behaviour is negative for an organizational actor is rather an empirical than a definitional question. Political behaviour is associated with multiple consequences; whether they are considered harmful or beneficial largely depends on the context, the perceptions and the subjective appraisal of those affected by it. It is therefore crucial for researchers on power and politics to not only pay attention to the interests and tactics of strategic actors pursuing their objectives but also to the consequences of these political actions and their assessment by the multiple stakeholders involved who might evaluate the outcomes of politics in highly diverse ways. The A-B-C-model by Buchanan and Badham (2008) neatly summarizes this concept of politics as a process of antecedents (A), behaviour (B) and consequences (C) which may be perceived as functional or dysfunctional depending on the subjective position of the actor considered. Meanwhile, many researchers agree that the narrow view of politics as illegitimate behaviour is inadequate (Fleming and Spicer 2014). Work by Pettigrew and others (Blazejewski and Dorow 2003; Pettigrew 1973/2001) has demonstrated that organizational politics is instrumental and even indispensable in conducting organizational change. Politics also plays a major role in sparking innovation, intrapreneurship and institutional entrepreneurship (Clemens and Cook 1999; Jones *et al.* 2001) when actors with idiosyncratic interests challenge or circumvent routines, established positions and paths. In our view, politics is therefore not only unavoidable in organizational contexts, it is an important driver of organizational dynamics (Buchanan and Badham 1999; Clegg, Courpasson, and Phillips 2006).

Actors

Organizational politics involves some form of enactment, behaviour or activity conducted by so called 'actors'. But who is this? A person? An organizational entity? Can anyone be a political actor? Quite rarely do authors in the field actually elaborate on the definition and characterization of the key acting agency in their research on politics; the 'actor' therefore often remains a rather abstract and elusive concept (Emirbayer and Mische 1998; Hitlin and Elder 2007). Even if researchers specify their approach as *micro*political and consequently focus on individual actors, it often remains unclear *how* these individual actors are understood and conceptualized. Based on the work by Friedberg and Crozier (Crozier and Friedberg 1980; Friedberg 1992) we view actors in organizational politics as concrete and identifiable, autonomous and at the same time contingent, bounded rational, reflective and self-referential humans. This definition in the first place refers to individual human beings but also allows for teams or groups of people, for instance, when they agree to politically pursue shared interests as a coalition. It does not, however, apply to unitary entities or abstract bodies such as 'the organization' or 'the MNC' that sometimes are treated as if they were a person with coherent homogeneous interests and a human-like ability to act and reflect (see the discussion of unitary organizational rationalities in Chapter 3). A necessarily inconclusive list of potential political actors will include employees, managers, customers, unionists, NGO members and corporate partners but organizational politics as a generic concept is not limited or even focused on any specific actor or group of actors. As Küpper and Ortmann (1986: 593; our translation) emphasize, 'Each actor in organizations is a micropolitician in his or her own way'. It is the researcher's task then to understand what his or her specific rationalities in his or her own, biographical and historical situation is or has been in order to disclose the contextual meaning of his or her political strategy. We now look at the components of our definition of the actor in more detail.

Organizational politics is concerned with the political behaviour of 'real' and human actors, i.e. embodied and concrete individuals (Clegg *et al.* 2006: 203; Fleming and Spicer 2014: 278; Granovetter 1985). These actors dispose of self-conceptualized, individually reconstructable identities and interests that make sense to them in their biographically situated context (even when they may seem foolish to a bystander). In this bounded and subjective sense actors act purposefully and rationally. Being 'human' also means to be potentially knowledgeable and reflective about the world, others and oneself. Self-reflection, in turn, allows conscious actors to distance themselves from routines, authorities and roles legitimately ascribed in their organization (Clegg *et al.* 2006; Goffman 1959/1990). Consequently, neither their identities nor their interests are ever fully determined by structures or institutionalized norms, although, as we discuss below, they are also never fully independent of their contingencies. For Friedberg and Crozier actors are therefore 'autonomous' in that they always retain an 'irreducible margin of liberty' (Crozier and Friedberg 1980:20) and are 'in no case' (Friedberg 1995: 197; our translation) determined by traditions, structures and institutions. Friedberg nicely summarizes this concept of actors as human, cognisant and purposive: 'The field of action consists of actors who think, even when they do not possess all the facts; who act intentionally, even when they do not always attain their goals; who are able to choose, even when their choices might be intuitive, and who can intelligently adapt to requirements of the situation – at least to their perception of it – and develop their behavioural strategies from there' (Friedberg 1995: 202; our translation). Although we define political actors as human agents here, we are aware that due to technological development non-human agency is on the rise and that power – as a key component of politics – does also reside in networks, discourses or technologies that go far beyond visible action or agency (Latour 1996; Munro 2009: see also our discussion on power below). Nevertheless, politics in the understanding developed here takes the perspective of the human actor as an anchor point without, however, disregarding his or her contextual embeddedness. As we discuss next, the actor's autonomy in political behaviour is well bounded by intersubjective rules and structures as well as subjective and perceptual limits.

Individual actors although cognisant and reflective are bounded by cognitive constraints in gathering, processing and making use of information (Lindenberg 2001; Simon 1955, 1957). Their rationality is delimited by their subjective, biographical perspective which might make them pursue political objectives that only make sense to them and eventually forgo allegedly 'real' interests that others might consider – from their idiosyncratic position – more pertinent (see the section on interests below). Actors' political behaviour is also contingent on others and their interdependent scopes of action which in organizations are additionally circumscribed by the formal and informal allocation of roles, positions and resources. The actor's scope of action is limited by his or her subjective perception of alternatives for action and the perceived availability of required resources, i.e. by his or her interpretation and processes of sensemaking about the situation at hand (Clark and Geppert 2011; Pettigrew *et al.* 2001; Weick 1995). In addition, there are also 'real' or objectified constraints of political action since one's strategies might encounter previously undisclosed or imperceptible barriers in the social and structural context or produce unexpected results which might indicate an incorrect evaluation of the situation in the first place or a suboptimal selection of political tactics (Crozier and Friedberg 1980; Osterloh 1983). This is particularly relevant in MNCs where the 'correct' estimation of available and successful routes for action are often hindered by the ambiguity of norms, rules and meanings in culturally and institutionally diverse organizational settings (Kostova *et al.* 2008; Kristensen and Zeitlin 2005). Crozier and Friedberg (1980) employ the 'game' metaphor to indicate that actors in organizational politics are free to chose their moves, but according to rules and constraints that are not always of their own making or choice. Actors are therefore autonomous but also clearly embedded in social, structural, economic, political, spatial and temporal contexts, norms and institutions – without ever being caught in the 'iron cage' of institutional or cultural 'dopes' (Clegg *et al.* 2006: 218). This consistent integration of the actor's perspective without forgoing the contextual constitution of the actor's scope of action, meaning and identity is in our view a core advantage of the organizational politics approach.

Interests

Even though 'interests' are a recurrent element of organizational politics definitions, the concept tends to remain unclear and underdefined in much of the power and politics literature. Authors often manage to circumvent a thorough definition by presenting a more or less extensive list of potential kinds of interests actors may pursue such as economic, social, cultural, biographical or identity-related interests. Actors seek to further their personal career (Dörrenbächer and Geppert 2009) or to protect their local work unit (Blazejewski 2009; Kristensen and Zeitlin 2005). At times, the word 'interests' is used interchangeably with related terms such as preferences, needs, motives or intentions, without specifying the relationship between these concepts. According to March (1988: 17), with the organizational politics approach 'we have a theory of wilful and intentional actors without a theory of will or intention'.

A brief look at other, related fields of research employing the interest concept such as psychology, political science or economics reveals that the term remains inconclusive and even contested across disciplines. Social and motivational theorists conceptualize interests as the 'cognitive representation of needs' (Rokeach 1973), implying a distinction between unconscious deep-structure motives or needs on the one hand, and interests on the other hand, i.e. conscious aspirations that the individual has learned to think might contribute to the satisficing of her or his underlying motives (Deci and Ryan 2000; Kehr 2004). Interests as explicit goals or aspirations are potentially subject to change depending on learning processes, social influences and sensemaking processes (Silvia 2001). Apart from cognizance, temporality is a second, disputed dimension of the interest concepts. Similar to classical economic definitions, some psychologists define interests as enduring preferences which form part of the individual's personality (Silvia 2001). Interests as preferences or standards of judgement are assumed to remain stable across situations (even though it is acknowledged that over time preferences might adjust). Consciousness and stability/malleability apart, the concept remains disputed regarding the beneficiary of interested action (self-serving vs. altruistic interests), the rationality or legitimacy of interests and the coherence between organizational and individually idiosyncratic interests in the corporate context. We discuss each of these dimensions from the viewpoint of the organizational politics literature below.

March as a key proponent of organizational politics as a theoretical approach maintains that interests are inconsistent and malleable through interaction, learning and the accumulation of experiences (March 1988). Actors will readjust their intentions or goals, e.g. when their level of aspiration rises (Simon 1979). In addition, according to Küpper and Felsch as well as Lindenberg (Lindenberg *et al*. 2006) interests and norms are in fact constructed *uno actu* (Küpper and Felsch 2000: 299) through situational definitions and situational selection. Actor's interests change depending on her or his assessment of the situational context and the framing of the situation. If a particular situation is perceived as threatening to ones' identity, actors are expected to focus their intentionality on protecting and maintaining their identity coherence and integrity and thus actualize their personal identity interests. This approach draws attention to the situational construction and relevance of actors' interests rather than to enduring preferences or underlying motives (Blazejewski 2012).

When we understand interests as a situational, malleable concept, it consequently contains an element of cognisance: interests are those goals and intentions that the actor is or becomes aware of in a specific context. In this sense, actors *know* their interests. Organizational politics thus focuses on and takes seriously interests that people think they have and consider relevant and important in a particular context rather than their 'real' interests (Clegg *et al*. 2006: 211). In his concept of the three faces of power, Lukes (2005) argues that actors' interests might be formed and dominated by institutional norms and powerful structures of which actors are unaware. Through the third face of power, actors are systematically kept from ever disclosing and pursing their 'real' interests. Legitimate, unavoidable norms, values and discourses make them follow intentions which are inherently against their own, genuine, deeply hidden interests. Based on Gramsci's idea of hegemonic power Buraway (1979) shows how consent is engineered in the capitalist factory system when managers and workers, because of the alignment of their interests with the interests of employers/owners, cannot see their 'real interests' and therefore show little interest in active forms of resistance, e.g. against exploitative work practices. There has been considerable criticism towards Luke's approach which, according to Clegg *et al.*, runs the danger of being 'arrogant' (Clegg *et al.* 2006: 214) in that it implies emancipation liberating actors from their 'false consciousness' and making them understand their 'real' interests must necessarily come from some position outside this system of power and norms. Against this 'arrogance' we sustain that in order to understand their behaviour we must take seriously that actors are potentially knowledgeable and self-reflective about their interests – even if in the course of life we often have to realize that our well-thought intentions did not produce a desired outcome and did not do us any good. Also, Lukes himself would maintain that 'real' interests can never refer to 'the last word on the matter', i.e. one's 'true' interests, but instead draws attention to the 'internalized illusions' (Lukes 2005: 149) which we through processes of manipulation and misleading information have come to consider our own and genuine interests. Human beings thus do maintain the ability to consent to dominating power while at the same time resenting the mode of its exercise (Lukes 2005).

Once we accept that actors' interests are as 'real' as they are 'real' and sensible to *them*, it seems reasonable to some authors to portray political actors as essentially egoistic. In fact, particularly the aspectual view of politics has suffered from a narrow understanding of interests as self-serving, anti-social and even malicious (Ferris *et al.* 1989; Ferris *et al.* 2007). Against this limited view, Drory and others argue that characterizing interests as 'self-serving' does not in any way exclude altruism and other pro-social behaviour – as long as the actor considers them important to her or him, legitimate and subjectively rational (Drory and Romm 1990; Neuberger 2006). Consequently, political behaviour in organizations does not preclude that actors act in the interest of the organization, i.e. pursue strategies that contribute to organizational objectives – as long as he or she can assume that these organizational goals are in congruence or instrumental to their own well-being or personal plans (Vroom 1964). *Whose* interests are served by political activities is ultimately dependent on the subjective assessment of those affected, and foremost on an empirical question. As Küpper and Felsch (2000) argue, organizational politics is concerned with those interests – whether self-serving, pro-social or formally legitimate – that we can perceive and disclose in the concrete political episode or action system.

On the organizational level, organizational politics approaches affirm that interests are – since they give primacy to idiosyncratic actor perspectives – most probably heterogeneous. The presumed heterogeneity of interests inside the organization is, in fact, the condition *sine qua non* of the organizational politics approach. This view does not preclude that many organizations seek to attain interest harmonization among their members through sophisticated incentive systems, the implementation of shared values and other vehicles of cultural and social integration. It only takes the somewhat realistic view, that these efforts might not always produce the desired effects and that therefore the assumption that individual and organizational interests potentially conflict in organizations is a more realistic view of the world than the assumption of a fully conforming 'organization man' (Whyte 1957/2013). According to March (March 1988: 17), 'the apparent coherence [in organizations] is often produced less by resolving inconsistencies than by obscuring them'. This is even more evident in MNCs where, on the one hand, personal biographies apart, actor interests are shaped by diverging cultural, institutional, structural and social influences (Wildavsky 1987) and, on the other hand, where there are potentially more opportunities to conceal non-compliant behaviour. The culturally and geographically dispersed constitution of the MNC gives more room for 'ceremonial adoption' where actors apparently adopt headquarters' (HQ) standards, values and routines, while in the subsidiary they in fact cultivate their own, local practices and interests (Björkman and Lervik 2007; Kostova and Roth 2002).

Power

Politics has frequently been defined as the strategic employment of power (Table 2.1) so it seems imminent to look more closely at this key concept in the social sciences at large and for our debate around organizational politics in particular. Since power is a core definitional element of politics, even to the extent that in some instances the terms seem to collapse and become conceptually indistinguishable, we also want to delineate where and how the concept of power goes beyond its usage in the organizational politics literature – particularly since much of the organizational politics literature has made only partial use of a much broader power concept prevalent in the social science. As we discuss below, the organizational politics approach has long been dominated by concepts emphasizing agentic or episodic power at the expense of systemic and discursive power concepts (see Table 2.2).

A plethora of definitions, theories and perspectives on power exists so that Lukes refers to a 'contested phenomenon' (Lukes 2005) whereas Haugaard and Clegg (2009: 3) consider this a 'requisite variety' enabling multiperspective research. Still, a number of attempts have been made to put some order into the field by classifying approaches and/or dimensions of power. We consider two of these classifications – power to/power over and episodic/systemic power – in the following.

The distinction between 'power to' and 'power over' is based on the observation that power works, depending on the situation, as either an enabling or a constraining force (Giddens 1984; Göhler 2009). Parsons (1963) has been influential in the debate in delineating power as a positive force creating, maintaining and eventually changing the institutional and organizational order as long as it is based on legitimate authority. In Giddens' (1984) concept 'power to' is related to the enabling, facilitative side of power that holds the capacity for action. 'Power to' thus captures the productive face of power; it 'empowers' actors to pursue their (legitimate) interests. In turn, 'power over' describes the restraining, prohibitive dimension of power. Power works as a constraint for action (Giddens 1984) and prevents actors from pursuing and attaining their interests, e.g. by delimiting their scope of action, coercion or manipulation. This is the power actors would tend to resist but also the power of domination when actors are involuntary complicit, e.g. through powerful discourses and socialization, with the dominating structures (Haugaard and Clegg 2009).

Although the 'power to' and 'power over' typology has been successfully employed in studies on power and politics in MNCs (cf. Blazejewski and Becker-Ritterspach 2011), we agree with Göhler (2009) that both faces of power are essentially two sides of the same coin and do not help to theoretically distinguish fundamental facets of the power concept. Göhler (2009) argues that the positive deployment of 'power to' by any actor to further his or her interests, invariably disenfranchises others, generating 'power over' and potential resistance to change. For instance, Khan *et al.* (2007) use the case of soccer ball production to demonstrate how MNCs use their power to provide for 'better' labour conditions in the Pakistan region of Sialkot, where up to 80 per cent of the global manufacturing of soccer balls takes place. Among the working women and their families in Sialkot, however, this initiative entails a number of negative consequences (work away from home where they could tend their children and gardens alongside their stitching, among others). For them, the MNCs' positive power to change their working situation turns into constraint and domination and prevents them from voicing and safeguarding their local and personal interests. In addition, Courpasson and Dany (2009) argue that resistance to power can also become creative and productive and effectively empower seemingly peripheral or 'powerless' actors. Here, a case in point is the Danish subsidiary of the MNC case company in the work by Kristensen and Zeitlin (2005) which through formally 'illegitimate' action and secret resistance to HQ strategic intents establishes itself as a strong competence centre that eventually enables the MNC to develop strategically. As Clegg and others maintain, whether power is productive or constraining, is 'strictly contingent' (Clegg *et al.* 2006: 191) and depends predominantly on the context, the perception of those involved and also their potential to emancipate from seemingly oppressive norms, discourses and structures.

The second attempt at structuring the field, the distinction between episodic and systemic power, is the more fruitful for our purposes. Table 2.2 provides an overview of power and politics approaches along these dimensions. Not only has the differentiation between systemic and episodic power, through the work of Clegg and others (Clegg 1989; Clegg *et al.* 2006; Fleming and Spicer 2014; Haugaard and Clegg 2009), become more or less endemic to the field of organizational studies, it also mirrors best the development of the organizational politics field from a focus on the political actor, his or her intentions and behavioural strategies – sometimes rooted in paradigmatic traditions of methodological individualism and voluntarism – to integrated views that take account of the embeddedness and the contextual constitution of political actors and political agency.

With its focus on actors' strategic behaviour the organizational politics literature has often retained an understanding of power as episodic and agentic (Allen *et al.* 1979; Buchanan and Badham 1999; Burns 1961; Dlugos *et al.* 1993; Mintzberg 1983; Pfeffer 1981; see Table 2.2). Power in this sense is manifest in concrete situations and concrete actions where different actors with different bundles of power sources available to them seek to protect their interests in interaction (Clegg 1989). Episodic power is the power which actors actually put to use in political processes – 'the direct exercise of power' (Fleming and Spicer 2014: 240) – and which comes about in 'identifiable acts that shape

the behaviour of others' (Fleming and Spicer 2014: 240). It is consistent with Lukes' description of the first face of power (Lukes 2005) and
also with the classical definition by Weber (1976) which served as a theoretical basis for many of the early proponents of the organizational
politics perspective: 'Power has typically been seen as the ability to get
others to do what you want them to, if necessary against their will, or
to get them to do something they would otherwise not do' (Hardy and
Clegg 1996: 623).

In its episodic face, the concept of power is associated with causality, control, power sources and power means. Causality is implied
when we define power as the ability to get others to do what we
want them to do. Power, then, is the ability to mobilize resources
in order to affect and/or change outcomes (e.g. the behaviour of
others) (Giddens 1984; Mintzberg 1983, 1985) even against potential resistance and even when there is agreement that political actors
usually cannot fully determine the outcome, e.g. when opponents
react in an unexpected way. Episodic power is also associated with
control: control over critical resources (Bacharach and Lawler 1980;
Dowding 2009; French and Raven 1960; Pfeffer 1992; Salancik and
Pfeffer 1974) and control over zones of uncertainty (Crozier and Friedberg 1980). While the proponents of the resource (dependence) theory of power identify different sources or bases of power (rewards,
titles, charisma, expert knowledge, network access, information etc.)
and delineate how actors strategically withhold or make use of these
power bases in tactical behaviour (threatening, manipulating, rewarding etc.), Crozier and Friedberg (1980) argue that power becomes available when actors experience ambiguity or insecurity. When the relationship between causes and effects is unclear in a specific situation,
those actors who are potentially able to contain or relieve others of
this insecurity become powerful. In MNCs, HQ is often unaware or
less knowledgeable about the local situation, culture and practices in
international subsidiaries than local employees. When institutional environments are thus ambiguous or disputed at least from the viewpoint
of the HQ, local actors might credibly portray HQ policies as being
incompatible with local business customs, and intentionally reinterpret
and readjust global standards according to their interests. The team
around Edward and Ferner (Almond and Ferner 2006; Ferner *et al.*
2004) demonstrates how European subsidiaries of US companies deliberately employ margins of interpretation and institutional ambiguity

in order to protect local practices in human resources (HR) management and resist the strategies of global standardization pursued by their HQ. Regarding the power-as-resources perspective, manifold literature exists in IB analysing the distribution of power bases between HQ and subsidiaries or among subsidiaries and also the evolution and change of this allocation of power when, for example, subsidiaries gain status and expertise as global competence centres (Birkinshaw and Hood 1998; Bouquet and Birkinshaw 2008). Similarly, the withdrawal of capital and production capacity can also offset and rearrange the balance of power between HQ and subsidiaries (Blazejewski 2009). In the MNC literature, language has been identified as a key resource or skill that actors make use of as a strategic power source (Logemann and Piekkari 2015; Welch *et al.* 2005). According to the resource-based view, power is relational, context dependent and dynamic. As demonstrated by Bouquet and Birkinshaw (2008), powerless actors might gain power over time, e.g. when they make sophisticated use of local expertise and networks. Also, Pfeffer (1992) among others, argues that power is relational and contingent in that the successful employment of a power base in a specific situation depends on the political skills of actors in selecting and enacting adequate tactics (Blickle *et al.* 2008; Ferris *et al.* 2007) and on the relevance of these power bases to the parties involved.

Based on earlier work by Bachrach and Baratz (1962, 1963) more recently authors emphasize that power even in its episodic understanding goes beyond the visible employment of power sources and power means (Dörrenbächer and Gammelgaard 2011; Kolb and Bartunek 1992). Non-action, non-information and non-decisions are important tactics of power withholding or withdrawing presumably valuable alternatives of action from potentially interested but ignorant parties. In this sense, episodic power does not only relate to Lukes' first face of power but also to his second face emphasizing power as preventing decision making or limiting choices available (Lukes 2005). Again, in MNCs language as a power source plays a crucial role in this sense: translations are an important and often non-observable tool for reinterpreting, reevaluating or withholding information exchanged between MNC subunits (Logemann and Piekkari 2015). Investigating the episodic deployment of these MNC-specific power bases still offers many avenues for further research even when from a theoretical point of view, the episodic perspective on power – 'the dull stuff' (Clegg *et al.* 2006) – is limited in a number of ways which we will discuss below.

Table 2.2 *Episodic and systemic power*

Circuits of power	Faces of power	Key proponents/theoretical foundation		Application in MNC politics research (example)
Episodic/agentic	Power tactics, identifiable acts of power use	French and Raven 1960; Mintzberg 1983; Pfeffer 1981; Salancik and Pfeffer 1974		Mudambi and Navarra 2004
	In-/non-action, hidden power, agenda setting, manipulation	Bachrach and Baratz 1962	Lukes, 2005	Logemann and Piekkari 2015
Systemic	Domination: reification of power structures, normalization of subjectivities and practices	Foucault 1977, 1982, 1988, 2003; Foucault and Gordon 1980	Clegg 1989; Clegg et al. 2006; Fleming and Spicer 2014	Frenkel 2008
	Subjectivity: construction of identities, meanings and			Gagnon and Collinson 2014

This is particularly the case when authors (Dörrenbächer and Gammel-gaard 2011; Dörrenbächer and Geppert 2009; Logemann and Piekkari 2015; Vaara *et al.* 2005; Welch *et al.* 2005) do not only delineate political tactics and related power bases in use in concrete human interaction but link the political behaviour of actors to their structural, systemic and discursive embeddedness. Episodic power relates to its structural and systemic context in at least two ways: (i) outcomes of power episodes do have effects on the context (e.g. on the reallocation of resources among parties); and (ii) structures, norms and discourses largely determine who has which kind of power available in an episode (e.g. who has access to rewards and sanctions; who is able to mobilize legitimate discourses in the situation).

Systemic power is power that reaches *beyond* the episode and resides *between* actors rather than being 'held' by any given party (Clegg 1990). Systemic power thus maintains that power is always there even if it is not currently employed in a circumscribed political episode. So, even if we may feel free to decide and act according to our interests in a certain situation, our freedom may be structured and contained by forces we are not aware of or cannot control. This view of power is associated with the influential work by Foucault (Foucault 1977, 1982; Foucault and Gordon 1980) who strongly emphasizes the systemic dimension of power: 'power is not something that is divided between those who have it and hold it exclusively, and those who do not have it and are subject to it. Power must, I think, be analysed as something that circulates, or rather that functions only when it is part of a chain... In other words, power passes through individuals' (Foucault 2003: 29). Power is therefore implicated in our everyday world, not just in episodes of (visible, discernible) political action; in this sense, 'Power does not show itself because it is implicated in all that we are and all that we inhabit' (Allen 2003: 65). Therefore systemic power is congealed in the institutions, cultures and norms that structure our discourses, our interests, our roles and identities (Fleming and Spicer 2014). In this way, actors, their goals, their power bases and power means are constituted through systemic power. It also determines who has access to the political games and who is prevented from entering the field – who, in other words, is unable to position him- or herself as an interested, political actor in a specific situation. In the case study of the Pakistanian soccer stitchers (Khan *et al.* 2007), for instance, the local community is – either purposively or involuntarily – precluded from access to the debate about their 'better' future of work initiated by the MNCs and global NGOs. In consequence, they neither have a chance to voice their interests, nor to undertake political action to protect those interests that seem relevant and 'real' to them. Using a different case, Frenkel (2008) traces such institutionalized power back to colonial structures of first world versus third world geopolitical relations which even nowadays define some discourses as relevant or legitimate while subduing others. Lukes (2005) terms this systemic dimension of power that is grounded in unquestionable norms and dominant discourses the 'third face' of power. While he seems to imply that there is no way out, no way of emancipation from these dominating structures because the actors are trapped in powerful norms unknowable to themselves, Clegg *et al.* (2006) argue that because these norms are man-made they are also potentially subject to man-made change initiatives. Following our argument that human actors always retain a margin of liberty, we also consent that they might use it in order to non-conform, reaffirm or to question, reinterpret and eventually modify dominant discourses and taken-for-granted rules and rulers. This argumentation parallels the debate around institutional entrepreneurship which consents that even 'powerless' actors might be able to tackle, adjust, hybridize or create institutions depending on their motivation and their ability to generate powerful coalitions and networks (Battilana 2006; Garud *et al.* 2007; Marti and Mair 2010). If we accept that systemic power as institutional power is subject to institutional work, it is evident that even when actors perceive them as insurmountable, structures and discourses of dominance are per se not eternally fixed but essentially in flux. Through actors' reflexive capacity and reproduction, reinterpretation and reassessment of rules and norms as they go along, they partake at structuring and restructuring the fields for political action.

Fleming and Spicer differentiate between two modes of systemic power: domination and subjectification (Fleming and Spicer 2014). Domination occurs when ideological values, practices, interpretations and technologies become hegemonic. They then shape actors and their 'perceptions, cognitions, and preferences in such a way that they accept the role in the existing order of things, either because they can see or imagine no alternative to it, or because they see it as natural and unchangeable' (Lukes 2005: 24). In some MNCs dominance becomes discernible when subsidiaries always turn to headquarters for advice, resources or direction, thus reproducing an inherent core-periphery-structure which, in turn, keeps them in their strategically marginal position (Boussebaa 2015; Boussebaa *et al.* 2014). The argument is similar to the work by Frenkel and others (Banerjee and Prasad 2008; Frenkel 2008) on neo-colonial power structures between 'Western' headquarters and their subunits in developing countries.

Subjectification is largely based on the work by Foucault (Foucault 1977; Hutton *et al.* 1988) who convincingly argued that we internalize roles, identities and norms shaped by structures of dominance power in such a way that we ourselves embody, control and maintain our own domination through self-monitoring and self-disciplining. If we internalize formerly external norms about 'what is good for us' through regulation processes (Deci 1992; Deci and Ryan 2000), we develop an identity or self-concept that even though the impulse for its development might originally be located outside – and represent outside interests – is perceived as authentically ours. Mumby and colleagues (Laclau and Mouffe 2001; Mumby 2001; Mumby and Stohl 1991) delineate the role of discourses in identity formation and development, for instance in constructing masculinity, as an underlying and self-reproducing albeit invisible power structure in organizations (Mumby 1998). Power as subjectification thus does not require coercive or manipulative action or dominance structures to 'get B doing what A wants'. When B has thoroughly internalized the 'right' behaviour as his or her own intrinsic motivation, there is no need for incentives, pressures, control, monitoring or any other perceptible political action or instrument. By infiltrating 'the very heart of the employee' (Fleming and Spicer 2014: 268), actors are ostensibly 'free' to choose their action according to their inherent interests, but their interests, identities and perception of alternatives for action have been shaped by norms and structures beyond their reach and consciousness. Even though the action is 'freely' chosen, it retains a quality of power that is, however, barely visible. At times, it becomes discernible in its consequences, e.g. when the prevalence of burn-out syndromes can be traced back to a long-term discongruity between internalized aspirations (about 'success', 'achievement', 'career' etc.) and the motivational deep structure that over time exhausts the human capacity for volition (Kehr 2004). For the case of the MNC we can suppose that the identity of 'global' or 'transnational' managers with its implications of boundaryless transferability and élite status is a potentially rewarding field for research on processes of subjectification (Cappellen and Janssens 2010; Gagnon and Collinson 2014).

Systemic and episodic power are interrelated: while systemic power shapes actors, interests, identities and the allocation of power sources, as well as the legitimacy of power means and structures and the arena in which politics takes place, each embedded power episode contributes to the stabilization or destabilization of its constitutive context. Clegg's circuits of power framework (Clegg 1989; Clegg *et al.* 2006) provides the most thorough theorization of this interrelationship. His framework integrates: (i) episodic or transitive power where actors employ available power bases to pursue their recognized interests in instances of organizational politics; (ii) systemic power as domination based on rules that fix relations of meaning and membership (i.e. define roles, positions, hegemonic values and norms); and (iii) systemic power as subjectification where techniques of production and discipline (i.e. internationalization and self-regulation) generate the social structures that, in turn, define who is an actor and which interests are pursued. Apart from differentiating the three faces or dimensions of power, Clegg's model is exemplary in emphasizing the multiple feedback loops between episodic and systemic power. Episodic outcomes reproduce or transform structures of domination which in turn facilitate or hinder the development of regimes of discipline or production. Systemic power defines who has access to the field of political activity, which power sources are relevant and how they are allocated, what the rules of the political game are and how legitimacy is constituted. In Clegg's framework, 'obligatory passage points' (channels, conduits) are instrumental for the flow of power through episodes and structures. Here, institutionalized structures and norms (systemic power) are used by controlling actors or agencies to define what the game in question is, that is, obligatory passage points represent and constitute the extant power positions, rules and relations.

The framework is hardly ever applied in full to the analysis of political games in MNCs; particularly the complex concept of the obligatory passage points seems to resist a smooth and lean application to MNC research. Vaara *et al.* (2005: see also Chapter 6) explicitly refer to the framework but essentially uses it only to differentiate between episodic and systemic dimensions of power. Similarly, even theoretical contributions such as the recent work by Fleming and Spicer (2014) – although they refer extensively to Clegg's work – do not discuss the more intricate elements of the model. More recently, Geppert *et al.*

(2014) apply Clegg's model for the study and comparison of micropolitical game-playing at Lidl stores across Europe but still focus on the three dimensions of power rather than on the dynamic linkages between them. A possible explanation for the selective use of the model in the IB field but also in the power and politics literature at large might lie in the iterative development of the field. As we emphasized at the beginning of this chapter, the organizational politics literature is rooted in the conception of politics as the employment of power by interested actors, i.e. as episodic. Early proponents of the perspective in organizational studies (Mintzberg 1983; Pfeffer 1981; Salancik and Pfeffer 1974) but also early work on power and politics in MNCs (Prahalad and Doz 1987) are basically limited to an agentic and episodic view of power. With the increased interest in power and politics in MNCs during the last decade, underlying conceptions of power have been growing in complexity and increasingly also take account of the systemic embeddedness of political agency and the feedback loops between the structural and the episodic dimension of power. In our own work, for instance, we have drawn attention to the interaction between power resources employed by actors in the field and the constitution of the field – and thus also the reconfiguration of power structures in MNCs – through previous and ensuing political action (Blazejewski 2009). With the integration of institutional perspectives into MNC research, the structural and systemic context of political agency has gained considerable attention in recent years. Maybe this development also prepares the field for a more thorough reception of the more complex conceptualizations of power in sociology and organizational studies in the future.

Conflicts

Some authors include conflict as a core element of organizational politics (Blazejewski 2006; Dlugos 1993; March 1962; Narayanan and Fahey 1982; Schotter and Beamish 2011). Drory and Romm (1990), for instance, maintain that politics as a behavioural quality is associated with conflict as a situational characteristic. On a macro level, Dahrendorf argues that politics create conflicts when actors resist the influencing attempts of others (Dahrendorf 1988). In turn, Neuberger (2006) argues that politics is not necessarily conflictual, for instance, when pro-social political behaviour does not produce any resistance. In our view, the debate about whether conflict is an element of politics or not largely hinges on the definition of conflict in use by respective authors. If we employ a narrow definition of conflict as a manifest episode in which actors fight, bargain and negotiate their opposing interests, it is in fact difficult to assert that political behaviour is necessarily conflictual. A broader and more adequate definition of conflict as incompatible interests in interdependent social situations which are perceived by at least one of the actors or parties involved (Boulding 1962; Dlugos *et al.* 1993; Thomas 1976), however, does also allow for conflicts to be latent, covert or hidden (Kolb and Bartunek 1992; Morrill *et al.* 2003). Such a definition of conflict does also more adequately correspond to our concept of power as both episodic and systemic. In an episodic perspective, conflicts occur when actors perceive that their interests are endangered by the political activities of others. They will then seek to make use of their own power bases to handle the conflict, i.e. stage resistance or negotiate a consensus. In the systemic perspective, power is employed to foreclose or silence potential resistance. The domination can be perceived by actors as oppressive but they might feel themselves unable to acknowledge, voice or even react against it; the situation would produce a latent or hidden conflict – which, however, when the dominating authority is challenged or actors develop an emancipatory impulse, might become manifest at any time. With subjectification actors would not even be aware of potentially conflictual interests; they have learned to identify with and internalize hegemonic interests and values. Especially this total absence of conflict should make the politics researcher suspicious: it is then highly interesting to understand how and through which political strategies actors in this field are prevented from holding conflictual interests in the first place.

The conflict construct therefore seems to us a useful correlate to the politics and power perspective as we have argued more extensively else- where (Blazejewski and Becker-Ritterspach 2011). Conflicts are necessarily conceptualized as processual and dynamic (Barki and Hartwick 2001; Pondy 1967; Thomas 1976; Wall Jr and Callister 1995): inside the episode the perception of conflict by at least one party triggers a process of (reciprocal) conflict handling. Beyond the episode the conse- quences of conflict-handling processes produce a new situation which in turn might give rise to further episodes or conflict escalation pro- cesses (Diehl 2006; Glasl 2010; Pearson d'Estrée 2003). The conflict concept thus emphasizes and supports a processual view of politics in organizations and takes account of the multiple interactional effects between political action, situation and the organizational or institutional context at large.

Conclusion

Power and politics is rather a conceptual field with many multifaceted definitions and constructs than a coherent theory in organization studies. Over time and from changing angles, organizational politics has been understood as a specific quality of – mostly dysfunctional – behaviour or as a generic approach to understanding organizations. Authors have limited their research endeavours to the identification of political tactics, skills or the consequences of political behaviour. Or they have broadened their perspective to look beyond the concrete episode of political activity to the institutional and contextual embeddedness of power and politics. In view of the multiple approaches and viewpoints – and their insightful application to many different empirical phenomena in the literature – it seems both useless and senseless to attempt to provide a general definition of organizational politics here. Instead, we have suggested that there are certain debates – around power, interests, actors and conflict – that are and always have been closely associated with politics and that help us to get a grasp on and structure our own understanding of the concept. In this sense, the chapter is intended to help the reader, first, to map his or her understanding of power and politics against the manifold perspectives already out there, and, second, to extend, develop or adjust this position through critically reassessing some of the arguments presented here. In the following chapters we revisit many of the debates and issues raised in this chapter; this chapter then may serve as a useful backdrop for navigating the field of power and politics in the multinational corporation.

References
Allen, J. 2003. *Lost Geographies of Power*. Oxford: Blackwell.
Allen, R. W., Madison, D. L., Porter, L. W., Renwick, P. A. and Mayes, B. T. 1979. Organizational politics: tactics and characteristics of its actors. *California Management Review*, 22(1): 77–83.

Almond, P. and Ferner, A. 2006. *American Multinationals in Europe: Managing Employment Relations across National Borders.* Oxford University Press.

Aristotle. 1984. *The Complete Works of Aristotle. The Revised Oxford Translation.* Edited by Jonathan Barnes. Princeton University Press.

Bacharach, S. B. and Lawler, E. J. 1980. *Power and Politics in Organizations.* San Francisco, CA: Jossey-Bass.

    1981. *Bargaining: Power, Tactics and Outcomes.* San Francisco: Jossey-Bass.

    1998. Political alignments in organizations: contextualization, mobilization, and coordination. In R. M. Kramer and M. A. Neale (eds.), *Power and Influence in Organizations*: 67–88. Thousand Oaks, CA: Sage.

Bachrach, P. and Baratz, M. S. 1962. Two faces of power. *American Political Review,* 56(4): 947–952.

    1963. Decisions and non-decisions: an analytical framework. *American Political Review,* 57(3): 641–651.

Banerjee, S. B. and Prasad, A. 2008. Special issue on 'Critical reflections on management and organizations: a postcolonial perspective'. *Critical Perspectives on International Business,* 4(2/3).

Barki, H. and Hartwick, J. 2001. Conceptualizing the construct of interpersonal conflict. *The International Journal of Conflict Management,* 15(3): 216–244.

Battilana, J. 2006. Agency and institutions: the enabling role of individuals' social position. *Organization,* 13(5): 653–676.

Birkinshaw, J. M. and Hood, N. 1998. Multinational subsidiary evolution: capability and charter change in foreign-owned subsidiary companies. *Academy of Management Review,* 23(4): 773–795.

Björkman, I. and Lervik, J. E. 2007. Transferring HR practices within multinational corporations. *Human Resource Management Journal,* 17(4): 320–335.

Blazejewski, S. 2006. Transferring value-infused organizational practices in MNCs: a conflict perspective. In M. Geppert, and M. Mayer (eds.), *Global, Local and National Practices in Multinational Companies.* Houndsmills, Basingstoke: Palgrave, 63–104.

    2009. Actors' interests and local contexts in intrafirm conflict: the 2004 GM and Opel crisis. *Competition and Change,* 13(3): 229–250.

    2012. Beyond or betwixt the lines of conflict? Biculturalism as situated identity in multinational corporations. *Critical Perspectives on International Business,* 8(2): 111–135.

Blazejewski, S. and Becker-Ritterspach, F. 2011. Conflict in headquarters–subsidiary relations. In C. Dörrenbächer and M. Geppert (eds.), *Politics and Power in the Multinational Corporation.* Cambridge University Press, 139–190.

Blazejewski, S. and Dorow, W. 2003. Managing organizational politics for radical change. *Journal of World Business,* 38(3): 204–223.

Blickle, G., Meurs, J. A., Zettler, I., Solga, J., Noethen, D., Kramer, J. and Ferris, G. R. 2008. Personality, political skill, and job performance. *Journal of Vocational Behavior,* 72(3): 377–387.

Boulding, E. K. 1962. *Conflict and Defense: a General Theory.* New York: Harper and Brothers.

Bouquet, C. and Birkinshaw, J. 2008. Managing power in the multinational corporation: how low power actors gain influence. *Journal of Management,* 34, 477–508.

Boussebaa, M. 2015. Control in the multinational enterprise: the polycentric case of global professional service firms. *Journal of World Business,* 50(4): 696–703.

Boussebaa, M., Sturdy, A. and Morgan, G. 2014. Learning from the world? Horizontal knowledge flows and geopolitics in international consulting firms. *The International Journal of Human Resource Management,* 25(9): 1227–1242.

Buchanan, D. and Badham, R. 1999. Politics and organizational change: the lived experience. *Human Relations,* 52(5): 609–629.

2008. *Power, Politics, and Organizational Change: Winning the Turf Game.* London: Sage.

Buraway, M. 1979. *Manufacturing Consent: Changes in the Labor Process under Monopoly Capitalism.* University of Chicago Press.

Burns, T. 1961. Micropolitics: mechanisms of institutional change. *Administrative Science Quarterly,* 6(3): 257–281.

Cappellen, T. and Janssens, M. 2010. Characteristics of international work: narratives of the global manager. *Thunderbird International Business Review,* 52(4): 337–348.

Clark, E. and Geppert, M. 2011. Subsidiary integration as identity construction and institution building: a political sensemaking approach. *Journal of Management Studies,* 48(2): 395–416.

Clegg, S. R. 1989. *Frameworks of Power.* London: Sage.

1990. *Modern Organizations: Organization Studies in the Postmodern World:* London: Sage.

Clegg, S. R., Courpasson, D. and Phillips, N. 2006. *Power and Organizations.* London: Sage.

Clemens, E. S. and Cook, J. M. 1999. Politics and institutionalism: explaining durability and change. *Annual Review of Sociology,* 25: 441–466.

Courpasson, D. and Dany, F. 2009. Cultures of resistance in the workplace. In S. R. Clegg and M. Haugaard (eds.), *The Sage Handbook of Power*. London: Sage, 332–347.

Crozier, M. and Friedberg, E. 1980. *Actors and Systems. The Politics of Collective Action*. Chicago University Press.

1993. *Die Zwänge kollektiven Handelns. Über Macht und Organisation*. Weinheim: Beltz Athenäum.

Cyert, R. M. and March, J. G. 1959. A behavioral theory of organizational objectives. In M. Haire (ed.), *Modern Organization Theory*. New York: Wiley, 76–90.

Dahrendorf, R. 1988. *The Modern Social Conflict: an Essay on the Politics of Liberty*. Berkeley: University of California Press.

Deci, E. L. 1992. The relation of interest to the motivation of behavior: a self-determination theory perspective. In A. Renninger, S. Hidi and A. Krapp (eds.), *The Role of Interest in Learning and Development*. Hillsdale, NJ: Lawrence Erlbaum Associates, 43–70.

Deci, E. L., and Ryan, R. M. 2000. The 'what' and 'why' of goal pursuits: human needs and the self-determination of behavior. *Psychological Inquiry*, 11: 227–268.

Diehl, P. F. 2006. Just a phase? Integrating conflict dynamics over time. *Conflict Management and Peace Science*, 23: 199–210.

Dlugos, G. 1993. Towards the business politics approach and the field of research. In G. Dlugos, W. Dorow and D. Farrell (eds.), *Organizational Politics*. Wiesbaden: Gabler, 75–91.

Dlugos, G., Dorow, W. and Farrell, D. 1993. *Organizational Politics*. Wiesbaden: Gabler.

Dörrenbächer, C. and Gammelgaard, J. 2011. Subsidiary power in multinational corporations: the subtle role of micro-political bargaining power. *Critical Perspectives on International Business*, 7(1): 30–47.

Dörrenbächer, C. and Geppert, M. 2009. A micro-political perspective on subsidiary initiative-taking: evidence from German-owned subsidiaries in France. *European Management Journal*, 27(2): 100–112.

Dowding, K. 2009. Rational choice approaches. In S. R. Clegg and M. Haugaard (eds.), *The Sage Handbook of Power*. London: Sage, 40–53.

Drory, A. and Romm, T. 1990. The definition of organizational politics: a review. *Human Relations*, 43: 1133–1154.

Emirbayer, M. and Mische, A. 1998. What is agency? *American Journal of Sociology*, 103(4): 962–1023.

Farrell, D. and Petersen, J. C. 1982. Patterns of political behavior in organization. *Academy of Management Review*, 7(3): 403–412.

Ferner, A., Almond, P., Clark, I., Colling, T., Edwards, T., Holden, L. and Müller-Carmen, M. 2004. The dynamics of central control and subsidiary autonomy in the management of human resources: case-study evidence from US MNCs in the UK. *Organization Studies*, 25(3): 363–391.

Ferris, G. R., Frink, D. D., Galang, M. C., Zhou, J., Kacmar, M. and Howard, J. L. 1996. Perceptions of organizational politics: prediction, stress-related implications, and outcomes. *Human Relations*, 49(2): 233–266.

Ferris, G. R., Hochwarter, W. A., Douglas, C., Blass, F. R., Kolodinsky, R. and Treadway, D. C. 2002. Social influence processes in organizations and human resource systems. In G. Ferris, and J. J. Marmocchio (eds.), *Research in Personnel and Human Resource Management*, Vol. 21. Stanford, CA: Elsevier, 65–127.

Ferris, G. R., Russ, G. S. and Fandt, P. M. 1989. Politics in organizations. In R. A. Giacalone and P. Rosenfield (eds.), *Impression Management in the Organization*. Hillsdale, NJ: Lawrence Erlbaum, 143–170.

Ferris, G. R., Treadway, D. C., Brouer, R., Perrewe, P. L., Douglas, C. and Lux, S. 2007. Political skill in organizations. *Journal of Management*, 33(3): 290–320.

Fleming, P. and Spicer, A. 2014. Power in management and organization science. *Academy of Management Annals*, 8(1): 237–298.

Foucault, M. 1977. *Discipline and Punish*. Toronto: Random House.

1982. The subject and power. *Critical Inquiry*, 8(4): 777–795.

1988. *Technologies of the Self: a Seminar with Michel Foucault*. University of Massachusetts Press.

2003. *Society Must Be Defended: Lectures at the Collège de France, 1975–1976*. New York: Picador.

Foucault, M. and Gordon, C. (eds.). 1980. *Power/Knowledge: Selected Interviews and Other Writings, 1972–1977*. New York: Pantheon.

French, J. R. P. and Raven, B. 1960. The bases of social power. In D. Cartwright and A. Zander (eds.), *Group Dynamics: Research and Theory*, 2nd edn. Evanston, IL: Row, Peterson and Company, 607–623.

Frenkel, M. 2008. The multinational corporation as a third space: rethinking international management discourse on knowledge transfer through Homi Bhabha. *Academy of Management Review*, 33(4): 924–942.

Friedberg, E. 1992. Zur Politologie von Organisationen. In W. Küpper and G. Ortmann (eds.), *Mikropolitik*, 2nd edn. Opladen: VS VerlagfürSozialwissenschaften, 39–52.

1995. *Ordnung und Macht*. Frankfurt/Main: Campus.

Gagnon, S. and Collinson, D. 2014. Rethinking global leadership development programmes: the interrelated significance of power, context and identity. *Organization Studies*, 35(5): 645–670.

Garud, R., Hardy, C. and Maguire, S. 2007. Institutional entrepreneurship as embedded agency: an introduction to the Special Issue. *Organization Studies*, 28(7): 957–969.

Geppert, M., Williams, K. and Wortmann, M. 2014. Micro-political game-playing in Lidl: a comparison of store-level employment relations. *European Journal of Industrial Relations*, 20(3): 1–17.

Giddens, A. 1984. *The Constitution of Society*. Berkeley, CA: University of California Press.

Glasl, F. 2010. *Konfliktmanagement*, 9th edn. Bern: Haupt.

Goffman, E. 1959/1990. *The Presentation of Self in Everyday Life*. London: Penguin.

Göhler, G. 2009. 'Power to' and 'power over'. In S. R. Clegg and M. Haugaard (eds.), *The Sage Handbook of Power*. London: Sage, 25–39.

Granovetter, M. 1985. Economic action and social structure: the problem of embeddedness. *The American Journal of Sociology*, 91(3): 481–510.

Greenberg, J. and Baron, R. A. 1997. *Behavior in Organizations*. Upper Saddle River, NJ: Prentice-Hall.

Hardy, C. and Clegg, S. 1996. Some dare call it power. In S. R. Clegg, C. J. Hardy and W. R. Nords (eds.), *The Handbook of Organization Studies*. London: Sage, 622–641.

Haugaard, M. and Clegg, S. R. 2009. Introduction: why power is the central concept of the social science. In S. R. Clegg and M. Haugaard (eds.), *The Sage Handbook of Power*. London: Sage, 1–24.

Hitlin, S. and Elder, G. H. 2007. Time, self, and the curiously abstract concept of agency. *Sociological Theory*, 25(2): 170–191.

Hutton, P. H., Gutman, H., Martin, L. H. and Foucault, M. 1988. *Technologies of the Self: a Seminar with Michel Foucault*. Amherst, MA: University of Massachusetts Press.

Jones, O., Conway, S. and Steward, F. (eds.). 2001. *Social Interaction and Organisational Change: Aston Perspectives on Innovation Networks*. London: Imperial College Press.

Kehr, H. M. 2004. Integrating implicit motives, explicit motives, and perceived abilities: the compensatory model of work motivation and volition. *Academy of Management Review*, 29(3): 479–499.

Khan, F. R., Munir, K. A. and Willmott, H. 2007. A dark side of institutional entrepreneurship: soccer balls, child labour and postcolonial impoverishment. *Organization Studies*, 28(7): 1055–1077.

Kolb, D. M. and Bartunek, J. M. (eds.). 1992. *Hidden Conflict in Organizations*. Newbury Park: Sage.

Kostova, T. and Roth, K. 2002. Adoption of an organizational practice by subsidiaries of multinational corporations: institutional and relational effects. *Academy of Management Journal*, 45(1): 215–233.

Kostova, T., Roth, K. and Dacin, M. T. 2008. Institutional theory in the study of multinational corporations: a critique and new directions. *Academy of Management Review*, 33(4): 994–1006.

Kristensen, P. H. and Zeitlin, J. 2005. *Local Players in Global Games. The Strategic Constitution of a Multinational Corporation.* Oxford University Press.

Küpper, W. and Felsch, A. 2000. *Organisation, Macht und Ökonomie. Mikropolitik und die Konstitution organisationaler Handlungssysteme.* Wiesbaden: Westdeutscher Verlag.

Küpper, W. and Ortmann, G. 1986. Mikropolitik in Organisationen. *Die Betriebswirtschaft*, 46(5): 590–602.

Laclau, E. and Mouffe, C. 2001. *Hegemony and Socialist Strategy: Towards a Radical Democratic Politics.* London: Verso.

Latour, B. 1996. On actor-network theory: a few clarifications. *Soziale Welt*, 47: 369–381.

Lindenberg, S. 2001. Social rationality versus rational egoism. In J. Turner (ed.), *Handbook of Sociological Theory.* New York: Kluwer, 635–668.

Lindenberg, S., Fetchenhauer, D., Flache, A. and Buunk, B. 2006. Solidarity and prosocial behavior: a framing approach. In D. Fetchenhauer, A. Flache, B. Buunk and S. Lindenberg (eds.), *Solidarity and Prosocial Behavior.* Springer, 3–19.

Logemann, M. and Piekkari, R. 2015. Localise or local lies? The power of language and translation in the multinational corporation. *Critical Perspectives on International Business*, 11(1): 30–53.

Lukes, S. 2005. *Power: a Radical View.* New York: Palgrave Macmillan.

Machiavelli, N. 1998. *The Prince* (edited by Harvey C. Mansfield). University of Chicago Press.

March, J. G. 1962. The business firm as a political coalition. *Journal of Politics*, 24(4): 662–678.

    1988. *Decisions and Organizations.* Oxford: Basil Blackwell.

March, J. G. and Olson, J. (eds.). 1994. *Ambiguity and Choice in Organizations.* Oslo: Scandinavian University Press.

March, J. G. and Simon, H. A. 1958. *Organizations.* New York: Wiley.

Marti, I. and Mair, J. 2010. Bringing change into the lives of the poor: entrepreneurship outside traditional boundaries. In T. B. Lawrence, R. Suddaby and B. Leca (eds.), *Institutional Work: Actors and Agency in Institutional Studies of Organizations.* Cambridge University Press, 92–119.

Mintzberg, H. 1983. *Power In and Around Organizations.* Englewood Cliffs, NJ: Prentice Hall.

    1985. The organization as political arena. *Journal of Management Studies*, 22(2): 133–154.

Morrill, C., Zald, M. N. and Rao, H. 2003. Covert political conflict in organizations: challenges from below. *Annual Review of Sociology*, 29: 391–415.

Mudambi, R. and Navarra, P. 2004. Is knowledge power? Knowledge flows, subsidiary power and rent-seeking within MNCs. *Journal of International Business Studies*, 35(5): 385–406.

Mumby, D. K. 1998. Organizing men: power, discourse, and the social construction of masculinity (s) in the workplace. *Communication Theory*, 8(2): 164–183.

2001. Power and politics. In L. L. Putnam and F. M. Jablin (eds.), *The New Handbook of Organizational Communication: Advances in Theory, Research, and Methods*. Thousand Oaks, CA: Sage, 585–623.

Mumby, D. K. and Stohl, C. 1991. Power and discourse in organization studies: absence and the dialectic of control. *Discourse and Society*, 2(3): 313–332.

Munro, R. 2009. Actor-network theory. In S. R. Clegg and M. Haugaard (eds.), *The Sage Handbook of Power*. London: Sage, 125–139.

Narayanan, V. K. and Fahey, L. 1982. The micro-politics of strategy formulation. *Academy of Management Review*, 7(1): 25–34.

Neuberger, O. 2006. *Mikropolitik und Moral in Organisationen*, 2nd edn. Stuttgart: Lucius and Lucius.

Osterloh, M. 1983. *Handlungsspielräume und Informationsverarbeitung*. Bern/Stuttgart/Wien: Hans Huber Verlag.

Parsons, T. 1963. On the concept of influence. *Public Opinion Quarterly*, 27(1): 37–92.

Pearson d'Estrée, T. 2003. Dynamics. In S. Cheldelin, D. Druckman and L. Fast (eds.), *Conflict*. London: Continuum, 68–87.

Perrow, C. 1972. *Complex Organizations: a Critical Essay*. Glenview, IL: Scott Foresman.

Pettigrew, A. M. 1973/2001. *The Politics of Organizational Decision-making*. London: Tavistock/Routledge.

Pettigrew, A. M., Woodman, R. W. and Cameron, K. S. 2001. Studying Organizational Change and Development: Challenges for Future Research. *Academy of Management Journal*, 44(4): 697–713.

Pfeffer, J. 1981. *Power in Organizations*. Marshfield, MA: Pitman.

1992. *Managing with Power. Politics and Influence in Organizations*. Boston: Harvard Business School Press.

Pondy, L. R. 1967. Organizational conflict: concepts and models. *Administrative Science Quarterly*, 12(2): 296–320.

Prahalad, C. K. and Doz, Y. L. 1987. *The Multinational Mission: Balancing Local Demands and Global Vision*. New York: The Free Press.

Rokeach, M. 1973. *The Nature of Human Values*. New York: The Free Press.

Salancik, G. R. and Pfeffer, J. 1974. The bases and use of power in organizational decision making. The case of a university. *Administrative Science Quarterly*, 19(4): 453–473.

Schotter, A. and Beamish, P. W. 2011. Intra-organizational turbulences in multinational corporations. In C. Dörrenbächer and M. Geppert (eds.), *Politics and Power in the Multinational Corporation. The Role of Interests, Identities and Institutions*. Cambridge University Press, 191–230.

Silvia, P. J. 2001. Interest and interests: the psychology of constructive capriciousness. *Review of General Psychology*, 5: 270–290.

Simon, H. A. 1955. A behavioral model of rational choice. *Quarterly Journal of Economics*, 69(1): 99–118.

1957. *Models of Man, Social and Rational: Mathematical Essays on Rational Human Behavior in a Social Setting*. New York: John Wiley and Sons.

1979. Rational decision making in business organizations. *The American Economic Review*, 69(4): 493–513.

Thomas, K. 1976. Conflict and conflict management. In M. D. Dunnette (ed.), *Handbook of Industrial and Organizational Psychology*. Chicago: Rand McNally College Publishing Company, 889–935.

Vaara, E., Tienari, J., Piekkari, R. and Säntti, R. 2005. Language and the circuits of power in a merging multinational corporation. *Journal of Management Studies*, 42(3): 595–623.

Vigoda, E. 2003. *Developments in Organizational Politics: How Political Dynamics Affect Employee Performance in Modern Work Sites*. Cheltenham/UK: Edward Elgar.

Vigoda-Gadot, E. and Drory, A. (eds.). 2006. *Handbook of Organizational Politics*, 1st edn. Cheltenham: Edward Elgar.

Vroom, V. H. 1964. *Work and Motivation*. Oxford: Wiley.

Wall Jr, J. A. and Callister, R. R. 1995. Conflict and its management. *Journal of Management*, 21(3): 515.

Weber, M. 1976. *Wirtschaft und Gesellschaft. Grundriss der verstehenden Soziologie. Mit textkritischen Erläuterungen hrsg. von Johannes Winckelmann*, 5th edn. Tübingen: Mohr.

Weick, K. E. 1995. *Sensemaking in Organizations*. Thousand Oaks, CA: Sage.

Welch, D., Welch, L. and Piekkari, R. 2005. Speaking in tongues: the importance of language in international management processes. *International Studies of Management and Organization*, 35(1): 10–27.

Whyte, W. H. 1957/2013. *The Organization Man*. Philadelphia: University of Pennsylvania Press.

Wildavsky, A. 1987. Choosing preferences by constructing institutions: a cultural theory of preference formation. *American Political Science Review*, 81(1): 3–21.

3 | The evolution of a politics perspective of the multinational enterprise – past developments and current applications

FLORIAN A. A. BECKER-RITTERSPACH AND
SUSANNE BLAZEJEWSKI

Introduction

When the field of international business and management (IB&M) saw its emergence about fifty years ago with the seminal contribution of Hymer (1960), the question of how politics, power and conflict influence the organizational behaviour in and of the multinational corporation (MNC) was not a central concern of research. However, since these early contributions of mainly economists, the consideration of power, politics and conflict has come a long way. At some general level we can say that its consideration has gone hand-in-hand with the overall development of the field of IB&M, that is, a broadening of perspectives from early economist perspectives to an increasing attention to the nature of the MNC through different firm and organization theoretical lenses. It is in particular the introduction of advances in organization studies to the field of IB&M that ultimately paves the way for seeing MNCs as political entities. The theorization of MNCs as political entities ultimately entails seeing them as constituted by diverse actors with different interests and sources of power and whose ability to realize their own interests or suppress the interests of others can only be understood in association with the environmental embeddedness of actors within and outside of the organization.

In this chapter we argue that understanding the past developments in the IB&M literature on politics, power and conflict broadly follows the trajectory of major paradigmatic shifts in organization theory and their introduction to the field of IB&M. These paradigmatic shifts can be identified with Scott (1998) on two dimensions, that is, from closed- to open-system models on the first and from rational- to natural-system models on the second dimension. The first dimension

51

entails a shift from seeing organizations as self-contained towards seeing them as 'embedded in – dependent on continuing exchanges with and constituted by – the environments in which they operate' (Scott 1998: 28). This shift towards seeing organizations as open system also implies viewing organization–environment relations as 'shifting, ambiguous and arbitrary' (Scott 1998: 27). The second dimension entails a shift from seeing organizations as monolithic, purpose- and goal-driven entities constituted by formal structure towards seeing them as having often *diffuse and conflicting goals*. It views organizations as 'collectives whose participants are pursuing multiple interests, both disparate and common' and where the 'informal structure of relations that develop among participants provides a more informative and accurate guide to understanding organizational behaviour than the formal' (Scott 1998: 26). We could also say, it is mostly the shift from *rational-* to *natural-system* perspectives that introduces politics, power and conflict perspectives through the recognition of interest diversity and contradiction, as well as the recognition of asymmetric abilities of different (groups of) actors to realize their interests or to suppress those of others. The shift from *rational-* to *natural-system* perspectives also brings with it a shift from rationalistic-managerialist perspectives to critical perspectives that take a broader stakeholder view, focusing particularly on weaker or marginalized stakeholders.

Theoretical shifts in IB&M

We will show that understanding the development of politics, power and conflict perspectives in IB&M can be adequately mapped by accounting for the influences from organization theory that mark a shift in both research fields from closed- to open- and from rational- to natural-system perspectives. Specifically, while the first recognition of power, politics and conflict in IB&M is mostly reflective of the advent of open-rational-system perspectives of MNCs – mainly through contingency, network and resource dependence perspectives originating in the field of organization studies – the full fledged recognition of politics, power and conflict in MNCs is connected to the introduction of open-natural-system perspectives as reflected in micropolitical and discursive perspectives (see Table 3.1).

In this chapter, we investigate the evolution of generic organizational politics perspectives in IB&M. Organizational politics perspectives see organizations as political systems that are constituted by diverse

Table 3.1 *IB&M theories in the open/closed and rational/natural system grid*

	Rational (economic constitution)	Natural (social constitution)
Closed	Hymer's industrial order approach Internalization theory Learning, knowledge and capability perspectives	–
Open	Contingency theory Business network perspective Subsidiary initiative perspective	New institutional theory Comparative capitalism Micropolitical perspective Critical discursive perspective

actors with idiosyncratic interests. In this view, conflicting interests and the strategic use of power are constitutive of organizational life (see Chapter 2). In the following mapping of the field, we present ten major perspectives, which are broadly aligned with the historical development of the field and are reflective of the paradigmatic shifts from closed to open and rational to natural models. We will show that this classification is very useful for the questions of how politics, power and conflict have developed in the field of IB&M. Specifically, we interrogate the respective perspectives as to whether actor diversity, goal and interest diversity, conflict and power asymmetry are considered and whether and how their environmental relation or constitution is theorized. We will show that the nature of actors and their behavioural orientation as well as the environmental constitution of actors and their agency vary substantially by perspective. As part of this discussion, we will also illustrate what the focal empirical phenomenon of organizational behaviour in the MNC is and how the units and levels of analysis shift. Finally, although we present the development of politics, power and conflict perspectives in IB&M as a historical trajectory, a word of caution is required. Rather than suggesting a linear trend or one perspective replacing the other over time, we see more of an addition and diversification through the introduction of new perspectives. Importantly, as we try to capture main developments and streams, we cannot do justice to all ramifications in the field. Starting with the early works in the field, we focus instead on the main developments that have contributed to the emergence of an organizational politics perspective on the MNC (see Table 3.2 for an overview).

Table 3.2 *Politics, power and conflict perspectives in IB&M*

Theory/approach	Unit of analysis	Nature of actors and behaviour orientation	Actor-context relations	Theorization of politics, power and conflict
Hymer and the internalization theory	MNCs as a homogenous class of firms	MNCs as unitary and coherent actors Rational actor perspective (respond to market imperfections)	Market imperfections constitute emergence of MNCs Actor-context or firm-environment relations not elaborated	Not explicitly theorized Limited aspectual politics perspective in form of opportunistic behaviour Power assumed at top of hierarchy
Learning, knowledge and capability perspective	MNC as whole/subsidiaries	Varies between MNCs as coherent and divergent organizational actors Rational actor perspective	Market imperfections constitute emergence of MNCs Emerging emphasis on relevance of local/host context for MNC behaviour	Not explicitly theorized
Contingency theory	MNC as whole/subsidiaries	MNCs as divergent organizational actors Rational actor perspective	Nature of task and market environment as crucial for constitution and behavioural orientation of MNCs	Aspectual politics perspective Power theorized to limited extent Recognises organizational interest divergence and conflict in MNCs
Business network perspective	Subsidiary/different units in MNC	MNCs as divergent organizational actors Between rational and natural actor perspective	Internal and external business networks embeddedness as crucial for constitution and behavioural orientation of MNC subunits	Generic politics perspective Organizational power and its roots considerably theorized Recognises organizational interest divergence and

perspective		individual actors Between rational and natural actor perspective	crucial for constitution and behavioural orientation of MNC subunits	roots considerably theorized Recognizes organizational interest divergence and conflict in MNCs
New institutionalism	MNC as whole/subsidiaries	MNCs as divergent organizational actors Emerging natural actor perspective	Dual institutional embeddedness in MNC and local/host context as crucial for constitution and behavioural orientation of MNC subunits	Not explicitly theorized Recognizes conflicting institutional pressures in subsidiaries
Comparative capitalism	MNC as whole/subsidiaries	MNCs as divergent organizational actors Emerging natural actor perspective	Home and host institutional embeddedness as crucial for constitution and behavioural orientation of MNC and its subunits	Emerging generic politics perspective Some theorization of power Some recognition of conflict in MNCs
Micropolitical perspective	Suborganizational level/individual actors	MNCs as divergent organizational and individual actors Natural actor perspective	Multilevel situatedness as crucial for constitution and behavioural orientation of individual actors	Generic politics perspective Individual actor power and its roots considerably theorized Developed conflict perspective at organizational and individual level
Critical discursive perspective	Different units in MNC/actor groups	MNCs as divergent organizational and groups of actors Natural actor perspective	Organizational situatedness and wider societal and discourses as crucial for constitution and discursive strategies of actor groups	Generic politics perspective Power of actor groups and its roots considerably theorized Developed conflict perspective at organizational and actor group level

From closed-rational to open-rational perspectives of the MNC

Following the seminal work of Hymer (1960) and Vernon (1966) in the 1960s, that marks the beginning of the field of IB&M, the 1970s saw the emergence of two dominant streams in IB&M – the internalization and the capability-based view of the MNC. The key focus of both streams is how and why firms internationalize. While the internalization stream sees the main answer to these questions in market failure, the capability-based view sees the answer in firm specific capabilities. Both of these streams are still present in a wide range of contributions to this day. Starting with Dunning's (1988) ownership–location–internalization (OLI) paradigm, there have been increasing efforts to integrate the two perspectives (e.g. Rugman *et al.* 2011; Dunning and Lundan 2008). We will start the discussion briefly with Hymer, who has been the first to theorize on the nature of MNCs, before we move on to the internalization and capability perspectives.

Economic perspectives

Hymer's theory of the multinational firm
Theory, proponents and empirical focus: Hymer's (1960) theory of foreign direct investment (FDI) is seen by many as seminal for the foundation of the field of IB&M (e.g. Forsgren 2008; Rugman *et al.* 2011; Ietto-Gilles 2012). Hymer's work is based on industrial organization theories 'showing that the MNC is an institution for international production rather than international exchange' (Rugman *et al.* 2011: 758). Hymer's (1960) early work centres on the question: why do MNCs engage in FDI or, put differently, why do firms internationalize? Rejecting earlier 'portfolio theory' with its explanatory focus on macroeconomic international capital movements, Hymer (1960) is among the first who shifts the analytical level in IB&M from the country level to the firm (Rugman *et al.* 2011).

Nature of actors and behavioural orientation: Hymer's (1960) industrial organization theory treats MNCs as unitary or monolithic actors. Seeing MNCs as rather homogenous types of firms, Hymer argues that they possess monopolistic advantages, which can be internationally exploited, outweighing their liability of foreignness in a host country (Rugman *et al.* 2011). While Hymer introduces a firm focus, MNCs are not treated in a differentiated way but rather as a class of firms that share similar properties. In this view the organizational behaviour, that is, the internationalization of the firm, is driven by opportunities to exploit market imperfections. These market imperfections provide MNCs with specific advantages that can be exploited abroad and serve to increase the firm's market power. Next to exploiting specific advantages, MNCs internationalize to remove impending or manifest conflict with rival firms through collusion or acquisitions in foreign markets (Ietto-Gilles 2012). Either way, firms are conceptualized as rationally acting entities that internationalize to exploit, secure and expand market power.

Actor-context relations: In Hymer's (1960) perspective the organizational environment is not extensively theorized. It involves different business environments, which comprise mainly market conditions/ imperfections and other firms (Forsgren 2008; Rugman *et al.* 2011). Specifically, drawing on industrial organization theory, Hymer (1960) sees the roots of firm-specific advantages in different market imperfections, which are particularly prominent in certain industries (Forsgren 2008; Rugman *et al.* 2011). Forsgren summarizes this as follows:

Firm-specific advantages reflect deviations from perfect competition, that is, market imperfections. Market imperfection offers some firms the ability to exploit an asset in a more profitable way than others (that is, than host country firms). This ability constitutes both a prerequisite and a trigger for such investments, as firms want to grow and earn more money by expanding to new markets. (Forsgren 2008: 28)

Hence, although theorized rather weakly, the environment conditions – output market imperfections in particular – are important to understand the internationalization behaviour of MNCs (Rugman *et al.* 2011).

Summary: Hymer's (1960) work marks the beginning of the field of IB&M through recognizing the MNC as a crucial unit of analysis and an important actor in border-crossing business activities. Hymer's (1960) perspective offers, however, no differentiated treatment of MNCs, let alone a focus on divergent actors, politics, power and conflict within them. Similarly, the firm environment receives no differentiated treatment. Nevertheless, the firm environment plays a role in understanding the organizational behaviour of the MNC. For it is the idea that market imperfections give rise to specific firm advantage, which serves as a prerequisite and a trigger for the expansion into international markets.

From internalization theory to Dunning's OLI paradigm
Theory, proponents and empirical focus: In the 1970s and 1980s we see a growing interest in the question of why MNCs come into being. It marks the beginning of a large and still developing body of work that falls under the label of internalization theory (e.g. Buckley and Casson 1976, 2009; Rugman 1981; Hennart 1982). The main theoretical foundation of this work has been transaction cost theory, building on the seminal work of Coase (1937). In contrast to Hymer (1960), the key interest in internalization theory is less about the prerequisites of firm internationalization as it is about the reasons why firms prefer to internalize border-crossing market transactions over arm's length market transaction (Forsgren 2008).

Nature of actors and behavioural orientation: The focal question in this stream is 'why firms become involved in international production' (Rugman *et al.* 2011: 759). In this view, the organizational behaviour of MNCs is based on the goal of maximizing profits by reducing transaction costs through internalization in imperfect markets. More specifically, internalization theorists argue that firms internationalize in order to reduce the higher costs involved in transactions in imperfect goods and factor markets (e.g. Buckley and Casson 1976; Casson 1979; Rugman 1981).

The essential argument of internalization theory is that firms aim at maximizing profit by internalizing their intermediate markets (typically the markets for intangible assets such as technology, production knowhow, brands, etc.) across national borders in the face of various market imperfections (such as the public goods externality associated with pricing an intermediate product like knowledge, the lack of future markets, information asymmetries between buyers and sellers, government intervention in the form of trade barriers or the ineffective application of the national patent system). (Rugman 2011: 759)

Complementarily, Hennart (1982, 2001, 2009) sees the existence of MNCs rooted in the higher firm efficiency and internalization advantage in imperfect markets:

An MNE will expand abroad when it can organize interdependencies
between agents located in different countries more efficiently than markets.
(Hennart 2001: 132)

In the internalization theory, the emergence of the MNC is a side-
effect of the firm's efforts in reducing cost/increasing efficiency in
those transactions that happen to be border-crossing (Rugman *et al.*
2011).

    While Hymer (1960) makes out structural market imperfections
as the prerequisite for firm internationalization, internalization theorists see transactional market imperfections as the driver of firm internationalization (Ietto-Gilles 2012). The latter implies a concern with
the MNC as an organizational entity because it starts asking about
the costs and benefits of internal as compared to external (market)
transactions. Firms are in this view hierarchies in which transactions
are coordinated through planning and direction (Ietto-Gilles 2012).
Internalization scholars also start viewing MNCs as hierarchies that
need to coordinate and control diverse actors including employees and
subsidiaries. In essence, the perspective starts conceding indirectly the
presence of diverse actors and interests through the need to monitor
and control opportunistic behaviour (i.e. their cheating and shirking
in particular) in MNCs (Forsgren 2008). In this sense, the approach
recognizes diverse actors and opportunistic behaviour that challenge
the organization as a rational system. At the same time, the rational
view of the MNC as a whole remains largely unchallenged. MNCs are
hierarchies in which internationalization choices are rationally made
based on an informed comparison of the costs and benefits of different
modes of transaction. Although power is not explicitly theorized, it is
implicitly assumed at the top of the hierarchy. Again, it manifests in
the managerial ability to rationally plan, direct and control the organizational behaviour in the MNC in line with the organization's goals.

    *Nature of the environmental constitution of actors and their
behavioural orientation:* Being a rather inward-looking perspective,
internalization theory does not theorize the firm's environment extensively. Yet, as background institutions, markets, or rather imperfect
markets, increase transaction costs for market transactions and lead
to preferences for border-crossing internalization. Similar to Hymer
(1960), a key explanation for MNC behaviour is found in market

imperfections, yet of a different kind. In this view, market imperfections are less related to monopoly rents (abnormal profits due to market structure or barriers to entry). Instead, they are transactional in nature (Ietto-Gilles 2012) such as small numbers bargaining, bounded rationality, opportunism and uncertainty in combination with the nature of the activities involved in the economic transaction (Forsgren 2008). More specifically, the more intangible and knowledge-intensive the activity, the higher the transaction costs and the more inefficient cross-border market transactions between independent market partners (Rugman *et al.* 2011).

The limited consideration of the environment in the internalization theory changes with its extension by John Dunning (1988). Dunning's (1988) 'eclectic framework' is among the first perspectives to theorize how the nature and variance of host environments constitute the organizational behaviour of the multinational firm. Specifically, next to the ownership/firm (*cf.* Hymer) and internalization advantages (*cf.* internalization scholar), Dunning's approach recognizes location-specific advantages as a crucial component in explaining firm internationalization. These location advantages include, for example, skilled labour or public infrastructure (Dunning 1998). Extending the internalization theory, Dunning's work clearly adds a differentiated concern for the MNC's business environments and how these affect firm internationalization and foreign market entry behaviour.

Summary: Although internalization perspectives start to adopt differentiated actor perspectives, as manifested in the problem of control of opportunistically behaving actors, the MNC remains a unitary actor that can maintain overall organizational rationality. Like other economist perspectives, the approach essentially retains an 'apolitical view' of the MNC, not least because the organizational hierarchy and its top managerial actors are seen as fully informed, goal rational and able to fully control organizational and individual behaviour (see also Geppert and Dörrenbächer 2014). There is no elaborate theorization of the external environment of the firm and as to how organizational environments constitute the organizational behaviour in and of the MNC. The environmental constitution of organizational behaviour is relegated to market imperfections that condition transaction cost reducing responses. While the emergence of Dunning's OLI framework marks a shift in IB&M from more closed- to open-system models of the MNC, economic perspectives, including the OLI perspective, leave little room for divergent actors and interests in the MNC, let alone for power struggles and conflict or the contextual constitution of politics, power and conflict.

Learning, knowledge and capability-based theory of the multinational enterprise

From the Uppsala model to Rugman's CSA-FSA framework
Theory, proponents and empirical focus: The development of the internalization school and the OLI framework at the end of the 1970s was paralleled by the emergence of another stream of research which we would like to broadly label the learning, knowledge and capability stream (see also Forsgren 2008). While this work builds on different theoretical roots, it shares a concern with understanding the organizational behaviour from within the firm. In addition, it is based on a refined understanding of the specific qualities, abilities and advantages of the internationalizing firm. These qualities and abilities are mainly knowledge related. Specifically, it is the MNC's knowledge base and capability to efficiently transfer, absorb and generate knowledge that constitutes the emergence of MNCs, their internationalization patterns and competitive advantages. We discuss here three streams that fall under this body of work. The first one emerged in the late 1970s and is generally associated with Johanson and Wiedersheim (1975) and Johnson and Vahlne's (1977, 1990) 'Uppsala model'. The model has been later taken up by other, mainly Scandinavian, scholars (Luostarinen 1980; Larimo 1985; Gandemo and Mattsson 1984; Juul and Walters 1987). It builds on Cyert and March's (1963/1992) behavioural theory of the firm but also on work by Penrose (1959). Empirically, this stream is primarily concerned with understanding how firms internationalize, that is, their process of internationalization. This involves, for instance, the questions of which foreign markets firms chose to enter, and how foreign investments and forms of market entry evolve over time. The second stream we discuss developed in the 1990s and is mainly associated with the contributions of Kogut and Zander (1992, 1993/2003), in particular their knowledge-based theory of the multinational corporation. Contesting internalization theory, they draw on the foundational work of Teece (1977) on technology transfer in multinationals. Their interest centres on the questions of which mode

of entry internationalizing firms choose in transferring different kinds of knowledge across borders, and relatedly, how this gives rise to the emergence of the MNC. The third stream is the competence-based or technology accumulation approach developed by Cantwell and colleagues (Cantwell 1989, 1994; Cantwell and Piscitello 1999; Cantwell and Santangelo 2000). This work builds on the resource-based view of the firm (e.g. Penrose 1959; Wernerfelt 1984; Barney 1991) and the related evolutionary view of the firm (Nelson and Winter 1982). Contributions that fall under this stream are interested in MNCs as evolving networks of innovation (Cantwell 1989). A guiding question in this body of work is: 'why it is that technology is developed in international networks' (Cantwell 2009: 424). This perspective also addresses the increasing geographical spread of innovation in MNCs (Cantwell and Zhang 2009). The fourth stream, which we cover only in brief, is the recent work by Rugman and colleagues (e.g. Rugman *et al.* 2011). This work is in a way an amalgam of the previous perspectives in that it not only integrates core ideas of the different learning, knowledge and capability streams, but also includes key ideas of internalization theory.

Nature of actors and behavioural orientation: In the Uppsala model, the organizational behaviour under investigation revolves around two issues: (i) the selection and sequence of foreign market entry; and (ii) the market commitment as expressed in shifting modes of entry. However, while there is some interest in the development of foreign investments in terms of increasing market commitment, there is little interest in subsidiary specific differences or initiatives. Foreign operations are seen as tightly aligned and coordinated by strategic considerations of the corporate headquarters. Although the external environment plays some role in this framework, it is firm internal conditions, that is, past internationalization experience, knowledge base and 'experiential market knowledge' (Johanson and Vahlne 1990) that drive the strategic choices of market entry and increased market commitment through changing modes of entry. Hence, the Uppsala model builds on the importance of market knowledge and experiential learning within the MNC. At the same time, it shows little consideration for how knowledge- or learning-related processes play out among the different actors that constitute an MNC. The perspective shows little concern for different actors, politics, power or conflict. The MNC remains a unitary actor that behaves rationally by engaging in a logical and sequential process of internationalization and market commitment.

Similar to the Uppsala model, Kogut and Zander (1993) see the MNC as a unitary and coherent unit that acts rationally in its internationalization efforts. For Kogut and Zander (1993: 625) firms are 'social communities that specialize in the creation and internal transfer of knowledge'. They argue that it is the community of employees, their shared understanding based on repeated interactions and their cooperation based on their identification with the firm that constitutes a superior capability in generating and transferring knowledge (Kogut and Zander 1993).

Cooperation within an organization leads to a set of capabilities that are easier to transfer within the firm than across organizations and constitute the ownership advantage of the firm. These capabilities consist as well of the capacity to grow and develop through the recombination of existing elements of the knowledge of the firm and its members. It is this notion of the firm as a repository of social knowledge that structures cooperative action that lies at the foundation of an evolutionary theory of the multinational corporation. (Kogut and Zander 1993: 627)

Foreign direct investment is essentially an organizational extension of the firm's community and knowledge-related coordination capabilities across borders. While both the MNC as networks of subsidiaries and their constitution by individuals or employees finds recognition, the focus on community, identification and cooperation implies little concern with potentially divergent behavioural orientations of the different actors within the MNC. In this perspective, the MNC is a seamless and frictionless entity. The MNC is a predominantly harmonious community in which knowledge is efficiently developed and readily shared across borders as long as it stays in the firm. While the approach sees MNCs as social communities, that is, as constituted by individual actors and their communication and interaction, this social behaviour is aligned with the behavioural orientation of the firm as a whole. Hence, although individual actors find recognition, it is the behaviour of the MNC as a whole that remains the main unit of analysis. The focal behavioural question is why do firms grow across borders?

Firms grow on their ability to create new knowledge and to replicate this knowledge so as to expand their market. Their advantage lies in being able to understand and carry out this transfer more effectively than other firms.

Horizontal foreign direct investment is, therefore, the transfer of knowledge within the firm and across borders, and in this regard, such transfers are the primary expression of the growth of the firm. (Kogut and Zander 1993: 639)

The behavioural driver of MNCs is their ambition to grow. Growth through foreign direct investment, in turn, is constituted by two conditions: first, the firm's superior organizational capability to transfer knowledge – in particular, knowledge that is difficult to understand and to codify – and second, the firm's 'combinative capability' (Kogut and Zander 1992). When expanding the organizational boundaries through foreign direct investment, this capability allows generating and internally exploiting new knowledge through recombining extant with new market knowledge (Kogut and Zander 1993).

Cantwell's (2009) competence-based approach shares the main contentions of Kogut and Zander (1993). He also understands MNC behaviour as constituted by firm-specific knowledge-related capabilities. These are to a large degree human-based, social and collective in nature and therefore not readily tradeable (Cantwell 1991, 2009). However, his perspective emphasises that learning and innovation in MNCs is not only firm- but also location-specific. He argues that the ability to continuously learn and innovate is crucially connected to entering foreign environments. This implies that the 'asset seeking' motive of MNCs becomes a key driver for foreign direct investment (Cantwell 1989). In this view, the MNC is an innovation network or system that ensures competitive advantage through its ability to build and coordinate international or multipolar learning.

The competitive advantage of established or mature MNCs increasingly stems... from their abilities to build and control a network of global flows of information, resources and people. This ability to create global networks, utilize geographically specialized resources and transfer knowledge between different knowledge-creating nodes lies at the core of many current conceptualizations of the MNC (Cantwell and Mudambi 2005; Hakanson 1993, 1995). (Cantwell 2013: 21)

While Cantwell's view entails some attention to the network of subsidiaries and subsidiaries as key sources and sites of knowledge development (see Cantwell and Mudambi 2005) and recently acknowledges (Cantwell 2009) that intersubsidiary differentiation may go hand-in-hand with different subsidiary power and influence, politics, power and conflict do not play a role in this perspective. Similarly, while the evolutionary perspective that underlies the approach entails that the development of international MNC networks of innovation evolve over time and 'are not the outcome of the introduction of some readily made and planned structure' (Cantwell 2009: 428), there is an underlying assumption that the respective steps taken are rational and that the MNC has the ability to orchestrate its internationally dispersed innovation processes.

Actor-context relations: Although firm behaviour is mainly explained through internal knowledge and learning, the environment plays a role in the Uppsala model. The differences of international market environments, that is, the lack of foreign market knowledge create a 'liability of foreignness' for the internationalizing firm (Rugman *et al.* 2011). Conceptualized as 'psychic distance' (Johanson and Vahlne 1977), the differences among foreign environments create barriers to internationalization. Johanson and Wiedersheim (1975: 18) define 'psychic distance' as 'factors preventing or disturbing the flows of information between firms and market'. These factors include a wide range of differences such as cultural, lingual and economic as well as political and legal differences. The environmental distance implies that firms internationalize incrementally, that is, entering first more familiar or proximate foreign markets and reaching out gradually to more distant ones as foreign market experience grows. As part of their incremental approach, firms also opt at first for low commitment modes of market entry and increase their market commitment as local market experience grows. Hence, in this view, organizational behaviour is driven by the interplay of firm exposure to new market environments (external) and experiential learning (internal).

Compared to the Uppsala model, the evolutionary perspective of the MNC by Kogut and Zander (1993) gives less attention to the external environment of the firm. Here, the environment is populated with competing firms, rather than composed of abstract markets. Similar to the work by Johanson and Vahlne (1977), the foreign market environment is a source of incremental learning. Importantly, we find in this work an emerging recognition of learning opportunities in foreign markets as a driver for firm internationalization.

The initial entry serves in this regard as a platform that recombines the firm's knowledge acquired in its home market with the gradual accumulation of learning in the foreign market. In a final stage of this process, the learning from the foreign market is transferred internationally and influences the accumulation and recombination of knowledge throughout the network of subsidiaries, including the home market. (Kogut and Zander 1993/2003: 523)

However, the learning from foreign markets and the firm–environment interaction in the recombination and generation of new knowledge is assumed rather than theorized in an elaborate way. The role of the external environment for understanding the organizational behaviour of MNCs remains undertheorized.

While Kogut and Zander (1993) do not pay too much attention to the nature of the external environments, this is different in Cantwell's work (1989). On the one hand, the external environment comes into the picture at a general level, that is, in the form of the technological competition among firms that drives their innovation orientation (Cantwell 2009). On the other hand, it is the different foreign environments, with their different 'local capabilities' or 'technological strengths' (Cantwell and Piscitello 1999) that provide the breeding ground for 'complementary innovations' (Cantwell 2009).

In the technological accumulation approach, innovation is not just essentially created in the home country and then diffused abroad, but rather created in multiple geographically dispersed centres of excellence and fed back into further innovation on other parts of the MNC corporate group. One implication is that different MNCs follow a variety of strategies with respect of the types of the activities they locate in a given site, depending on their existing corporate capabilities and hence specialized nature of their absorptive capacity. (Cantwell and Zhang 2009: 56)

The expansion of international production thereby brings gains to the firms as a whole, as the experience gained from adapting its technology under new conditions feeds back new ideas for development to the rest of its system. (Cantwell 2009: 427)

Different countries and world regions are vested with different levels of technological strengths which structure the locational choices in research and development. Divergent local opportunities co-evolve with firm capabilities. In other words, different local environmental conditions in combination with firm capabilities become key incentives and drivers for firm internationalization and location choices. What is more, in some of Cantwell's contributions, abstract conceptions of local technology environments are replaced with specific considerations about the relations between foreign investors and local firms (e.g. Cantwell and Iammarino 1998, 2000; Cantwell and Santangelo 2000).

The emergence of the knowledge, learning and capability stream in IB&M marks the beginning of a deeper conceptualization of MNCs as unique organizational entities based on their knowledge and learning abilities. While Johanson and Vahlne (1977) introduce the crucial notion of knowledge, learning and distance for the behaviour of MNCs, Kogut and Zander (1993) and Cantwell (1989), emphasize the firm-specific and location-specific nature of knowledge and learning in MNCs respectively. The on-going relevance of these streams manifests not only in the growing body of knowledge transfer and learning literature in IB&M, but most prominently in recent efforts to combine internalization and resource-based views. Rugman and Verbeke's recent CSA-FSA framework is in many ways an integration of the three streams discussed above. Rugman *et al.* (2011) argue that the organizational behaviour of the MNC is driven by the combinations and interactions of country-specific advantages (CSAs) and firm-specific advantages (FSAs). While CSAs can involve the home and host country, FSAs can be either location bound (LB FSAs) or transferable, that is, non-location bound (NLB FSAs). A key challenge for MNCs is to turn home or host country CSAs and related LB FSAs into NLB FSAs. This transformation is the prerequisite for a new round of asset generation wherein MNCs exploit NLB FSAs in new contexts by recombining them with new CSA and related LB CSAs. For Rugman *et al.* (2011) 'the key scholarly and managerial challenge in IB, irrespective of the unit of analysis selected, is to understand properly how "distance" affects the transferability, deployability, recombination and profitable exploitation across borders of (quasi-) proprietary know-how, whether in the form of stand-alone competences or higher-order capabilities' (Rugman *et al.* 2011: 768). MNC's organizational behaviour is essentially driven by the opportunities and constraints to internationally leverage CSAs and FSAs and recombine them.

Summary: While the beginning of this stream treats the MNC as a unitary rational actor, this perspective modifies over time – largely due to an adoption of other parallel developments in the IB&M literature. Integrating insights from contingency theory, business network and subsidiary initiative literature (see discussion below), the stream acknowledges that MNCs are constituted by networks of subsidiaries, that individual subsidiaries can play a pivotal role in knowledge generation and learning and that it is individuals and their interaction that make up much of what constitutes the knowledge or capability and organizational behaviour of the MNC. At the same time, there is only little recognition that the different actors in the MNC follow divergent interests, engage in politics and conflict and use power to realize their interests. This has also gone hand-in-hand with a criticism as to how individual behaviour on the micro-level constitutes knowledge processes in MNCs (Foss and Pedersen 2004). In the learning, knowledge and capability stream, the MNC is, as Forsgren (2008) succinctly puts it, 'one big happy family'. This perspective also implies that the overall rationality of the MNC is largely assumed, which is also true for its most integrated and recent derivatives (e.g. Rugman *et al.* 2011). While the learning, knowledge and capability streams clearly view the MNC as a rational system, they mark a shift from closed to open system approaches. Moving beyond internalization theory's limited consideration of the environment, this stream involves an increasing refinement of the nature and role of external environments for the behaviour of the MNC.

From open-rational to open-natural perspectives of the MNC

In the 1980s and 1990s the field of IB&M sees the introduction of a range of organization theories that propel the shift from closed- to open-system models. At the heart of these perspectives lies a strong theorization of the firm–environment nexus. The perspective that we discuss first is the contingency theory. Heralding the beginning of open-rational perspectives in IB&M, contingency theory is increasingly extended, combined and partly replaced by other theoretical perspectives such as the network, intraorganizational power, resource dependence and agency perspectives. While these additions to and replacements of contingency theory increasingly acknowledge that MNCs are made up of divergent actors and interests and that politics, power and conflict are parts of organizational life, they do not entail the adoption of a developed natural-system perspective. Similarly, while power and conflict become an integral part of theorization and are seen as a natural concomitant of managing complex organizations across diverse environments, there is still a belief that organizational rationality can be maintained.

Contingency theory

The environment-strategy-structure paradigm

Theory, proponents and empirical focus: The contingency perspective is probably first introduced into IB&M by the work of Stopford and Wells (1972) in the 1970s. Their key observation is that internationalizing firms go through different structural configurations as their international product diversity and the importance of foreign operations increases. While early work in this stream shares with the work of Johansson and Vahlne (1977) an interest in the evolution of the internationalizing firm, the focus of attention shifts towards the strategic management of the international firm (Westney and Zaheer 2009). Resembling the foundational work of Chandler (1962) and Lawrence and Lorsch (1967), the empirical focus of the contingency perspective rests on understanding the relationship between environmental demands and strategy and between strategy and organizational structure or processes (Prahalad and Doz 1987; Bartlett and Ghoshal 1989). Labelled also as the 'environment–strategy–structure paradigm' (e.g. Harzing 1999), contributions relate the organizational behaviour of MNCs and their subsidiaries to the variation in their internal and external environments.

Nature of actors and behavioural orientation: The contingency perspective gives up the unitary and coherent entity perspective of the MNC. Even early perspectives that adopt a hierarchical perspective of the MNC recognize that the different, often conflicting environmental pressures give rise to conflicting internal managerial perspectives within the MNC (e.g. Doz *et al.* 1981). Contingency theorists are among the first to explicitly account for interest divergence and conflict in MNCs. These divergent interests and conflict potentials are initially seen to unfold vertically between headquarters and subsidiaries (e.g. Doz *et al.* 1981; see also Roth and Nigh 1992; Pahl and Roth 1993) and also laterally between different units. These units compete with each other for resources, attention, strategic roles or mandates in MNCs (see below work on subsidiary initiatives). Starting in the mid-1980s, a developed divergent actor perspective emerges that gives up the hierarchical view of the MNC. This shift is introduced by the seminal contribution of Hedlund (1986), who sees MNCs as a 'heterarchy', and the work by Bartlett and Ghoshal (1989), who conceptualize MNCs as 'differentiated networks' or 'integrated networks'. Rather than seeing MNCs as hierarchies and the actor-relations within them as vertical dependencies, these contributions foster a new understanding of MNCs as networks of diverse actor relations. This also implies a clear recognition of actor and interest diversity in MNCs as well as a recognition of an asymmetric distribution of resources and power among those actors (Forsgren 2008). However, while there is recognition that the MNC is constituted by different actors, who have different behavioural orientations, the MNC is still seen as capable of integrating, that is, of managing diverse actors and behavioural orientations through appropriate organizational design and, more importantly, through mechanisms of social or normative integration (Bartlett and Ghoshal 1989; Nohria and Ghoshal 1997). In most of this work, which is published throughout the 1980s and 1990s, the organizational behaviour of the MNC is driven by the effort to produce strategic fit, that is, to adapt the organizational strategy and structure as well as processes to specific constellations of environmental pressures. What is more, while there is an acknowledgement of the enormous managerial challenge for the MNC, especially when different and conflicting pressures have to be responded to at the same time, there is also optimism that the overall organizational rationality can be maintained through appropriate organizational design and integration mechanisms. As we will demonstrate below for the business network and subsidiary initiative perspective, this overall organizational rationality assumption begins to fade as the unit of analysis shifts to the subsidiary and its local environment.

Actor-context relations: Contingency theory emphasizes the environmental constitution of organizations and their behavioural orientation. The very early work (e.g. Stopford and Wells 1972) sees organizational behaviour, that is, the structural evolution constituted by the changing internal task environment (e.g. foreign product diversity, dependence on foreign operations or ratio of foreign sales) of the MNC. Over time, however, the contingency perspective shifts its attention to the external market environment, to 'external selection pressures' (Westney and Zaheer 2009). It is the nature of the environment that forms the most important condition for understanding the behaviour of the international firm. The environmental situation of the MNC is captured most prominently by the global integration-local responsiveness dilemma facing MNCs. It essentially describes the question to which extent MNCs are exposed to and have to respond to the different environmental pressures 'for global integration' and 'for local responsiveness' (Prahalad and Doz 1987). Drawing on the developing learning, knowledge and capability perspective of the MNC, Bartlett and Ghoshal (1989) later also add a third set of environmental pressures, that is, the 'forces for world-wide innovation'. However, irrespective of the number of environmental forces included, the basic rationale of the approach remains the same. It is the rationale that different environmental pressures constitute the organizational behaviour of the MNC in the form of optimal strategic responses and organizational design solutions. Correspondingly, conflicting environmental pressures are also identified as a major source of conflict in MNCs. In essence, the pressures for global integration and local responsiveness lead to different goals, interests and conflict among the different subunits, that is, headquarters tilting more towards responding to organizational needs of global integration and subsidiaries towards the needs of local responsiveness (Doz and Prahalad 1984; Roth and Nigh 1992; Pahl and Roth 1993). In this view, divergent actors follow different organizational rationales or have different interests based on their organizational position that corresponds with the exposure to certain types of environmental pressures. As the level of analysis shifts from the MNC as a whole to intersubsidiary relations and subsidiary initiatives, the relevant environment includes both internal and external environment conditions. However, both early and more recent approaches (as we shall see below) share the view that the key actors and their behavioural orientations are based on environmental determinants. Non-economic and individual behavioural orientations that are disconnected from organizational goals and environments are not considered. The view also entails that actors adapt to environmental pressures but do not proactively influence their environments.

In summary: Contingency theory develops a differentiated understanding of organizational actors and behavioural orientations based on their organizational and environmental embeddedness. Although contingency perspectives recognize divergent actors in MNCs, mainly in the form of subsidiaries or their managerial representatives (e.g. Doz and Prahalad 1984), the approach rarely moves below the organizational level to non-managerial or individual stakeholders. While politics, power and conflict are not the main building block of the contingency approach, there is recognition that environment pressures constitute divergent actor orientations and conflict, which constitutes a major managerial challenge and calls for organizational solutions. In this view, conflict has a negative connotation. It is viewed as an

aberration from organizational efficiency that has to be managed
by means of appropriate organizational design and integration
mechanisms. However, where early approaches appear confident
that MNCs can reconcile divergent interests to maintain the overall
organizational rationality, more recent and theoretically extended
contingency approaches come to call this into question (e.g. Ambos
and Schlegelmilch 2007).

Integration of network, resource and intraorganizational power perspectives

In the 1990s, we see the development of two streams, the *business
network* and the *subsidiary initiative* perspective. Both streams build
on the 'differentiated network' perspective of the MNC and combine this perspective with other theoretical perspectives, most important of which is the intraorganizational power perspective and the
resource dependency perspective. In both streams, power, politics and
conflict become central to understanding the organizational behaviour
of MNCs and of subsidiaries in particular. Importantly, the construct of power is conceptualized explicitly in both streams. However,
the streams also differ in important ways. Where business network
approaches provide us with a fine-grained power and politics perspective of the subsidiary behaviour – which is largely understood through
the structural embeddedness of the subsidiary in network relations –
the subsidiary initiative stream starts moving beyond a mere structural
embeddedness perspective of politics and power in MNCs. To understand subsidiary power and politics, the subsidiary initiative stream
adopts a more individual-level perspective of subsidiary managerial
behaviour. This entails more attention to managerial interaction patterns, strategizing, games and politicking.

Business network perspective
Theory, proponents and empirical focus: The business network perspective emerges during the late 1990s. While building on earlier
notions of the MNC as a 'differentiated network' and the 'heterarchi-
cal' perspective of the MNC (e.g. Doz and Prahalad 1991; Nohria and
Ghoshal 1997; Hedlund 1993), business network scholars deepen the
network perspective by drawing more elaborately on network theory
(Håkansson 1982; Turnbull and Valla 1986; Cowley 1988; Håkansson
and Snehota 1995; Uzzi 1996, 1997) and other theory perspectives.

Among the latter, resource dependence theory (e.g. Pfeffer and Salancik 1978) and the intraorganizational power perspective (e.g. Astley and Sachdeva 1984) are of particular interest. Empirically, business network research stretches from understanding patterns of MNC internationalization (Forsgren *et al.* 2005) to the behaviour of MNC subunits. The latter involves a wide array of themes ranging from a scrutiny of subsidiary network embeddedness, subsidiary role and competence development (Andersson and Forsgren 2000; Andersson *et al.* 2001, 2002) or more generically subsidiary influence, strengths and importance (Anderson *et al.* 2007; Yamin and Andersson 2011) to a closer concern with headquarter roles and headquarter behaviour in more recent work.

Nature of actors and behavioural orientation: The business network approach radically departs from seeing the MNC as a harmonious and rational entity that can be efficiently coordinated and controlled by a central authority. MNCs are 'heterogeneous, loosely coupled organizations' in which headquarters are 'considered to be one player among several' (Forsgren 2008: 122). In this view, the MNC is full of struggles in which 'headquarters has to compete with different subunits for strategic influence' (Forsgren 2008: 122). Interest divergence and conflict is mainly seen between headquarters and subsidiaries but also among subsidiaries. Organizational behaviour in MNCs manifests as 'incessant bargaining processes . . . in which different subsidiaries and the headquarters use their power basis to gain influence' (Forsgren 2008: 122; see also Andersson *et al.* 2007). Rather than understanding the behaviour of the MNC as a whole, the business network view focuses on the behavioural rational of specific subunits (Andersson and Forsgren 2000; Andersson *et al.* 2007). For instance, while from a subsidiary's point of view the main behavioural goal is increasing strategic influence vis-à-vis headquarters and other subsidiaries, headquarters aims at diminishing the influence of powerful subsidiaries (Andersson *et al.* 2007). Much of the business network perspective has focused on subsidiary behaviour and the subsidiary as the focal unit of analysis. The subsidiary behaviour which finds attention in this stream involves, for instance, competence development and market performance of subsidiaries (Andersson and Forsgren 2000; Andersson *et al.* 2001, 2002) as well as more generic explorations into the bases of subsidiary influence in the MNCs (Andersson *et al.* 2007). It is important to note that more recent work in this stream has shifted attention from the subsidiary to the headquarters' behaviour (Ciabuschi *et al.* 2012; Andersson and Holm 2010; Forsgren and Holm 2010).

While the business network perspective's concern with politics, power and conflict is not very elaborate in the beginning, we see an increasing theorization of these constructs over time. Andersson *et al.* (2007) draw, for example, on a Weberian concept of power and define it as 'the ability of headquarters and subsidiaries to get things done, regardless of the motivation of and resistance from others within the MNC' (Andersson *et al.* 2007: 805). Drawing on resource dependence theory, Andersson *et al.* suggest that 'a subunit's access to resources that are crucial for other subunits in the federative MNC is the primary base of power'. Furthermore, they see not only network embeddedness or centrality but also 'knowledge about relevant networks' (Andersson *et al.* 2007: 806) as a crucial source of power. Forsgren *et al.* (2005) draw on both resource-dependence theory and intra-organizational power perspectives (e.g. Hickson *et al.* 1971) and see subsidiary power as based on both 'net dependencies of parties' with regard to resource exchanges between units (internally and externally) and power that is based on the 'position of the unit in a functional system' (Hickson *et al.* 1971: 143). The business network perspective not only entails that power in the MNC is unequally distributed, but also that different types of subunits can leverage different bases of power (Forsgren 2008). For instance, while subsidiaries can leverage their local business networks and their importance to other units within the MNC, headquarters may exploit, apart from its formal authority, its own network and its knowledge about other units' networks (Andersson and Forsgren 2000; Andersson *et al.* 2007; Forsgren 2008).

Politics and conflict among the different players in the MNC are an integral part of understanding the organizational behaviour in MNCs in the business network perspective. Accordingly, it gives up the contention that MNC headquarters or the MNC as a whole can maintain overall organizational rationality and normatively integrate the centrifugal behaviour of the divergent actors (Forsgren *et al.* 2005). In fact, the business network perspective even questions whether an overarching organizational rationality even exists or can exist. This contrasts sharply with contingency theory's assumption of powerful and knowledgeable headquarters. The notion of headquarters as orchestrating centres that fully oversee and understand environmental conditions throughout the MNC is dropped in the business network approach (Forsgren 2008). At the same time, business network scholars maintain the notion of organizational rationality at the level of organizational subunits. In this view, the subunits (subsidiaries and headquarters) act rationally in pursuing their own unit's interest and goals.

Actor-context relations: From early on scholars from the business network perspective emphasize (e.g. Andersson and Forsgren 2000) the environmental constitution of subunits goals and power. As Forsgren puts it:

> The impact of the environment on the organization is reflected, rather, in the interest that the different sub-units choose to pursue and in the resources they can use in the bargaining process. (Forsgren 2008: 102)

A core feature of the business network perspective is the fine-grained analysis of the nature of local or external network relationships of subsidiaries and how these constitute their organizational behaviour (Andersson *et al.* 2002, 2007). Focusing initially on the individual subsidiary, the firm's environment is conceived of as the subsidiary's business networks. While business network contributions consider both internal and external environments, there is a strong focus on network embeddedness in the external and local business context (Andersen and Forsgren 2000; Andersson *et al.* 2001, 2002; Forsgren 2008). Unlike in contingency theory, the external environment is also not conceived of as abstract market conditions or as 'general, aggregate characteristics', but rather as relationships between a focal unit and other specific economic actors (Andersson *et al.* 2007; Forsgren 2008). These comprise first and foremost customers and suppliers (Forsgren 2008).

In this view, subunit interests are derived from their network embeddedness. Subunit conflicts with other subunits are attributed to conflicting expectations that stem from their potentially dual embeddedness in corporate (internal) and (external) business network contexts (Forsgren 2008). In a similar vein, the subunits' power to carry through their interests is structured by their embeddedness in different networks. For it is the embeddedness in the internal and external network – and their interplay – that structures what knowledge and strategic resources can be leveraged (Forsgren 2008). Exploring, for instance, the 'network infusion' effect, Andersson and Forsgren (2000: 334) argue that 'the relationship with specific external counterparts constitutes an important base for the subsidiary's influence within the MNC' (see also Andersson *et al.* 2002).

In more recent studies business network scholars also considered the reverse relationship suggesting that subsidiaries' strongly tied into local networks may be more orientated towards developing and expanding within these, which implies both less headquarter influence on subsidiary behaviour but also less internal network bargaining power of the subsidiary (Andersson *et al.* 2007). Overall, the firm–environment relations in focus are the subsidiary–network partner relations, which are potentially transgressing both MNC and country borders. These relations are mainly conceptualized as resource exchange relationships that differ in depth. Understanding the behaviour of subsidiaries (or subunits), that is, their interests and their power to pursue them, depends in this stream on analyzing the position of organizational actors within networks and the structure and kind of the relationships with other actors.

Summary: The business network perspective sees MNCs as multiactor networks in which power is distributed unequally. While the social relationships among actors and the political nature of these relationships is central to the approach, this does not extend to microlevel actors and agency. The environment is constituted by other economic actors within and outside the MNC. The firm–environment relationship, that is, the contextual constitution of internationalization and behaviour, is based on understanding the nature of the network relationships of a focal unit with other economic actors inside and outside the MNC. The political perspective is considerably developed in this perspective given its focus on diverse actors who are embedded in business relations that structure actor interest, actor power and conflict among actors. At the same time, the political constitution of the MNC is limited to the focus on relationships among organizational-level actors. There is little concern with micro-level actors and agency at the subsidiary level, let alone with how individual-level actors and agency is constituted by the wider societal context.

Subsidiary initiative perspective
Theory, proponents and empirical focus: Starting in the late 1990s, we see the emergence of another research stream that can be broadly labelled the subsidiary initiative literature. The subsidiary initiative stream also combines the differentiated network perspective with a wider range of other theoretical perspectives that focus more explicitly on politics, power and conflict. These are, on the one hand,

resource-related perspectives, including resource- or knowledge-based views (Buckley and Casson 1976; Wernerfelt 1984; Barney 1991) and the resource-dependence approach (Pfeffer 1992, 1981; Salancik and Pfeffer 1977; Pfeffer and Salancik 1978). On the other hand, they revolve around intraorganizational power perspectives (Hickson *et al.* 1971; Hinings *et al.* 1974) and agency theory (Jensen and Meckling 1976). The empirical focus of these contributions centres on subsidiary initiatives (e.g. Birkinshaw *et al.* 1998; Birkinshaw and Ridderstrale 1999; Birkinshaw *et al.* 2005; Ambos *et al.* 2010; Williams and Lee 2011). More specifically, it centres on their antecedents, patterns and consequences. Contributions that fall under this stream include studies on the bargaining power of subsidiaries (Mudambi and Navarra 2004), headquarter attention for and issue-selling of subsidiaries (Ling *et al.* 2005; Bouquet and Birkinshaw 2008; Ambos and Birkinshaw 2010), subsidiary mandate/role or charter evolution (Birkinshaw and Hood 1998; Birkinshaw 2000) or intrafirm competition (Birkinshaw and Lingblad 2005). While subsidiary initiative contributions vary to some degrees in the theories they combine and in their empirical focus, they tend to have two features in common: they build on the concept of the MNC as a differentiated network and see politics, power and conflict as central for understanding organizational behaviour in MNCs.

Nature of actors and behavioural orientation: Subsidiary initiative approaches see MNCs alternatively as socio-political organizational systems (Birkinshaw and Ridderstrale 1999), socially constructed communities of subsidiary members (Bouquet and Birkinshaw 2008), cooperative systems of shifting coalitions (Ambos and Birkinshaw 2010) or political coalitions (Mudambi and Navarra 2004; Williams and Lee 2011) that are full of competition, conflicts and cooperation. Contributions in this stream move beyond a mere contingency theory and structural or network-based understanding of the behavioural orientation of actors in MNCs. While structural contingencies continue to play a role (particularly in the guise of a strategic contingency theory of intraorganizational power) in understanding organizational behaviour in MNCs, subsidiaries and their managers are seen to have a great deal of freedom to further their own goals and interests. Specifically, MNC units are perceived as semiautonomous or as actors with mixed motives (Ambos and Birkinshaw 2010; Ambos *et al.* 2010). Ambos *et al.* (2010) illustrate this in the context of subsidiary initiative as follows:

The headquarters views the initiative-taking subsidiary with ambivalence, as it seeks to ensure that it is in control (and on top of any risks the subsidiary might take) while also encouraging the subsidiary to fulfil its potential. The subsidiary – for its part – is interested in enhancing its own standing within the MNE network and increasing its degrees of freedom in decision-making, while also being seen to be a good corporate citizen. (Ambos *et al.* 2010: 1100)

While the subsidiary remains the key unit of analysis in the subsidiary initiative research, there is – in comparison to business network perspectives – a shift towards paying more attention to individual actors, their proactivity, communication, interaction, networking or behavioural strategies (e.g. Birkinshaw and Ridderstrale 1999; Williams and Lee 2011). The individual actors that are typically considered are headquarters executives and subsidiary managers. Their behavioural orientation is geared towards furthering the cause of the subsidiary. This has been framed in different ways ranging from specific goals of enhancing subsidiary roles or charters (Birkinshaw and Hood 1998) to more generic goals such as increasing bargaining power or expanding subsidiary autonomy as well as influence over corporate decisions and other corporate units (Bouquet and Birkinshaw 2008; Ambos *et al.* 2010). While the subsidiary initiative approaches stand out in their concern for the behavioural orientation of individual actors, individual-based orientations and variance therein find only little consideration. For the most part, the behavioural orientation of subsidiary managers or headquarters executives is equated with the behavioural orientation of the organizational unit they represent (Mudambi and Navarra 2004; Ambos *et al.* 2010). The work of Birkinshaw and Ridderstrale (1999) is an exception here in that it acknowledges the role of personal traits and circumstances of managers. There is, for instance, a consideration that ethnocentricity, self-interest, threat to status or lack of trust have an influence as to whether and how corporate managers resist subsidiary initiatives (Birkinshaw and Ridderstrale 1999).

Contributions that fall under this stream recognize the importance of politics and power for the organizational behaviour in MNCs (e.g. Birkinshaw and Ridderstrale 1999; Williams and Lee 2011). For example, subsidiary roles are seen as negotiated and underwritten by the power balance between headquarters and subsidiaries (Birkinshaw *et al.* 2000). This entails a closer attention to the constructs and sources of power. Depending on the power perspective, at least two of the following three sources of power are identified (c.f. Hickson *et al.* 1971; Astley and Zajac 1991). First, there is power that is generated through formal authority and rooted in property rights. More congruent with the hierarchical model of the MNC, power is generally located at corporate headquarters and manifests itself in different degrees and kinds of corporate control of subsidiaries by headquarters. Second, there is systemic or structural power, which is constituted by the position or network centrality of a unit within the internal network of value creation or, as Astley and Zajac (1991: 399) put it, the 'workflow interdependencies between units located in the division of labour'. Third, there is power that is related to unique and non-substitutable resources, knowledge assets or capabilities, which are held or are accessible by a unit and exchanged with other units. While much of this research holds on to intraorganizational or resource-based power perspectives – meaning that the most powerful units are those which are vested with formal authority or those which enjoy net dependencies of other units or monopolize unique and non-substitutable resources – there is an increasing recognition that even structurally weak or low power actors may have a substantial influence by employing creative strategies and political games (Bouquet and Birkinshaw 2008).

It is important to note that contributions in the subsidiary initiative stream are among the first to focus on the political strategies of individual actors. Birkinshaw and Ridderstrale (1999) show, for instance, how corporate managers draw on different political strategies including lobbying and delaying to resist subsidiary initiatives. Subsidiary managers for their part engage in strategies such as lobbying and leveraging external relationships and internal contacts as well as their reputation to further their cause (Birkinshaw and Ridderstrale 1999). In a similar vein, Bouquet and Birkinshaw (2008) and Williams and Lee (2011) emphasize the importance of political strategies such as initiative taking, profile building, rule breaking and entering different types of political games or the power-enhancing role of interpersonal and cross-boundary networking. It is evident that this perspective leaves little room for an overarching organizational rationality of the MNC. Subsidiaries behave 'opportunistically' from an agency perspective (Mudambi and Navarra 2004) and follow at least in part their idiosyncratic local goals and agendas. These are not necessarily in alignment with the goals of the firm as a whole (Birkinshaw *et al.* 2000; Mudambi and Navarra 2004; Mudambi and Pedersen 2007). At the same time, the behavioural rationality at the subsidiary level is maintained, as the same reasoning of semiautonomous actors with mixed motives is generally not extended to below the subsidiary level.

Actor-context relations: The subsidiary, which remains the focus of analysis in this stream of research, faces two kinds of environment, the internal and the external environment. Both types of environment are either conceptualized as more abstract market conditions, such as market importance, dynamism, heterogeneity, uncertainty (Birkinshaw and Lingblad 2005), or in terms of specific actors, such as customers, suppliers and competitors (Birkinshaw *et al.* 2005). Subsidiaries are embedded in these environments through interdependencies, resource exchange relationships and competition with other units. In the context of subsidiary entrepreneurship, Birkinshaw *et al.* suggest that the:

MNC subsidiary faces two distinct competitive arenas that the subsidiary must respond to – the external competitive arena consisting primarily of customers, suppliers and competitors in the local marketplace, and the internal competitive arena consisting of the various customers, suppliers and competing entities that are part of the same MNC. (Birkinshaw *et al.* 2005: 228)

While some contributions consider the social nature of the environment, for instance by considering interpersonal relations, interaction and coalition-building among managers, the nature of environments remains largely economic (e.g. Birkinshaw and Ridderstrale 1999). The nature of internal and external environments, and more specifically, the locations of subsidiaries within these, are crucial as they structure the unit's goals and means to pursue them. Birkinshaw *et al.* (2005) argue, for instance, that the internal and external competitive arenas represent threats and opportunities that structure the strategic options of subsidiary managers (see also Birkinshaw and Ridderstrale 1999).

The relative strength of these competitive environments shapes the subsidiary's options; and it is then up to subsidiary managers to take the initiative to respond to the threats and opportunities to secure the subsidiary's performance. (Birkinshaw *et al.* 2005: p. 227)

Similar to contingency perspectives and business network perspectives, behavioural orientations, that is interests and sources of power, remain largely structured by positions, roles, interdependencies and resource exchanges in internal and external networks (e.g. Birkinshaw *et al.* 2000). In this view, internal interdependencies, network centrality or access to resources in or relations to the host environment structure the power of subsidiaries to further their goals (Birkinshaw and Ridderstrale 1999; Mudambi and Navarra 2004). Birkinshaw and Ridderstrale (1999) show, for example, that subsidiaries mobilize internal and external relationships to fight resistance to their initiatives. Mudambi and Navarra (2004) illustrate how the bargaining power of subsidiaries is dependent on the degree of knowledge in and outflows from and to other subsidiaries (see Chapter 4). Hence, it is internal and external economic embeddedness, and the different degrees of being embedded in either internal and external environments, that structure the actor's goals and their means to achieve them. It is important to underline that the subsidiary initiative stream moves away from seeing subsidiaries as passive respondents to organizational environments. Instead, environments are seen to provide opportunities and constraints with which actors proactively engage. Or, with Birkinshaw *et al.*:

They are both competitive arenas in which players fight – through their own proactive entrepreneurial initiatives – to establish and defend advantageous positions, and ultimately secure competitive advantage. (Birkinshaw *et al.* 2005: p. 228)

Actors are not determined by their environments but can proactively use them to change their situation, that is, their competitive position, role or mandate. In this sense, subsidiaries and their managers are clearly not passive dopes or determined by their structural position in the environment but proactive players who can overcome and creatively circumvent structural constraints and exploit opportunities in their internal and external environments. It is also this proactive behaviour that ultimately impacts and changes the environment in which actors are embedded (Ambos *et al.* 2010).

Summary: Subsidiary initiative contributions see MNCs as political multi-actor systems in which power and politics play a crucial role in understanding the causes, patterns and consequences of subsidiary initiative. MNCs are seen as full of competition, conflict and coalitions among actors. Seeing MNC actors as semiautonomous players with mixed motives implies that an overarching organizational rationality is not expected. At the same time, local subsidiary-level rationality is maintained. Although individual actors find consideration, their behavioural orientation is generally aligned with the goals of the units in which they are embedded (e.g. Mudambi and Navarra 2004). While classical contingencies continue to play a strong role in explaining the behavioural orientation – the intended linkage between means and ends – of actors, they are not determined by structural conditions of their internal and external embeddedness. Instead, actors proactively use opportunities in their structural environments or creatively circumvent them through political tactics and strategies. It is also in this latter respect that these approaches herald a shift towards recognizing the relevance of the non-economic environments through exploring the role of social interaction among individual players.

From open-natural to critical perspectives of the MNC

The introduction of organization perspectives to the field of IB&M gives rise to the development of a differentiated understanding of MNCs and their organizational behaviour. It is not until the introduction of contingency theory and network perspectives that MNCs are seen as constituted by diverse actors, who differ in their interests, whose interest and behavioural orientations may conflict, and who are vested with different means to pursue their goals. Simultaneously, these perspectives herald a much more fine-grained perspective in understanding how organizational behaviour, that is, how actor interests and power are environmentally constituted. While these developments mark a fundamental leap towards understanding MNCs as open-natural systems, there remain clear limitations in this development. On the one hand, the goal rationality of organizational actors stays generally intact, by shifting this rationality to the level of the subsidiary or subunits. Excepting the work of Birkinshaw and Ridderstrale (1999), the diverse actor perspective remains confined to the organizational level. How individual behaviour or politics, power and conflict at the micro-level impact behaviour at the organizational level are not part of the emerging natural system view of the MNC. In a similar vein, the emerging open-system perspective tends to focus rather narrowly on functional and economic environmental conditions, as exemplified by the focus on task and market environments or specific economic actors in the external environment. This implies that the wider societal, cultural or political constitution of organizational behaviour of and in MNCs is only marginally considered in the perspectives presented thus far.

This is not to deny that the field of IB&M has seen over the years the emergence and strengthening of a range of streams that centre on the political, cultural and institutional structuration of the behaviour in and of MNCs. Cases in point are the development of a strong culturalist stream, strongly building on the work of Hofstede and others (1984, 1994; see also Schwartz 1992, 1994; Trompenaars and Hampden-Turner 1997, 1998; House *et al.* 2004; Kogut and Singh 1988; Shenkar 2001) or political hazard perspectives. The latter has been presented by scholars such as Delios and Beamish (1999), Henisz (2000a, 2000b), Delios and Henisz (2003a, 2000b) or more recently Henisz and Zelner (2004) and Uhlenbruck *et al.* (2006). These scholars have asked, for instance, how political hazard – often understood as frequent and arbitrary changes in the political system and/or the policy environment – influences market entry and entry mode decisions of MNCs.

Hence, while these contributions are important developments in the field of IB&M in that they consider the influence of socio-political factors on the organizational behaviour of the MNC, we shall dispense with these streams in the following discussion because their contribution to a politics, power and conflict perspective of the MNC remains marginal. Specifically, while they alert us to the relevance of social environments for organizational behaviour, these contributions tend to retain a hierarchical and unitary perspective of the MNC. In essence, they conceptualize MNCs as rationally behaving actors who include cultural (e.g. cultural distance) and political variables (e.g. level of political hazard in the host country) in their strategic choices. In other words, while culturalist and political hazard approaches are important developments in seeing MNCs as open systems they retain to a large extent rational system conceptualizations of the MNC. Instead, we shall focus our discussion on two institutionalist perspectives. These perspectives not only give up the assumption that organizations are rational systems but they also feed into the micropolitical and critical discursive perspective, which centre on a generic political perspective of the MNC.

Institutionalist perspectives of the MNC

Within the field of IB&M institutionalist approaches investigate the relationship between institutional environments and the organizational behaviour of MNCs. We will focus here on two variants of institutionalism, namely the new institutionalism and comparative capitalism, as these approaches have found the widest application to MNCs (Geppert *et al.* 2006; Morgan and Kristensen 2006).

New institutionalist perspective

Theory, proponents and empirical focus: New institutionalist theory found its first entry into IB&M research in the early 1990s with the work of Rosenzweig and Singh (1991), Westney (1993) and Rosenzweig and Nohria (1994). However, it was not until the 2000s, with the contributions of Kostova (1999) and Kostova and Roth (2002), that new institutional theory moved more into the mainstream of IB&M research. The theoretical roots of the new institutional approach lie in sociology and organizational theory. The literature often referred to in this body of work includes seminal contributions by Meyer and Rowan (1977), DiMaggio and Powell (1983) and Scott (1995). New institutional theory has typically focused on institutional or isomorphic pressures (coercive, mimetic and normative) within organizational fields, which give rise to organizational diffusion and homogenization of organizational structures, forms or practices (DiMaggio and Powell 1983). Drawing on Scott's (1995) definition of institutions as normative, cognitive and regulatory systems, institutions comprise in this view formal (macro) and informal (micro) elements. Empirically, new institutional thought has mainly focused on the diffusion and adoption of structures, practice and innovations in MNCs (Westney 1993; Rosenzweig and Nohria 1994; Kostova and Roth 2002) as well as on strategic issues, such as host country selection and market entry choices (Xu and Shenkar 2002).

Nature of actors and behavioural orientation: The new institutionalist perspective sees MNCs as complex and heterogeneous organizations (Kostova *et al.* 2008). This complexity is largely based on the multitude of institutional environments in which MNCs are embedded. The new institutionalist perspective acknowledges that MNCs are constituted by different organizational actors, such as headquarters and subsidiaries (Kostova and Roth 2002). At the same time, the new institutional perspective is only marginally concerned with actors and agency below the organizational level. While micro-level actors come into the picture as carriers of the external institutional environment, that is, as carriers of cognitive and normative frameworks, new institutionalists pay little attention to the patterns of social interaction among micro-level actors. While politics and power do not play a strong role in this approach, there is a clear understanding that subsidiaries experience tension based on their dual embeddedness in the internal environment of the MNC and in the environment of the respective host context. The main unit of analysis is the subsidiary as it is here where the dual environmental pressures play out. The organizational behaviour of the subsidiary is driven by the need to respond to different institutional pressures. Somewhat similar to the contingency perspective or business network perspective, these responses can be geared either more towards the internal MNC environment or more towards the external environment. The new institutionalist perspective does not assume the existence of an overarching organizational rationality of the MNC. This does not suggest, however, that the organizational behaviour of subsidiaries follows an erratic pattern. Instead, the subsidiary responds rationally to the pressures in its institutional environment. So rather than behaving economically rationally, the subsidiary behaves rational vis-à-vis the institutional pressures to which it is exposed.

Actor-context relations: New institutionalists understand an organization's environment as composed of different types of institutions. Drawing on Scott (1995), Kostova and Roth (2002) distinguish, for example, regulatory, cognitive and normative institutions that vary in the different national environments of MNCs. In this view, institutions induce different types of pressures. In line with the work of DiMaggio and Powell (1983), coercive (e.g. based on law and regulations), mimetic (e.g. based on uncertainty) and normative (e.g. based on norms and values of professional groups) pressures are distinguished (Rosenzweig and Singh 1991; Kostova and Roth 2002). With the subsidiary being the focal point of much new institutionalist research on MNCs, two kinds of environments are considered. While the first tends to be the external or local institutional context of the subsidiary, the second is the internal institutional context within the MNC (Rosenzweig and Singh 1991; Kostova and Roth 2002). Put differently, subsidiaries are institutionally embedded in the MNC (reflecting largely home country institutional conditions) and, at the same time, in the institutional environment of their host context. Accordingly, much of the new institutionalist understanding of firm–environment relations in MNCs focuses on the contextual constitution of the subsidiary. The basic idea is that subsidiaries are exposed to multiple institutional environments (parent and host context). Subsidiaries need to respond to these different institutional pressures to achieve and maintain legitimacy. However, the 'dual institutional pressure' or 'institutional duality' (Rosenzweig and Singh 1991; Kostova and Roth 2002) creates tensions within the subsidiary as the different institutional pressures may contradict each other. How these different pressures play out in the subsidiary's behaviour depends, for example, in the case of practice transfer, not only on 'institutional distance' between the home and host institutional context of the practice, but also on mediating conditions such as the nature of the industry or the firm. The latter include typical strategies in the industry, entry modes (Rosenzweig and Singh 1991) or the culture within the subsidiary (Kostova 1999). Overall, MNCs or subsidiaries have been conceived of as rather passive respondents to environmental pressures. While some new institutionalist contributions have recognized the role of organizational agency (Kostova and Roth 2002) and the ability of actors to change institutions, particularly when exposed to contradicting institutional logics, this new development is yet to be reflected in IB&M research (Kostova *et al.* 2008).

Summary: The new institutionalist perspective sees MNCs as constituted by different organizational actors. While there is some recognition of agency and actors within the MNC at the organizational level, this does not extend to the micro-level (*cf.* Blazejewski 2008). There is also little consideration of the diverse actors in MNCs' external environments. The new institutionalist understanding of the firm environment centres on the rather anonymous institutional pressures within and outside the MNC (Forsgren 2008). New institutionalists pay close attention to the social constitution of MNCs, particularly to how institutional distance and duality affect transfer and diffusion processes to subsidiaries. However, this perspective is not much concerned with the question of how such organization-level outcomes are constituted by micro-level actors and agency. While conflict and tension – mainly experienced in the subsidiary – are a crucial element of the theoretical framework, the new institutionalist perspective is not a theory that centres on politics and power in MNCs. Different actor interests and politics in MNCs are largely defined away as actors are assumed to homogeneously follow one or the other institutional script.

Comparative capitalist perspective

Theory, proponents and empirical focus: Similar to the new institutional perspective, comparative institutionalists are initially not concerned with MNCs. As the label comparative capitalist suggests, the prime focus rests on comparing and explaining differences in socioeconomic organizations across countries (Hotho and Pedersen 2012). This body of literature draws on a wide range of seminal contributions. The most prominent include the 'societal effect approach' (e.g. Maurice *et al.* 1980; Sorge 1991), the 'national business system' approach (e.g. Whitley 1992), the 'industrial order' approach (Lane 1994), the 'social systems of production' approach (Hollingsworth and Boyer 1997) or the 'varieties of capitalism' approach (Hall and Soskice 2001). Starting in the late 1990s, scholars from this research tradition also began asking how national institutional contexts and diversity shape the organizational behaviour of firms that are organized across institutional and national divides (Whitley 1998; Lane 2000, 2001; Morgan 2001; Morgan and Whitley 2003). Concrete empirical studies in this research stream involve the questions of how home and host institutions impact patterns of internationalization (Whitley 1998, 2001; Morgan and Quack 2005), strategy and control in MNCs (Geppert *et al.* 2003; Harzing and Sorge 2003). Other questions include to what extent processes of globalization (e.g. of financial markets) reduce nationally distinct patterns of organizational behaviour in MNCs (Lane 2000, 2001). Questions that are raised at the subsidiary level include how national institutional contexts influence the design of work systems (Matten and Geppert 2004) or the ability to tab into host context research and development (Lam 2003). While comparative capitalist perspectives find a wide range application, most studies revolve around the transfer of organizational forms and human resources management (HRM) practices in MNCs (e.g. Ferner 1997; Ferner and Quintanilla 1998; Ferner *et al.* 2004; Ferner *et al.* 2005a; Becker-Ritterspach *et al.* 2010). Hence, research in this stream centres on two core questions. First, how are MNCs and their subsidiaries contextually constituted, given their embeddedness in different national institutional contexts? And second, how does the difference between home and host countries or other institutional contexts impact the transfer of practices in MNCs?

Nature of actors and behavioural orientation: Comparative capitalists see MNCs and their subsidiaries as constituted by their institutional environments. While there is a general recognition that

MNCs are constituted by the institutional diversity they face in the international business context, early contributions have tended to emphasize the influence of the home institutional contexts or the so-called 'country-of-origin-effect' (e.g. Ferner 1997; Ferner and Quintanilla 1998; Ferner *et al.* 2001; Quintanilla and Varul 2001; Geppert *et al.* 2003; Whitley 2001). As organizational behaviour investigated ranges from the contextual constitution of the MNC as a whole (e.g. Whitley 1998, 2001; Lane 2000, 2001; Morgan 2001) to the transfer of practices to subsidiaries (Sharpe 1997; Saka 2003; Becker-Ritterspach 2009) or the local constitution of work systems in subsidiaries (Matten and Geppert 2004), the focal unit of analysis also varies between the whole MNC and the subsidiary level. Although there is recognition that MNCs are constituted by different organizational actors, micro-level actors receive only modest attention (see Sharpe 1997 and Saka 2003 as exceptions). Similarly, while it is realized that MNCs, their subsidiaries or the transfer of practices are subject to diverse institutional environments, there is only limited attention to politics, power and conflict. A notable exception in this regard is the work of Sharpe (1997), who considers how institutional diversity (also below the national level) structures resistance in transfer processes. Apart from these early studies recognizing conflict, the issue of power in MNCs finds some consideration through asking how national institutional contexts – based on typical modes of corporate governance and economic relations in home countries – shape authority relations in MNCs and the control of subsidiaries. Cases in point are the contributions by Whitley (2001) and Harzing and Sorge (2003). Whitley (2001) argues, for instance, that the home institutional embeddedness of MNCs influences internationalization propensity, country preferences and control modes in subsidiaries. In comparative capitalist perspectives, the organizational behaviour of actors – irrespective of whether we look at the MNC as a whole, subsidiaries or individual actors – is driven or shaped by their institutional embeddedness. Hence, similar to the new institutionalist perspective the interest is not so much about an overarching economic goal rationality of the MNC as it is about (rational) responses and adaptations to the requirements and demands of different institutional settings.

Actor-context relations: The constitution of organizations by their institutional environments is at the heart of actor-context relations in comparative capitalist perspectives on MNCs. In the comparative capitalist perspective, the MNC's environment consists mainly of national institutional configurations. Comparative capitalist environment perspectives build on describing and classifying how economic activities are organized or coordinated differently in different countries. This leads to the identification of nationally distinct configurations of market economies. Accounting for such configurations centres on the adoption of an open system perspective that asks how MNCs, their subunits or organizational practices are shaped by the institutional environments of different market economies. Specifically, despite the variety of approaches, comparative capitalist approaches share a focus on a wide range of macro-institutional domains, such as, certain types of political systems, financial systems, or skill-formation systems (e.g. Whitley 1999) that shape structures and practices in organizations. The relationship between different institutional domains but also between organizations and their institutional environment is typically viewed as complementary, interrelated and path dependent (Jackson and Deeg 2008; Hotho and Pedersen 2012).

While there is some variance with regard to how institutional environments relate to organizational actors, comparative capitalist perspectives have tended to emphasize a strong structuring – if not determining – effect of institutional environments on the organizational behaviour (e.g. Whitley 2001, 2009). In a similar vein, the institutional embeddedness considered focuses on the national level in many studies. Increasingly, however, institutional embeddedness has been seen as multilayered and interacting. There is also a growing emphasis in comparative capitalism on how firms proactively shape their institutional environment (e.g. Morgan and Quack 2005; Campbell 2004; Crouch 2005; Hall and Thelen 2009; Streeck and Thelen 2005). However, these more recent insights in the comparative capitalism literature are yet to be fully applied to the organizational context of MNCs.

Summary: Similar to new institutionalists, scholars from comparative capitalism see MNCs as constituted by the diverse institutional environments into which they are embedded. While this institutional embeddedness can involve different levels (national, regional, organizational) as well as diverse country contexts (home, host, third country institutions) there has been a bias towards a strong structuring effect of national and home country institutions. Similarly, while contributions in this stream of research adopt a diverse actor perspective, only few contributions extend this perspective to the micro-level. The organizational behaviour in and of MNCs is largely conceptualized as structured or determined by institutional settings. While this does not imply the assumption of an overarching organizational goal rationality, it does entail a rather passive view of organizational actors and their behaviour vis-à-vis institutional environments. Nevertheless, micro-level actor perspectives, issues of politics, power and conflict start to emerge in this stream and feed increasingly into the micropolitical approaches that we discuss below. It is particularly the work of actor-centred institutionalists, which provides us with the theoretical foundations for the development of micropolitical perspectives on the MNC.

Micropolitical perspective

Theory, proponents and empirical focus: Politics, power and conflict have been considered to some extent in IB&M literature all along. However, their treatment is limited in a number of ways. On the one hand, politics, power and conflict are either only implicitly addressed (e.g. Bartlett and Ghoshal 1998) or they are treated as aspectual, that is, politics are only an aspect or a limited phenomenon in organizational life (see Chapter 2). In this view, politics tends to be seen as aberrations that are at worst dysfunctional and at best controllable through appropriate organizational design and processes. On the other hand, there are only a few theoretical perspectives that adopt generic politics perspectives or we could also say full-blown natural system perspectives of the MNC, and even fewer that explicitly theorize politics, power or conflict at the micro-level. This clearly changes with the advent of micropolitical contributions (Kristensen and Zeitlin 2001, 2005; Dörrenbächer and Geppert 2006; Ferner *et al.* 2005b; Almond and Ferner 2006; Edwards *et al.* 2007) that have their roots in actor-centred comparative institutionalist perspectives. The common rationale in these contributions is that we can only understand organization-level outcomes and behaviour in MNCs if we understand the political nature of agency at the micro-level in conjunction with the social and societal constitution of such agency. We could also say, we see with these IB&M contributions for the first time the combination of natural- and open-system perspectives with an explicit micro-level focus, that is, a focus on individual actors or groups of actors. Moreover, building on actor-centred institutionalist concepts (e.g. Sorge 1985; Scharpf 1997), these approaches move not only beyond considering national institutions as the prime social contexts but increasingly explore genuine power and conflict perspectives (e.g. Dörrenbächer and Geppert 2006; Becker-Ritterspach and Dörrenbächer 2011; Geppert and Dörrenbächer 2011; Ferner *et al.* 2012).

Micropolitical perspectives draw on power and conflict perspectives from social theory, organizational theory and organizational psychology (e.g. Dahl 1963; French and Raven 1960; Burns 1961; Etzioni 1964; Pondy 1967; Hickson *et al.* 1971; Deutsch 1973; Pfeffer and Salancik 1974; Crozier and Friedberg 1980; Mintzberg 1983; Thomas 1992; Astley and Zajac 1990; Rothman and Friedman 2001; Lukes 2005; Clegg *et al.* 2007). The empirical themes that are considered range from practice transfers and learning (e.g. Sharpe 1997; Clark and Geppert 2006; Geppert and Williams 2006; Blazejewski 2008; Fenton O'Creevy *et al.* 2011), to subsidiary role development and charter change (Dörrenbächer and Gammelgaard 2006; Dörrenbächer and Geppert 2009a, 2009b), and from restructuring and production relocation (Blazejewski 2009) to intrafirm competition (e.g. Becker-Ritterspach and Dörrenbächer 2011).

Nature of actors and behavioural orientation: Micropolitical perspectives conceptualize MNCs as natural systems that are full of political struggle and conflict (Geppert and Dörrenbächer 2011). Authors in this stream typically view MNCs as 'contested terrains' (Collinson and Morgan 2009; Edwards and Bélanger 2009) or even 'battlefields' (Kristensen and Zeitlin 2001) in which the interests of different actors collide. Micropolitical approaches adopt a differentiated actor perspective in and around the MNC. These differentiated actor perspectives involve, on the one hand, different analytical levels of actors. Bélanger and Edwards (2006) and Becker-Ritterspach and Dörrenbächer (2009) distinguish actors at the macro-, meso- and micro-level. While macro-actors are actors outside the MNC, such as trade unions, national, regional or local governments or media, meso actors are divergent organizational-level actors within the MNC, such as headquarters and subsidiaries. However, the main units of analysis are individual actors or groups of actors whose behavioural rationales cannot be equated with the behavioural rationale of an organizational-level actor (Becker-Ritterspach and Dörrenbächer 2011). In this view, actors are not simply organizational-level constructs, but rather individual actors or coalitions of actors. Actors follow different types of strategies (Becker-Ritterspach and Dörrenbächer 2011; Williams and

Geppert 2011; Maclean and Hollinshead 2011) or play different games in pursuance of their goals (Morgan and Kristensen 2006; Dörrenbächer and Geppert 2009b). Actors behave rationally towards the realization of individual goals (which may be personal goals) or the goals of a group with whom they share a common interest. To achieve their goals actors mobilize resources through social relationships or by referring to broader societal or institutional rules. While contributions in this stream differ in the extent to which they theorize politics, power and conflict, they tend to implicitly or explicitly understand political behaviour of actors in MNCs as interest-driven and intentional or strategic. Power is seen as based on the ability to mobilize resources. Resources for their part are typically based on or realized through social rules and relations. For example, Becker-Ritterspach and Dörrenbächer (2011) define power based on Giddens (1984) as the ability of actors to influence an organizational process in their interest. Moreover, drawing on Weber (1947) and Crozier and Friedberg (1980), they see power as 'constituted by relationships that allow the exchange of resources' (Becker-Ritterspach and Dörrenbächer 2011: 542). Moreover, while power is not seen as a property of actors, there is recognition that sources of power differ in kind and that actors differ in their ability to mobilize them.

However, while we also reject the notion of power as a property, we do recognize that the resources exchanged may be of different kinds and that both the availability of resources and the ability to engage in *resource exchange relationships* in organizations is not a coincidence but position dependent and structured by the internal and external context of the organization as has been suggested by the substantial body of literature on intra-organizational power (e.g. Hickson *et al.* 1971) and also social exchange theory (e.g. Thye 2000). (Becker-Ritterspach and Dörrenbächer 2011: 542)

Hence, this view also entails that not all actors are equally powerful in impacting organizational behaviour in their interest as the ability to mobilize resources is connected to the social embeddedness of actors.

In line with Scott (1998), we can say that approaches that combine actor-centred institutionalism with micropolitical perspectives complete the shift from seeing organizations as purpose- and goal-driven entities, towards seeing them as entities that follow *often diffuse and conflicting goals* because they are constituted by 'collectives whose participants are pursuing multiple interests, both disparate and common' (Scott 1998: 26). In this view, conflicts and politics are no longer unhealthy aberrations, but rather a *sine qua non* of organizational life.

Actor-context relations: Micropolitical perspectives agree that the social embeddedness of actors is crucial to understanding politics, power and conflict in MNCs. The social embeddedness is fundamental because it informs actor's interests, structures similarities and differences of actor interests and the ability of actors to realize their interests through resource mobilization. At the same time, approaches in this stream differ in what the relevant social context is and how determining it is with regard to the political behaviour of actors. Earlier work in the stream takes its vantage point from seeing national institutional contexts as strongly structuring politics, power and conflict in MNCs (e.g. Ferner *et al.* 2005a; Almond and Ferner 2006; Kristensen and Zeitlin 2001, 2005; Morgan and Kristensen 2006). Morgan and Kristensen (2006) hold for instance that 'institutional diversity', that is, diversity at the national or regional level of the MNC's home and host context, constitutes politics, power and conflict in MNCs (see also Kristensen and Zeitlin 2001, 2005). Morgan and Kristensen argue that:

Institutions enter into these processes, firstly as co-constitutors of the set of actors/groupings and their mutual roles and identities, secondly as forms of restriction on the choices actors make, thirdly as resources that empower actors and finally as rule-givers for the games that emerge. (Morgan and Kristensen 2006: 1473)

In a similar vein, Edwards *et al.* argue that:

Institutions set constraints within which political activity within firms can operate, shaping the preference of actors and the feasibility of certain courses of action, but they do not determine outcomes on their own. (Edwards *et al.* 2006: 72)

A range of micropolitical contributions also discuss the role of structural embeddedness of actors within the organization for the political behaviour in MNCs. Edwards and Kuruvilla (2005) illustrate, for instance, how the organizational embeddedness within the MNC (e.g. headquarters vs. subsidiary) structures both the interests of different actors and the resources they can mobilize (see also Edwards *et al.* 2006).

While early micropolitical perspectives tend to emphasize the structuring role of macroinstitutions from a top-down or a determinist perspective, more recent work reverses this view and opts for an open, dynamic and bottom-up approach to understand how politics, power and conflict are contextually constituted (e.g. Edwards *et al.* 2007; Blazejewski 2009; Fenton O'Creevy *et al.* 2011). Blazejewski and Becker-Ritterspach (2011) suggest, for example, that different contexts including 'organizational, cultural, and national or regional institutional, geopolitical, etc. – may affect the occurrence of conflict and may be relevant and referred to by actors in different situations over time'. They continue to argue, 'it is above all an empirical question which context is relevant and how it is interpreted in a given situation' (Blazejewski and Becker-Ritterspach 2011: 178). Such a micropolitical perspective puts actors and their agency centre stage and reconstructs which context constitutes political behaviour (interests and resources) in a specific event, on a specific issue or occasion (see also Chapter 7 in this book for a detailed explanation). In this view, the relevant context may be the macroinstitutional level, the organizational or even the personal situation of an individual (Becker-Ritterspach 2006; Blazejewski 2009). The latter can involve the career path and organizational position, personal social relations and/or dispositions such as career aspirations (Becker-Ritterspach and Dörrenbächer 2011; Fenton O'Creevy *et al.* 2011).

The structural determinism of organizational behaviour of the MNC that we find most strongly articulated in the early comparative institutionalist work is increasingly reversed as the question is raised how the political agency of actors affects their social context (Ferner *et al.* 2012). Geppert and Dörrenbächer suggest for instance:

The analysis of micro-political game playing starts from the bottom and asks how different identities and interests of key actors stabilize and destabilize established institutional, cultural and organizational structures, and not the other way round as in mainstream institutionalist approaches. (Geppert and Dörrenbächer 2011: 24–25).

In summary: Despite some variation, micropolitical perspectives see MNCs as first and foremost populated by individual actors who behave politically, that is, intentional and interest-driven in social interaction. In this perspective, the MNC is a terrain of conflicts, struggles and power games. Actor behaviour is structured, but not determined, by the social environment into which actors are embedded. Depending on the perspective, the social embeddedness involves macroinstitutions, organizational embeddedness, personal situations or a combination thereof. Hence, the organizational behaviour in MNCs is underwritten by the political or intentional agency of specific actors whose behaviours and rationales can only be understood in relation to social context.

Critical discursive perspectives
Theory, proponents and empirical focus: Next to the individual actor-centred micropolitical approaches, the 2000s have seen the emergence of another stream in IB&M that puts politics, power and conflict central to the understanding of the organizational behaviour in MNCs. Or, put differently, it is a second stream that combines a generic and a systemic perspective on politics in MNCs (see Chapter 2). The different approaches that fall under this stream can be broadly clustered under the label of critical discursive perspectives (Balogun *et al.* 2011; Vaara and Monin 2010; Frenkel 2008; Vaara *et al.* 2005, 2006; Vaara and Tienari 2002, 2004, 2008). As the self-attribution 'critical' of many perspectives in this stream indicates, it is the goal to depart from 'rationalistic and managerialist' understandings of organizational behaviour of MNCs (Balogun *et al.* 2011). Instead the objective is to develop a genuine critical orientation based on an 'interest in power and inequality' (Balogun *et al.* 2011; see also Vaara and Tienari 2008; Frenkel 2008; Böhm *et al.* 2008) in IB&M. So, while micropolitical approaches with their different roots including labour process theory partly introduce critical perspectives to IB&M, this becomes more explicit and outspoken in critical discourse perspectives. Discourse perspectives have their origins in critical theory, that is, particularly in seminal contributions of post-modernists and post-structuralists (e.g. Foucault 1973, 1980; Derrida 1978, 1982; Lyotard 1979). Scholars applying discourse perspectives to MNCs typically draw on critical discourse analyses (e.g. Fairclough 2003; Phillips and Hardy 2002; Phillips *et al.* 2008; Wodak and Meyer 2002; van Dijk 1998; Rojo and van Dijk 1997; van Leeuwen and Wodak 1999; Boje 1991) that have been previously developed and applied in organization and management studies. Other critical discourse perspectives employed (e.g. Frenkel 2008; Levy 2008; Böhm *et al.* 2008; Vaara *et al.* 2005) include post-colonial

approaches (Said 2003; Bhabha 1990), labour process theory (Ackroyd and Thompson 1999) or (neo)Gramscian perspectives (Gramsci 1971; Laclau and Mouffe 1985). Studies that adopt critical discursive perspectives focus on organizational behaviour in and around MNCs that is contested or controversial. The empirical focus of these studies revolves around organizational change and related dynamics of control and resistance (e.g. Balogun *et al.* 2011; Vaara and Tienari 2008; Böhm *et al.* 2008). Cases in point are studies that are interested in the discursive struggles over mergers and acquisitions (Vaara and Tienari 2011), corporate restructurings and shutdowns (e.g. Geppert 2003), charter reduction of subsidiaries (Balogun *et al.* 2011) or practice transfers (Frenkel 2008).

Nature of actors and behavioural orientation: The critical discourse perspective sees MNCs as open-natural systems that are discursively and narratively constructed. As such, they are full of discursive struggles and competing efforts of sensemaking. Within the context of the MNC discursive struggles can have different roots. While Frenkel (2008) discusses the conflict potential rooted in geopolitical hierarchies between the first and the third world, Balogun *et al.* (2011) as well as Vaara and Tienari (2011) see the global and local tension as a root cause for such discursive struggles. The latter often plays out between headquarters and subsidiaries in the form of what Balogun *et al.* (2011) call competing independence-interdependence narratives or discursive struggles around corporate control and local resistance. In this view, different actor groups use discourses to pursue their interests and to construct, defend and maintain their identities or organizational worldviews. While discourses are always constitutive for organizations by way of creating organizational reality through social constructions, their political nature and their relation to power become particularly evident in controversial events and processes of organizational change where dominant discourses become challenged and resisted by counter-discourses (Balogun *et al.* 2011). For instance, in situations of organizational change such as mergers, corporate shutdowns or restructuring, discourses are used to give sense, purpose and legitimacy to organizational behaviour (Geppert 2003; Riad 2005; Vaara and Tienari 2011). Such discourses do not go unchallenged, however, as those actors' identities and interests affected or potentially affected by the change employ alternative discourses to resist the change. Critical discourse perspectives adopt a divergent actor perspective of the MNC (e.g. Tienari and Vaara 2012). They are, however, typically not interested in individual actors but rather in (opposing) groups or coalitions of actors whose identities and interests are implicated in or aligned with the different sides of a discursive struggle. The main units of analyses are the discourses and the discursive struggles between different actor groups. These discourses are often situated in or between organizational entities, for instance, between headquarters and subsidiaries (Balogun *et al.* 2011) or between acquiring and acquired firm in post-merger situations (Vaara and Tienari 2011). It goes without saying that power, politics and conflict are central to critical discourse perspectives. Discourses are viewed, for instance, as being 'part of the battle over power and hegemony in the MNC context' (Balogun *et al.* 2011: 769; see also Frenkel 2008; Levy 2008). Critical discourse perspectives theorize the relation between discourses and power as one of mutual influence or constitution (e.g. Vaara and Tienari 2002). On the one hand, dominant discourses and the domination of certain discourses in discursive struggles reproduce and reflect power relations and structures of domination. Competing discourses, on the other hand, challenge dominant discourses and bear the potential of shifting power relations and structures of domination (e.g. Böhm *et al.* 2008; Levy 2008). The medium of discourses is language enacted through communication (Vaara and Tienari 2011), which also points to the power implications of language skills and the conflict implications of language policies in MNCs (Marschan-Piekkari *et al.* 1999a, 1999b; Vaara *et al.* 2005). The resources or means mobilized to construct a discourse are linguistic artefacts including vocabularies, arguments, narratives and stories (Geppert 2003; Vaara and Tienari 2011; Balogun *et al.* 2011). While discourses co-exist and compete, they are not equally powerful or dominant. In many discursive perspectives, the dominance of a discourse over other discourses tends to be connected to the legitimating potential or implications of the respective discourse (Vaara and Monin 2010; Vaara *et al.* 2006; Geppert 2003). For instance, a certain narrative used in discourses might give voice to certain actors and legitimate their sensemaking and interest while delegitimating, marginalizing or silencing those of others (Vaara and Tienari 2002, 2008, 2011; Vaara *et al.* 2005; Riad 2005).

Furthermore, this analysis helps us understand the inherent political nature of such discursive legitimation: it is through subtle textual strategies that particular interests and voices are reproduced and others silenced. (Vaara and Tienari 2008: 991)

To realize the legitimating potential, actors use different discursive strategies, which 'means that specific actors try to persuade and convince others through various kinds of rhetorical moves' (Vaara *et al.* 2006: 793). Drawing on the work of van Leewen and Wodak (1999), Vaara and Tienari (2008, see also Vaara *et al.* 2006) show, in the example of a production unit's shutdown, how different discursive strategies draw on different sources of legitimization. Also understood as different 'semantic-functional strategies' of legitimization, they refer to authority (authorization), utility (rationalization) and morals or values (moralization), as well as the past and future (mythopoesis) as sources of legitimization. In the critical discourse perspective, organizational behaviour of the MNC and of their actors is largely driven by discourses and processes of legitimization. Discourses are constitutive for organizational behaviour because they are connected to action; they have 'performative power' (Vaara and Tienari 2011) and behavioural implications (Balogun *et al.* 2011). Specifically, discourses construct behavioural expectations, rights and constraints (Balogun *et al.* 2011). Discourses are effectively used to legitimate or resist organizational change (Vaara and Tienari 2011; Riad 2005).

Legitimation in the MNC context thus usually entails complex interdiscursive dynamics where specific discourses and ideologies provide alternative and often competing ways to legitimate or delegitimate particular actions. (Vaara and Tienari 2008: 987)

Hence, discourses not only serve to defend, construct and promote identities (e.g. sense of superiority or inferiority) but also to impact the material interests and situations of different actor groups (e.g. job loss or career opportunities) (Vaara *et al.* 2005; Vaara and Tienari 2002). It becomes evident that the critical discourse perspective does not imply any organizational goal rationality. Rather the organizational behaviour of the MNC is driven by the hegemonic claims and contestations of different actor groups.

Actor-context relations: Critical discourse perspectives consider the role of context for discursive struggles in two ways. Context relates first to the situatedness of actors within the MNC or rather within the discursive field inside the organization. Put simply, it matters for the discursive strategies and preferences whether actors are situated in the headquarters or subsidiary, or the acquiring or acquired firm. At the same time, critical discourse perspectives adopt an open system perspective vis-à-vis the external environment. In fact the boundaries between the organization and the external environment dissolve in this perspective. As organizations are constituted by discourses and as organizational discourses stretch well beyond the legal boundaries of the organization, the organization–environment boundary increasingly blurs. The following quote is illuminating in this respect. Vaara and Tienari (2002) state within the context of media discourses around organizational change:

We believe, however, that it is extremely important to transcend the imagined boundaries of organizations when trying to understand how organizational phenomena become justified, legitimized and naturalized in wider socio-cultural contexts. (Vaara and Tienari 2002: 278)

It becomes clear that in this view organizational discourses in MNCs are not confined to the organization but are embedded in the wider (national) institutional environments (Geppert 2003) or societal discourses, for example, in the form of public media discourses (Vaara and Tienari 2002; Vaara *et al.* 2006). Such an embeddedness perspective extends in some contributions to the international level in considering the embeddedness of discursive struggles in geopolitical hierarchies (Frenkel 2008) or interstate structures (Levy 2008).

Conceptualized as 'intertextuality' (Balogun *et al.* 2011: 769) or 'interdiscursivity' (Vaara and Tienari 2008), different organizational discourses, discursive strategies and narratives are interconnected and legitimated by or interact with the wider societal discourses and ideologies. Vaara and Tienari (2011) show, for instance, that actors draw on discourses or different types of legitimating narratives related to either globalization (e.g. inevitability of internationalization, realization of synergies), nationalism (e.g. preserving national interests) or even regionalism (e.g. construction of pan-Nordic interests and identity) that reflect broader societal discourses, history and ideologies. Cases in point are the collective memory of a particular socio-historical context (e.g. colonial history) or competing societal or global discourses embedded in the ideologies of neoliberalism and global capitalism or alternatively in radical humanism or marxism (Vaara and Tienari 2011; Levy 2008; Frenkel 2008; Vaara *et al.* 2005, 2006). While organizational discourses and struggles are embedded in wider discourses and struggles, such a perspective also implies that discourses originating in organizations shade into and influence discourses in the wider societal context. Vaara and Tienari (2008) show in the context of the foreign acquisition of a state-owned Norwegian bank that:

The public discussion was not only about the legitimacy of the particular acquisition but also about foreign ownership in general in the previously nationally controlled sector. The discussion in the media was characterized by complex discursive dynamics that could only be understood by realizing that the power positions of both politicians and corporate representatives were at stake. (Vaara and Tienari 2008: 987)

In other words, organizational discourses influence for their part wider societal discourses with implications for actors outside the organization such as politicians.

Summary: Critical discourse perspectives adopt a natural- and open-system perspective of the MNC. Rather than being cohesive, coherent and goal-rational entities, they are constituted by discursive struggles and competing efforts of sensemaking. At the core of these struggles lie battles of different actor groups over power and hegemony. This implies that individual actors and how their specific organizational or societal embeddedness enables and constrains political behaviour do not find much consideration. Instead, there is a broader concern with how the outcomes of discursive struggles affect certain groups of actors in terms of their identities and material situations. Discourses and structures of domination are conceptualized as mutually consti-tuting. The dominance or power of discourse is connected to its legit-imacy. This legitimacy is typically constructed through reference to broader societal conceptions, values and ideologies. The open-system perspective of the approach is manifest, in particular, in the condition that organizational and societal discourses are connected and mutually influencing.

Conclusion

The goal of this literature review is to illustrate that the emergence of the political perspectives of the MNC can be understood as a journey that essentially parallels major paradigm shifts in organization studies, namely from open-rational to open-natural and ultimately to critical perspectives. This journey should of course not be misunderstood as a unidirectional development towards the truer and the better. Until this date, all perspectives discussed are present in IB&M and it is the wealth of these different perspectives that defines the richness and maturation of the field IB&M. A part of this maturation involves that politics, power and conflict perspectives have been introduced to the field and come, as we can see, in a variety of shades and colours. Although politics, power and conflict perspectives have still not become a mainstream perspective, they have become an integral part of the field's development and are increasingly employed to understand a wide range of empirical domains of the organizational behaviour in and of the MNC.

References

Ackroyd, S. and Thompson, P. 1999. *Organizational Misbehavior.* Sage: London.

Almond, P. and Ferner, A. (eds.) 2006. *American Multinationals in Europe: Managing Employment Relations Across National Borders.* Oxford University Press.

Ambos, B. and Schlegelmilch, B. 2007. Innovation and control in the multinational firm: political and contingency approaches. *Strategic Management Journal,* 28(5): 473–486.

Ambos, T. C. and Birkinshaw, J. 2010. Headquarters' attention and its effect on subsidiary performance. *Management International Review,* 50(4): 449–469.

Ambos, T. C., Andersson, U. and Birkinshaw, J. 2010. What are the consequences of initiative-taking in multinational subsidiaries? *Journal of International Business Studies,* 41(7): 1099–1118.

Andersson, U., and Forsgren, M. 2000. In search of centre of excellence: Network embeddedness and subsidiary roles in multinational corporations. *Management International Review,* 40(4): 329–350.

Andersson, U. and Holm, U. 2010. *Managing the Contemporary Multinational: the role of headquarters.* Cheltenham: Edward Elgar.

Andersson, U., Forsgren, M. and Holm, U. 2001. Subsidiary embeddedness and competence development in MNCs: a multilevel analysis. *Organization Studies,* 22(6): 1013–1034.

2002. The strategic impact of external networks: subsidiary performance and competence development in the multinational corporation. *Strategic Management Journal,* 23(11): 979–996.

2007. Balancing subsidiary influence in the federative MNC: a business network view. *Journal of International Business Studies,* 38(5): 802–818.

Astley, W. G. and Sachdeva, P. S. 1984. Structural sources of interorganizational power: a theoretical synthesis. *Academy of Management Review*, 9(1): 104–113.

Astley, W. G. and Zajac, E. J. 1990. Beyond dyadic exchange: functional interdependence and sub-unit power. *Organisation Studies*, 11(4): 481–501.

  1991. Intraorganizational power and organizational design: reconciling rational and coalitional models of organization. *Organization Science*, 2(4): 399–411.

Balogun, J., Jarzabkowski, P. and Vaara, E. 2011. Selling, resistance and reconciliation: a critical discursive approach to subsidiary role evolution in MNCs. *Journal of International Business Studies*, 42(6): 765–786.

Barney, J. B. 1991. Firm resources and sustained competitive advantage. *Journal of Management*, 17(1): 99–120.

Bartlett, C. A. and Ghoshal, S. 1989. *Managing Across Borders: the Transnational Solution*, Boston: Harvard Business School Press.

  1998. *Managing Across Borders: the Transnational Solution*, Boston: Harvard Business School Press.

Becker-Ritterspach, F. 2006. The social constitution of knowledge integration in MNEs: a theoretical framework. *Journal of International Management*, 12(3): 358–377.

  2009. *Hybridization of MNE Subsidiaries: the Automotive Sector in India*. Basingstoke: Palgrave Macmillan.

Becker-Ritterspach, F. and Dörrenbächer, C. 2011. An organizational politics perspective on intra-firm competition in multinational corporations. *Management International Review*, 51(4): 533–559.

Becker-Ritterspach, F., Saka-Helmhout, A. and Hotho, J. 2010. Learning in multinational enterprises as the socially embedded translation of practices. *Critical Perspectives on International Business*, 6(1): 8–37.

Bélanger, J. and Edwards, P. 2006. Towards a political economy framework: TNCs as national and international players. In A. Ferner, J. Quintanilla and C. Sànchez-Runde (eds.), *Multinationals, Institutions and the Construction of Transnational Practices*. Basingstoke: Palgrave Macmillan, 24–52.

Bhabha, H. K. 1990. *Nation and Narration*. London and New York: Routledge.

Birkinshaw, J. 2000. *Entrepreneurship in the Global Firm*. London: Sage.

Birkinshaw, J. and Hood, N. 1998. Multinational subsidiary evolution: capability and charter change in foreign-owned subsidiary companies. *Academy of Management Review*, 23(4): 773–795.

Birkinshaw, J. and Lingblad, M. 2005. Intrafirm competition and charter evolution in the multibusiness firm. *Organization Science*, 16(6): 674–686.

Birkinshaw, J. and Ridderstrale, J. 1999. Fighting the corporate immune system: a process study of subsidiary initiatives in multinational corporations. *International Business Review*, 8(2): 149–180.

Birkinshaw, J., Holm, U., Thilenius, P. and Arvidsson, N. 2000. Consequences of perception gaps in the headquarters–subsidiary relationship. *International Business Review*, 9(3): 321–344.

Birkinshaw, J., Hood, N. and Jonsson, S. 1998. Building firm-specific advantages in multinational corporations: the role of subsidiary initiative. *Strategic Management Journal*, 19(3): 221–241.

Birkinshaw, J., Hood, N. and Young, S. 2005. Subsidiary entrepreneurship, internal and external competitive forces, and subsidiary performance. *International Business Review*, 14(2): 227–248.

Blazejewski, S. 2008. Normative control in MNC. In M. P. Feldman and G. D. Santangelo (eds.), *New Perspectives in International Business Research*, Vol. 3. Bingley: Emerald Group Publishing, 83–111.

2009. Actors' interests and local contexts in intrafirm conflict: the 2004 GM and Opel crisis. *Competition and Change*, 13(3): 229–250.

Blazejewski, S. and Becker-Ritterspach, F. 2011. Conflict in headquarter-subsidiary relations: a critical literature review and new directions. In M. Geppert and C. Dörrenbächer (eds.), *Politics and Power in the Multinational Corporation: the Role of Interests, Identities, and Institutions.* Cambridge University Press, 139–190.

Böhm, S., Spicer, A. and Fleming, P. 2008. Infra-political dimensions of resistance to international business: a neo-Gramscian approach. *Scandinavian Journal of Management*, 24(3): 169–182.

Boje, D. M. 1991. The storytelling organization: a study of story performance in an office-supply firm. *Administrative Science Quarterly*, 36: 106–126.

Bouquet, C. and Birkinshaw, J. 2008. Managing power in the multinational corporation: how low-power actors gain influence. *Journal of Management*, 34(3): 477–508.

Buckley, P. J. and Casson, M. 1976. *The Future of the Multinational Enterprise*. London: Macmillan.

2009. The internalisation theory of the multinational enterprise – a review of the progress of a research agenda after 30 years. *Journal of International Business Studies*, 40(9): 1563–1580.

Burns, T. 1961. Micropolitics: mechanisms of institutional change. *Administrative Science Quarterly*, 6(3): 257–281.

Campbell, J. L. 2004. *Institutional Change and Globalization*. Princeton University Press.

Casson, M. 1979. *Alternatives to the Multinational Enterprise*. London: Macmillan.

Cantwell, J. A. 1989. *Technological Innovation and Multinational Corporations*. Oxford: Basil Blackwell.

(ed.)1994. *Transnational Corporations and Innovatory Activities*. Routledge, London.

2009. Innovation and information technology in the MNE. In A. M. Rugman (ed.), *Oxford Handbook of International Business* (2nd edn). Oxford/New York: Oxford University Press, 417–446.

2013. Blurred boundaries between firms, and new boundaries within (large multinational) firms: the impact of decentralized networks for innovation. *Seoul Journal of Economics*, 26(1): 1–32.

Cantwell, J. A. and Iammarino, S. 1998. MNCs, technological innovation and regional systems in the EU: some evidence in the Italian case. *International Journal of Economics and Business*, 5(3): 383–408.

2000. Multinational corporations and the location of technological innovation in the UK regions. *Regional Studies*, 34(4): 317–332.

Cantwell, J. A. and Mudambi, R. 2005. MNE competence creating subsidiary mandates. *Strategic Management Journal*, 26(12): 1109–1128.

Cantwell, J. A. and Piscitello, L. 1999. The emergence of corporate international networks for the accumulation of dispersed technological capabilities. *Management International Review*, 39(1): 123–147.

Cantwell, J. A. and Santangelo, G. D. 2000. Capitalism, profits and innovation in the new techno economic paradigm. *Journal of Evolutionary Economics*, 10(1): 131–157.

Cantwell, J. A. and Zhang, Y. 2009. The co-evolution of international business connections and domestic technological capabilities: lessons from the Japanese catch-up experience. *Transnational Corporations*, 18(2): 37–68.

Cantwell, J. A., Dunning, J. H. and Lundan, S. M. 2010. An evolutionary approach to understanding international business activity: the co-evolution of MNEs and the institutional environment. *Journal of International Business Studies*, 41(4): 567–586.

Chandler, A. D. 1962. *Strategy and Structure: Chapters in the History of Industrial Enterprise*. Cambridge University Press.

Ciabuschi, F., Dellestand, H. and Holm, U. 2012. The role of headquarters in the contemporary MNC. *Journal of International Management*, 18(3): 213–223.

Clark, E. and Geppert, M. 2006. Socio-political processes in international management in post-socialist contexts: knowledge, learning and transnational institution building. *Journal of International Management*, 12(3): 340–357.

Clegg, S., Courpasson, R. D. and Phillips, N. 2007. *Power and Organizations*. London: Sage.

Coase, R. H. 1937. The nature of the firm. *Economica*, 1 (Nov): 386–405.

Collinson, S. and Morgan, G. 2009. *Images of the Multinational Firm*. Chichester: John Wiley and Sons.

Cowley, P. R. 1988. Market structure and business performance: an evaluation of buyer/seller power in the PIMS database. *Strategic Management Journal*, 9(3): 271–278.

Crouch, C. 2005. *Capitalist Diversity and Change: Recombinant Governance and Institutional Entrepreneurs*. Oxford University Press.

Crozier, M. and Friedberg, E. 1980. *Actors and Systems: the Politics of Collective Action*. University of Chicago Press.

Cyert, R. M. and March, J. G. 1963/1992. *A Behavioral Theory of the Firm* (2nd edn). Englewood Cliffs, NJ: Prentice Hall.

Dahl, R. A. 1963. *Modern Political Analysis*. Englewood Cliffs, NJ: Prentice-Hall.

Delios, A. and Beamish, P. W. 1999. Ownership strategy of Japanese firms: transactional, institutional, and experience influences. *Strategic Management Journal*, 20(10): 915–933.

Delios, A. and Henisz, W. J. 2003a. Policy uncertainty and the sequence of entry by Japanese firms, 1980–1998. *Journal of International Business Studies*, 34(3): 227–241.

2003b. Political hazards, experience, and sequential entry strategies: the international expansion of Japanese firms, 1980–1998. *Strategic Management Journal*, 24(11): 1153–1164.

Derrida, J. 1978. *Writing and Difference*. London: Routledge and Kegan Paul.

1982. *Positions*. London: Athlone Press.

Deutsch, M. 1973. *The Resolution of Conflict*. London: Yale University Press.

DiMaggio, P. J. and Powell, W. W. 1983. The iron cage revisited: institutional isomorphism and collective rationality in organizational fields. *American Sociological Review*, 48(2): 147–160.

Dörrenbächer, C. and Gammelgaard, J. 2011. Subsidiary power in multinational corporations: the subtle role of micro-political bargaining power. *Critical Perspectives on International Business*, 7(1): 30–47.

Dörrenbächer, C. and Geppert, M. 2006. Micro-politics and conflicts in multinational corporations: current debates, re-framing, and contributions of this special issue. *Journal of International Management*, 12(3): 251–265.

2009a. A micro-political perspective on subsidiary initiative-taking: evidence from German-owned subsidiaries in France. *European Management Journal*, 27(2): 100–112.

2009b. Micro-political games in the multinational corporation: the case of mandate change. *Management Revue*, 20(4): 373–391.

Doz, Y. and Prahalad, C. K. 1984. Patterns of strategic control within multinational corporations. *Journal of International Business Studies*, 15(2): 55–72.

1991. Managing DMNCs: a search for a new paradigm. *Strategic Management Journal*, 12(1): 145–164.

Doz, Y. L., Bartlett, C. A. and Prahalad, C. K. 1981. Global competitive pressures and host country demands: managing tensions in MNCs. *California Management Review*, 23(3): 63–73.

Dunning, J. H. 1988. The eclectic paradigm of international production: a restatement and some possible extension. *Journal of International Business Studies*, 19(1): 1–31.

1998. Location and the multinational enterprise: a neglected factor? *Journal of International Business Studies*, 29(1): 45–66.

Dunning, J. H. and Lundan, S. M. 2008. Institutions and the OLI paradigm of the multinational enterprise. *Asia Pacific Journal of Management*, 25(4): 573–593.

Edwards, P. K. and Bélanger, J. 2009. The MNC as a contested terrain. In S. Collinson and G. Morgan (eds.), *Images of the Multinational*. Oxford: Wiley, 193–216.

Edwards, T. and Kuruvilla, S. 2005. International HRM: national business systems, organizational politics and the international division of labour in MNCs. *International Journal of Human Resource Management*, 16(1): 1–21.

Edwards, T., Coller, X., Ortiz, L., Rees, C. and Wortmann, M. 2006. National industrial relations systems and cross-border restructuring: evidence from a merger in the pharmaceuticals sector. *European Journal of Industrial Relations*, 12(1): 69–87.

Edwards, T., Colling, T. and Ferner, A. 2007. Conceptual approaches to the transfer of employment practices in multinational companies: an integrated approach. *Human Resource Management Journal*, 17(3): 201–217.

Etzioni, A. 1964. *Modern Organizations*. Englewood Cliffs, NJ: Prentice-Hall.

Fairclough, N. 2003. *Analysing Discourse Textual Analysis for Social Research*. London and New York: Routledge.

Fenton-O'Creevy, M., Gooderham, P., Cerdin, J-L. and Ronning, R. 2011. Bridging roles, social skill and embedded knowing in multinational organizations. In C. Dörrenbächer and M. Geppert (eds.), *Politics and Power in the International Corporation: the Role of Institutions, Interests and Identities*. Cambridge University Press, 101–136.

Ferner, A. 1997. Country of origin effects and HRM in multinational companies. *Human Resource Management Journal*, 7(1): 19–37.

Ferner, A. and Quintanilla, J. 1998. Multinationals, national business systems and HRM: the enduring influence of national identity of a process of 'Anglo-Saxonization'. *International Journal of Human Resource Management*, 9(4): 710–731.

Ferner, A., Almond, P., Clark, I., Colling, T., Edwards, T. and Holden, L. 2004. The dynamics of central control and subsidiary autonomy in the management of human resources: case-study evidence from US MNCs in the UK. *Organization Studies*, 25(3): 363–392.

Ferner, A., Almond, P. and Colling, T. 2005a. Institutional theory and the cross-national transfer of employment policy: the case of 'workforce diversity' in US multinationals. *Journal of International Business Studies*, 36(3): 304–321.

Ferner, A., Almond, P., Colling, T. and Edwards, T. 2005b. Policies on union representation in US multinationals in the UK: Between micro-politics and macro-institutions. *British Journal of Industrial Relations*, 43(4): 703–728.

Ferner, A., Edwards, T. and Tempel, A. 2012. Power, institutions and the cross-national transfer of employment practices in multinationals. *Human Relations*, 65(2): 163–187.

Ferner, A., Quintanilla, J. and Varul, M. Z. 2001. Country-of-origin effects, host-country effects, and the management of HR in multinationals: German companies in Britain and Spain. *Journal of World Business*, 36(2): 107–127.

Forsgren, M. 2008. *Theories of the Multinational: a Multidimensional Creature in the Global Economy*. Cheltenham: Edward Elgar.

Forsgren, M. and Holm, U. 2010. MNC headquarters' role in subsidiaries' value-creating activities: a problem of rationality or radical uncertainty. *Scandinavian Journal of Management*, 26(4): 421–430.

Forsgren, M., Holm, U. and Johanson, J. 2005. *Managing the Embedded Multinational: a Business Network View*. Cheltenham: Edward Elgar.

Foss, N. J. and Pedersen, T. 2004. Organizing knowledge processes in the multinational corporation: an introduction. *Journal of International Business Studies*, 35(5): 340–349.

Foucault, M. 1973. *The Order of Things: an Archaeology of the Human Sciences*. New York: Vintage Books.

1980 *Power/Knowledge Selected Interviews and Other Writings, 1972–7*. Edited by Colin Gordon. New York: Pantheon Books.

French, J. P. R. and Raven, B. 1960. The bases of social power. In D. Cartwright and A. Zander (eds.), *Group Dynamics*. New York: Harper and Row, 607–623.

Frenkel, M. 2008. The multinational corporation as a third space: rethinking international management discourse on knowledge transfer through Homi Bhabha. *Academy of Management Review*, 33(4): 924–942.

Gandemo, B. and Mattsson, J. 1984. Internationalisation of firms – patterns and strategies. *Bedriftsykonomen*, 6: 314–317.

Geppert, M. 2003. Sensemaking and politics in MNCs: a comparative analysis of vocabularies within the global manufacturing discourse in one industrial sector. *Journal of Management Inquiry*, 12(4): 312–329.

Geppert, M. and Dörrenbächer, C. 2011. Politics and power in the multinational corporation: an introduction. In Dörrenbächer, C. and Geppert, M. (eds.), *Politics and Power in the International Corporation: the Role of Institutions, Interests and Identities*. Cambridge University Press, 1–38.

2014. Politics and power within multinational corporations: mainstream studies, emerging critical approaches and suggestions for future research. *International Journal of Management Reviews*, 2(2): 226–244.

Geppert, M. and Williams, K. 2006. Global, national and local practices in multinational corporations: towards a socio-political framework. *International Journal of Human Resource Management*, 17(1): 49–69.

Geppert, M., Matten, D. and Walgenbach, P. 2006. Transnational institution building and the multinational corporation: an emerging field of research. *Human Relations*, 59(11): 1451–1465.

Geppert, M., Williams, K. and Matten, D. 2003. The social construction of contextual rationalities in MNCs: an Anglo-German comparison of subsidiary choice. *Journal of Management Studies*, 40(3): 617–641.

Giddens, A. 1984. *The Constitution of Society: Outline of the Theory of Structuration*. Cambridge: Polity Press.

Gramsci, A. 1971. *Selection from Prison Notebooks*. London: Lawrence and Wishart.

Håkansson, H. (ed.) 1982. *International Marketing and Purchasing of Industrial Goods*. Chichester: Wiley.

Håkansson, H. and Snehota, I. 1995. *Developing Relationships in Business Networks*. London: Routledge.

Hall, P. A. and Soskice, D. 2001. An introduction to varieties of capitalism. In P. A. Hall and D. Soskice (eds.), *Varieties of Capitalism: The Institutional Foundations of Comparative Advantage*. Oxford University Press, 1–68.

Hall, P. A. and Thelen, K. 2009. Institutional change in varieties of capitalism. *Socio-Economic Review*, 7(1): 7–34.

Harzing, A-W. 1999. *Managing the Multinationals. An International Study of Control Mechanisms.* Cheltenham: Northampton, Edward Elgar.

Harzing, A.-W. and Sorge, A. 2003. The relative impact of country-of-origin and universal contingencies on internationalization strategies and corporated control in multinational enterprises: world-wide and European perspectives. *Organization Studies,* 24(2): 187–214.

Hedlund, G. 1986. The hypermodern MNC: a heterarchy? *Human Resource Management,* 25(1): 9–35.

1993. Assumptions of hierarchy and heterarchy, with applications to the management of the multinational corporation. In D. E. Westney and S. Ghoshal (eds.), *Organization Theory and the Multinational Corporation.* New York: St Martin's Press, 221–236.

Henisz, W. J. 2000a. The institutional environment for multinational investment. *Journal of Law, Economics and Organization,* 16(2): 334–364.

2000b. The institutional environment for economic growth. *Economics and Politics,* 12(1): 1–31.

Henisz, W. J. and Zelner, B. A. 2004. Explicating political hazards and safeguards: a transaction cost politics approach. *Industrial and Corporate Change,* 13(6): 901–915.

Hennart, J. F. 1982. *A Theory of Multinational Enterprise.* Ann Arbor: University of Michigan Press.

2001. Theories of the multinational enterprise. In A. M. Rugman and T. L. Brewer (eds.), *Oxford Handbook of International Business.* Oxford University Press, 127–149.

2009. Theories of the multinational enterprise. In A. M. Rugman (ed.), *The Oxford Handbook of International Business* (2nd edn). Oxford University Press, 125–145.

Hickson, D. J., Hinings, C. R., Lee, C. A., Schneck, R. E. and Pennings, J. M. 1971. Strategic contingencies' theory of intraorganizational power. *Administrative Science Quarterly,* 16(2): 216–229.

Hinings, C. R., Hickson, D. J., Pennings, J. M., Schneck, R. E. 1974. Structural conditions of intraorganizational power. *Administrative Science Quarterly,* 19(1): 22–44.

Hofstede, G. 1984. *Culture's Consequences: International Differences in Work-related Values.* Newbury Park, CA: Sage.

1994. *Cultures and Organizations: Software of the Mind.* London: Harper Collins Publishers.

Hollingsworth, J. R. and Boyer, R. 1997. Coordination of economic actors and social systems of production. In J. R. Hollingsworth and R. Boyer (eds.), *Contemporary Capitalism. The Embeddedness of Institutions.* Cambridge University Press, 1–47.

Hotho, J. and Pedersen, T. 2012. Beyond the 'rules of the game': three institutional approaches and how they matter for international business. In G. Wood and M. Demirbag (eds.), *Handbook of Institutional Approaches to International Business*. Cheltenham: Edward Elgar, 236–273.

House, R. J., Hanges, P. J., Javidan, M., Dorfman, P. and Gupta, V. 2004. *Leadership, Culture, and Organizations: the GLOBE Study of 62 Societies*. Thousand Oaks: Sage Publications.

Hymer, S. H. 1960. The international operations of national firms: a study of direct foreign investment. PhD thesis, MIT.

Ietto-Gillies, G. 2012. *Transnational Corporations and International Production. Trends, Theories, Effects* (2nd edn). Cheltenham, UK and Northampton, MA: Edward Elgar.

Jackson, G. and Deeg, R. 2008. Comparing capitalisms: understanding institutional diversity and its implications for international business. *Journal of International Business Studies*, 39(4): 540–561.

Jensen, M. and Meckling, W. 1976. Theory of the firm: managerial behavior, agency costs and ownership structure. *Journal of Financial Economics*, 3(4): 305–360.

Johanson, J. and Vahlne, J.-E. 1977. The internationalization process of the firm: a model of knowledge development and increasing foreign market commitments. *Journal of International Business Studies*, 8(1): 23–32.

  1990. The mechanism of internationalization. *International Marketing Review*, 7(4): 11–24.

Johanson, J. and Wiedersheim, P. F. 1975. The internationalization of the firm – the four Swedish cases. *Journal of Management Studies*, 12(3): 305–322.

Juul, M. and Walters, P. G. P. 1987. The internationalization of Norwegian firms – a study of the UK experience. *Management International Review*, 27(1): 58–66.

Kogut, B. and Singh, H. 1988. The effect of national culture on the choice of entry mode. *Journal of International Business Studies*, 19(3): 411–432.

Kogut, B. and Zander, U. 1992. Knowledge of the firm, combinative capabilities and the replication of technology. *Organization Science* 3(3): 383–397.

  1993/2003. Knowledge of the firm and the evolutionary theory of the multinational corporation. *Journal of International Business Studies*, 24(4): 625–645.

Kostova, T. 1999. Transnational transfer of strategic organisational practices: a contextual perspective. *Academy of Management Review*, 24(2): 308–324.

Kostova, T. and Roth, K. 2002. Adoption of an organizational practice by subsidiaries of multinational corporations: institutional and relational effects. *Academy of Management Journal*, 45(1): 215–233.

Kostova, T., Roth, K. and Dacin, M. 2008. Institutional theory in the study of MNCs: a critique and new directions. *Academy of Management Review*, 33(4): 994–1007.

Kristensen, P. H. and Zeitlin, J. 2001. The making of a global firm: local pathways to multinational enterprise. In G. Morgan, P. H. Kristensen and R. Whitley (eds.), *The Multinational Firm. Organizing Across Institutional and National Divides*. Oxford University Press, 172–195.

2005. *Local Players in Global Games*. Oxford University Press.

Laclau, E. and Mouffe, C. 1985. *Hegemony and Socialist Strategy: Towards a Radical Democracy*. Verso: London.

Lam, A. 2003. Organizational learning in multinationals: R&D networks of Japanese and US MNEs in the UK. *Journal of Management Studies*, 40(3): 673–703.

Lane, C. 1994. Industrial order and the transformation of industrial relations: Britain, Germany and France. In R. Hyman and A. Ferner (eds.), *New Frontiers in European Industrial Relations*. Oxford: Blackwell, 167–195.

2000. Understanding the globalization strategies of German and British multinational companies: is a 'societal effects' approach still useful? In M. Maurice and A. Sorge (eds.), *Embedding Organizations. Societal Analysis of Actors, Organizations and Socio-economic Context*. Amsterdam, PA: John Benjamins Publishing Company, 189–208.

2001. The emergence of German transnational companies: a theoretical analysis and empirical study of the globalization process. In G. Morgan, P. H. Kristensen and R. Whitley (eds.), *The Multinational Firm. Organizing Across Institutional and National Divides*. Oxford University Press, 69–96.

Larimo, J. 1985. The foreign direct manufacturing investment behaviour of Finnish companies. Paper presented at the European International Business Association Conference, Glasgow, December.

Lawrence, P. and Lorsch, J. 1967. *Differentiation and Integration. Administrative Science Quarterly*, 12(1): 1–30.

Levy, D. L. 2008. Political contestation in global production networks. *Academy of Management Review*, 33(4): 943–963.

Ling, Y., Floyd, S. W. and Baldridge, D. C. 2005. Toward a model of issue-selling by subsidiary managers in multinational organizations. *Journal of International Business Studies*, 36(6): 637–654.

Lukes, S. 2005. *Power: a Radical View*. Basingstoke: Palgrave.

Luostarinen, R. 1980. Internationalisation of the firm. *Acta Academica Series A: 30*. Helsinki School of Economics.

Lyotard, J.-F. 1979. *The Postmodern Condition: a Report on Knowledge* (trans. G. Bennington and B. Massumi). Minneapolis: University of Minnesota Press.

Maclean, M. and Hollinshead, G. 2011. Contesting social space in the Balkan region: the social dimensions of a 'red' joint venture. In C. Dörrenbächer and M. Geppert (eds.), *Politics and Power in the International Corporation: the Role of Institutions, Interests and Identities*. Cambridge University Press, 380–411.

Marschan-Piekkari, R., Welch, D. and Welch, L. 1999a. Adopting a common corporate language: IHRM implications. *International Journal of Human Resource Management*, 10(3): 377–390.

    1999b. In the shadow: the impact of language on structure, power and communication in the multinational. *International Business Review*, 8(4): 421–440.

Matten, D. and Geppert, M. 2004. Work systems in heavy engineering: the role of national culture and national institutions in multinational corporations. *Journal of International Management*, 10(2): 177–198.

Maurice, M., Sorge, A. and Warner, M. 1980. Societal differences in organizing manufacturing units: a comparison of France, West Germany, and Great Britain. *Organization Studies*, 1(1): 59–80.

Meyer, J. W. and Rowan, B. 1977/1991. Institutionalized organizations: formal structure as myth and ceremony. In W. W. Powell and P. J. DiMaggio (eds.), *The New Institutionalism in Organizational Analysis*. University Chicago Press, 41–62.

Mintzberg, H. 1983. *Power in Organizations*. Englewood Cliffs: Prentice-Hall.

Morgan, G. 2001. The multinational firm: organizing across institutional and national divides. In G. Morgan, P. Kristensen and R. Whitley (eds.), *The Multinational Firm: Organizing Across Institutional and National Divides*. Oxford University Press, 1–24.

Morgan, G. and Kristensen, P. H. 2006. The contested space of multinationals: varieties of institutionalism, varieties of capitalism. *Human Relations*, 59(11): 1467–1490.

Morgan, G. and Quack, S. 2005. Institutional legacies and firm dynamics: the internationalization of British and German law firms. *Organization Studies*, 26(12): 1765–1785.

Morgan, G. and Whitley, R. 2003. Introduction. *Journal of Management Studies*, 40(3): 609–616.

Mudambi, R. and Navarra, P. 2004. Is knowledge power? Knowledge flows, subsidiary power and rent seeking within MNCs. *Journal of International Business Studies*, 35(5): 385–406.

Mudambi, R. and Pedersen, T. 2007. Agency theory and resource dependency theory: complementary explanations for subsidiary power in multinational corporations. SMG Working Paper No. 5.

Nelson, R. R. and Winter, S. G. 1982. *An Evolutionary Theory of Economic Change*. Cambridge, MA: Harvard University Press.

Nohria, N. and Ghoshal, S. 1997. *The Differentiated Network: Organizing Multinational Corporations for Value Creation*. San Francisco: Jossey-Bass.

Pahl, J. M. and Roth, K. 1993. Managing the headquarters–foreign subsidiary relationship: the roles of strategy, conflict, and integration. *The International Journal of Conflict Management*, 4(2): 139–165.

Penrose, E. 1959. *The Theory of the Growth of the Firm*. New York: Wiley.

Pfeffer, J. 1981. *Power in Organizations*. Marshfield, MA: Pitman.

1992. *Managing with Power: Politics and Influence in Organizations*. Harvard Business School Press.

Pfeffer, J. and Salancik, G. R. 1974. Organizational decision making as a political process: the case of a university budget. *Administrative Science Quarterly*, 19(2): 135–151.

1978. *The External Control of Organizations*. New York: Harper and Row.

Phillips, N. and Hardy, C. 2002. *Discourse Analysis: Investigating Processes of Social Construction*. London: Sage.

Phillips, N., Sewell, G. and Jaynes, S. 2008. Applying critical discourse analysis in strategic management research. *Organizational Research Methods*, 11(4): 770–789.

Pondy, L. R. 1967. Organizational conflict: concepts and models. *Administrative Science Quarterly*, 12(2): 296–320.

Prahalad, C. K. and Doz, Y. L. 1987. *The Multinational Mission*. New York: The Free Press.

Quintanilla, J. and Varul, M. Z. 2001. Country-of-origin effects, host-country effects, and the management of HR in multinationals: German companies in Britain and Spain. *Journal of World Business*, 36(2): 107–127.

Riad, S. 2005. The power of 'organizational culture' as a discursive formation in merger integration. *Organization Studies*, 26(10): 1529–1554.

Rojo, L. and van Dijk, T. 1997. 'There was a problem, and it was solved!': legitimating the expulsion of 'illegal' migrants in Spanish parliamentary discourse. *Discourse and Society*, 8(4): 523–566.

Rosenzweig, P. M. and Nohria, N. 1994. Influences on human resource management practices in multinational corporations. *Journal of International Business Studies*, 25(2): 229–251.

Rosenzweig, P. M. and Singh, J. V. (1991). Organizational environments and the multinational enterprise. *Academy of Management Review*, 16(2): 340–361.

Roth, K. and Nigh, D. 1992. The effectiveness of headquarters–subsidiary relationships: the role of coordination, control, and conflict. *Journal of Business Research*, 25(4): 277–301.

Rothman, J. and Friedman, V. J. 2001. Identity, conflict and organizational learning. In M. Dierkes, A. Berthoin Antal, J. Child and I. Nonaka (eds.), *The Handbook of Organizational Learning and Knowledge*. Oxford University Press, 582–597.

Rugman, A. M. 1981. *Inside the Multinationals: the Economics of Internal Markets*. New York: Columbia Press. Reissued in 2006 as *Inside the Multinationals*, (25th Anniversary Edition). Basingstoke: Palgrave Macmillan.

Rugman, A. M., Verbeke, A. and Nguyen, Q. T. K. 2011. Fifty years of international business theory and beyond. *Management International Review*, 51(6): 755–786.

Said, E. W. 2003. *Orientalism*. London: Penguin Books. First published in 1978 by Routledge and Kegan Paul.

Saka, A. 2003. *Cross-national Appropriation of Work Systems, Japanese Firms in the UK*. Cheltenham, Northampton: Edward Elgar.

Salancik, G. R. and Pfeffer, J. 1977. Who gets power and how they hold on to it: a strategic contingency model of power. *Organizational Dynamics*, 5(3): 3–21.

Scharpf, F. 1997. *Games Real Actors Play. Actor-centered Institutionalism in Policy Research*. Boulder, Cumnor Hill: Westview Press.

Schwartz, S. H. 1992. Universals in the content and structure of values: theoretical advances and empirical tests in 20 countries. In M. P. Zana (ed.), *Advances in Experimental Social Psychology*, 25. New York: Academic Press, 1–65.

    1994. Cultural dimensions of values: towards an understanding of national differences. In U. Kim, H. C. Triandis, C. Kagitcibasi, S. C. Choi and G. Yoon (eds.), *Individualism and Collectivism: Theoretical and Methodological Issues*. Thousand Oaks, CA: Sage, 85–119.

Scott, W. R. 1995. *Institutions and Organizations*. Thousand Oaks: Sage.

    1998. *Organizations: Rational, Natural and Open System*. New Jersey: Prentice-Hall.

Sharpe, D. R. 1997. Compromise solutions: a Japanese multinational comes to the UK. In R. Whitley and P. H. Kristensen (eds.), *Governance at*

Work: the Social Regulation of Economic Relations. Oxford University Press, 171–189.

Shenkar, O. 2001. Cultural distance revisited: towards a more rigorous conceptualization and measurement of cultural differences. *Journal of International Business Studies*, 32(3): 519–535.

Sorge, A. 1985. *Informationstechnik und Arbeit im sozialen Prozeß. Arbeitsorganisation, Qualifikation u. Produktivkraftentwicklung*. Frankfurt and New York: Campus.

1991. Strategic fit and the societal effect: interpreting cross-national comparisons of technology, organization and human resources. *Organization Studies*, 12(2): 161–190.

1995. Cross-national differences in personnel and organization. In A. W. Harzing and J. V. Ruysseveldt (eds.), *International Human Resource Management*. London: Sage, 99–123.

Stopford, J. M. and Wells, L. T. 1972. *Managing the Multinational Enterprise: Organization of the Firm and Ownership of the Subsidiaries*. New York: Basic Books.

Streeck, W. and Thelen, K. 2005. *Beyond Continuity – Institutional Change in Advanced Political Economies*. Oxford University Press.

Teece, D. J. 1977. Technology transfer by multinational corporations: the resource cost of transferring technological know-how. *Economic Journal*, 87(346): 242–261.

Tienari, J. and Vaara, E. 2012. Power and politics in mergers and acquistions. In D. Faulkner, S. Teerikangas and R. J. Joseph (eds.), *The Handbook of Mergers and Acquisitions*. Oxford University Press.

Thomas, K. W. 1992. Conflict and conflict management: reflections and update. *Journal of Organizational Behavior*, 13(3): 265–274.

Trompenaars, F. and Hampden-Turner, C. 1997. *Riding the Waves of Culture: Understanding Cultural Diversity in Business* (2nd edn). London: Nicholas Brealey.

1998. *Riding the Waves of Culture: Understanding Cultural Diversity in Global Business*. New York: McGraw-Hill.

Turnbull, P. W. and Valla, J.-P. 1986. *Strategies for International Industrial Marketing: the Management of Customer Relationships in European Industrial Markets*. London: Croom Helm.

Uhlenbruck, K., Rodriguez, P., Doh, J. and Eden, L. 2006. The impact of corruption on entry strategy: evidence from telecommunication projects in emerging economies. *Organization Science*, 17(3): 401–414.

Uzzi, B. 1996. The sources and consequences of embeddedness for the economic performance of organizations: the network effect. *American Sociological Review*, 61(4): 674–698.

1997. Social structure and competition in interfirm networks. The paradox of embeddedness. *Administrative Science quarterly*, 42(1): 35–67.

Vaara, E. and Monin, P. 2010. A recursive perspective on discursive legitimation and organizational action in mergers and acquisitions. *Organization Science*, 21(1): 3–22.

Vaara, E. and Tienari, J. 2002. Justification, legitimization and naturalization of mergers and acquisitions: a critical discourse analysis of media texts. *Organization*, 9(2): 275–304.

2004. Critical discourse analysis as methodology for critical international business studies. In R. Marschan-Piekkari and C. Welch (eds.), *Handbook of Qualitative Research Methods for International Business*. Edward Elgar.

2008. A discursive perspective on legitimation strategies in MNCs. *Academy of Management Review*, 33(4): 985–993.

2011. On the narrative construction of MNCs: an antenarrative analysis of legitimation and resistance in a cross-border merger. *Organization Science*, 22(2): 370–390.

Vaara, E., Tienari, J. and Laurila, J. 2006. Pulp and paper fiction: on the discursive legitimation of global industrial restructuring. *Organization Studies*, 27(6): 789–810.

Vaara, E., Tienari, J., Piekkari, R. and Säntti, R. 2005. Language and the circuits of power in a merging multinational corporation. *Journal of Management Studies*, 42(3): 595–623.

van Dijk, T. 1998. *Ideology: a Multidisciplinary Approach*. London: Sage.

van Leeuwen, T. and Wodak, R. 1999. Legitimizing immigration control: a discourse-historical perspective. *Discourse Studies*, 1(1): 83–118.

Vernon, R. 1966. International investment and international trade in the product life cycle. *The Quarterly Journal of Economics*, 80(2): 190–207.

Weber, M. 1947. *The Theory of Social and Economic Organization*, translated by A. M. Henderson and Talcott Parsons. Edited with an introduction by Talcott Parsons. New York: Free Press.

Werner, S. 2002. Recent developments in international management research: a review of 20 top management journals. *Journal of Management*, 28(3): 277–305.

Wernerfelt, B. 1984. A resource-based view of the firm. *Strategic Management Journal*, 5(2): 171–180.

Westney, D. E. 1993. Institutionalization theory and the multinational corporation. In S. Ghoshal and D. E. Westney (eds.), *Organization Theory and the Multinational Corporation*. New York: St. Martins Press, 53–76.

Westney, D. E. and Zaheer, S. 2009. The multinational enterprise as an organization. In A. M. Rugman (ed.), *The Oxford Handbook of International Business*. Oxford University Press, 341–366.

Whitley, R. (ed.) 1992. *European Business Systems. Firms and Markets in their National Contexts*. London: Sage.

Whitley, R. 1998. Internationalization and varieties of capitalism: the limited effects of cross-national coordination of economic activities on the nature of business systems. *Review of International Political Economy*, 5(3): 445–481.

1999. *Divergent Capitalism*. Oxford University Press.

2001. How and why are international firms different? The consequences of cross-border managerial coordination for firm characteristics and behavior. In G. Morgan, P. H. Kristensen, R. Whitley (eds.), *The Multinational Firm. Organizing Across Institutional and National Divides*. Oxford University Press, 27–68.

2009. The multinational company as a distinct organisational form. In D. Collinson and G. Morgan (eds.), *Images of the Multinational Firm*. Oxford: Blackwell Publishing, 145–166.

Williams, C. and Lee, S. H. 2011. Political heterarchy and dispersed entrepreneurship in the MNC. *Journal of Management Studies*, 48(6): 1243–1268.

Williams, K. and Geppert, M. 2011. Bargained globalization: employment relations providing robust 'tool kits' for socio-political strategizing in MNCs in Germany. In C. Dörrenbächer and M. Geppert (eds.), *Politics and Power in the International Corporation: the Role of Institutions, Interests and Identities*. Cambridge University Press, 72–100.

Williamson, O. E. 1985. *The Economic Institutions of Capitalism: Firms, Markets and Relational Contracting*. New York: Free Press.

Wodak, R. and Meyer, M. 2002. *Methods of Critical Discourse Analysis*. London: Sage.

Xu, D. and Shenkar, O. 2002. Institutional distance and the multinational enterprise. *The Academy of Management Review*, 27(4): 608–618.

Yamin, M. and Andersson, U. 2011. Subsidiary importance in the MNC: what role does internal embeddedness play? *International Business Review*, 20(2): 151–162.

PART II

Seminal contributions

Introduction

In the previous chapters, we discussed the emergence of politics, power and conflict perspectives in the field of international business and management (IB&M). We covered this development from two ends, that is, first by discussing seminal contributions on politics, power and conflict in organization studies, and second by tracing the emergence and introduction of politics, power and conflict perspectives to the field of IB&M. We argued that the adoption of the two paradigmatic shifts in organization studies, that is, from closed- to open-system perspectives and importantly from rational- to natural-system perspectives of the organization paved the way for the development of politics, power and conflict perspectives in IB&M. Specifically, while the natural-system perspectives entail a recognition of actor and interest diversity in organizations, that is, adopting a generic politics perspective, the open-system perspective opens our horizon to external and systemic conditions that play a role in structuring the interest and divergent behavioural rationales of actors in multinational corporations (MNCs).

In Chapter 3, we discussed a range of streams that, while moving us closer to the emergence of politics, power and conflict perspectives in IB&M, are not genuine politics, power and conflict perspectives. Furthermore, while certain streams may come to recognize actor and interest diversity in MNCs as well as their external contextual constitution, they may not directly engage with the concepts of politics, power and conflict. In our understanding, however, a fully developed politics, power and conflict perspective requires a direct concern with these concepts as either explanans or explanandum of organizational behaviour in MNCs as well as some theoretical consideration of these terms.

119

Politics, power and conflict perspectives do not emerge until the introduction of organization theories and more specifically with the shift from open-rational to open-natural perspectives. Based on our above understanding, we distinguish broadly three genuine power, politics and conflict schools within the field of IB&M. They include: (i) the rationalistic-managerialist (or functionalistic) school based on the network, the intraorganizational power and the resource dependency perspective; (ii) the institutionalist and micropolitics school based on different institutionalist perspectives and/or micropolitics perspectives; and (iii) the critical-management school based on various critical perspectives.

In the following Chapters 4, 5 and 6, we will take a closer look at seminal and widely recognized contributions within these three schools of research. We discuss three seminal contributions in Chapter 4 and four seminal contributions in Chapters 5 and 6. The selection of these contributions was based on the following two criteria. First, they are widely cited contributions that have acted as signposts in the evolution of politics, power and perspectives in the field of IB&M in recent years. Second, they are contributions that exemplarily represent these major schools while, at the same time, illustrating the variety within these different schools.

To highlight similarities and differences between these contributions, we apply a common grid to our discussion. The grid starts with the empirical focus of the contribution. We then explore in what way politics, power or conflict are related to organizational behaviour of MNCs and how central they are for the understanding of the organizational behaviour of MNCs. The theoretical focus explores the main theoretical roots of the contribution and in particular the conceptualization of MNCs, politics, power and conflict (generic vs. aspectual concept of politics; episodic vs. systemic concept of power). This analysis includes asking how actors and their behavioural orientations (interests and sources of power) are conceptualized. The final dimension covers the actor-context relations. This includes asking what defines the relevant context and how it structures actor interests and power sources as well as the question of how reactive or proactive and dependent or independent actors are conceptualized vis-à-vis their context (see Table 4.1 defining core questions and elements of our analytical grid).

Table 4.1 *Analytical grid applied to seminal contributions*

Analytical dimension	Relevant questions
Empirical focus	What aspect of organizational behaviour in MNCs is the empirical focus? What aspect of organizational behaviour in MNCs is related to politics, power or conflict?
Centrality of politics, power and conflict	How central are politics, power and conflict to understand the organizational behaviour of MNCs? Are politics, power and conflict explanans and/or explanandum?
Theoretical focus	What are the main theoretical roots of the contribution? What theories are employed to conceptualize politics, power and conflict in MNCs?
Concept of MNC	How are MNCs conceptualized? Are they conceptualized as rational systems (i.e. MNCs as monolithic, purpose- and goal-driven entities constituted by formal structure) or as natural systems (i.e. MNCs as collectives whose participants are pursuing multiple interests, both disparate and common and having often diffuse and conflicting goals)?
Concept of politics, power and conflict	Is the concept of politics aspectual (i.e. approaches which view organizational politics as an aspect, a phenomenon in organizational life) or generic (i.e. approaches which see politics as constitutive of organizational life, i.e. organizations as political systems)? Is the concept of power episodic (i.e. where actors employ available power bases to pursue their recognized interests in instances of organizational politics) or is it systemic (i.e. power as domination embedded in institutions, cultures and norms that structure discourses, interests and power sources, roles and identities)? How does the paper conceptualize conflict (e.g. incompatible interests, resistance; conflict as overt, hidden or latent)?

(cont.)

Table 4.1 *(cont.)*

Analytical dimension	Relevant questions
Concept of actors and behavioural orientation	What kind of actors are considered (individual actors or organizational units; managerial vs. comprehensive actor perspective)? How are actors conceptualized (e.g. autonomous vs. contextually determined; perfectly rational vs. bounded rational; strategic vs. situational rationality)? How are actors' behavioural goals/ends conceptualized (e.g. kind of interests, intentions or preferences, etc.; consciousness, consistency and contradiction of goals or interests; degree of alignment between individual and organizational goals or interests)? How are actors' means, i.e. their sources of power conceptualized (kind of power basis: resources, rules, relations discourses, etc.)? How are actors' means–ends orientations, i.e. their behavioural orientations conceptualized?
Concept of actor-context relation	What MNC internal and external behavioural context is considered? What kind of contextual conditions (e.g. individual biographical, systemic, structural or discursive) constitute actors and their behavioural orientations (their goals/ends and means/sources of power)? Are actors seen as passive, responsive, proactive or in a recursive relationship with their context (e.g. does the outcome of power episodes have an effect on the context)?

4 | Seminal contributions of the rationalistic-managerialist school

FLORIAN A. A. BECKER-RITTERSPACH
AND JENS GAMMELGAARD

Is knowledge power? Knowledge flows, subsidiary power and rent-seeking within MNCs, by Ram Mudambi and Pietro Navarra, published in the *Journal of International Business Studies* in 2004

Empirical focus

Mudambi and Navarra's (2004) starting point is the dilemma that is connected to the increasing strategic independence of subsidiaries in multinational corporations (MNCs). On the one hand, subsidiary independence constitutes a vital prerequisite of learning and competitive advantage of MNCs. On the other hand, strategic independence and strong bargaining power enhances the subsidiaries' ability to seek and appropriate rents that challenge the shareholder value of the MNC as a whole.

Thus subsidiary strategic independence, designed to enhance the competitiveness of outputs (market knowledge) and inputs (asset-seeking and learning), can be corroded when the pursuit of subsidiary objectives encourages rent-seeking. (Mudambi and Navarra 2004: 385)

The paper aims at understanding the determinants of the political behaviour of rent-seeking by subsidiaries in MNCs. The paper addresses the question to what extent subsidiary rent-seeking is related to subsidiary bargaining power, and to what extent subsidiary bargaining power, in turn, is constituted by knowledge flows. In the model presented by Mudambi and Navarra (2004) subsidiary power assumes a central role as subsidiary power is used as both explanandum (explained by knowledge flows) and explanans (explaining rent-seeking). The empirical analysis conducted largely confirms that knowledge flows within MNCs are strong predictors for subsidiary

123

power and that subsidiary power is a strong predictor for the subsidiary managers' ability to appropriate rents. In particular, subsidiaries vested with knowledge that is vital for the MNC as a whole and subsidiaries with large knowledge outflows to other MNC units tend to command a high bargaining power within the MNC and therefore a higher ability to appropriate rents.

Theoretical focus

The paper adopts a rational-system perspective of the MNC, which is blended with a natural-system perspective. While the natural-system perspective finds expression in seeing MNCs as political systems full of interest diversity, bargaining and conflict, the rational-system perspective appears to take precedence over the former. The rational-system perspective is reflected in the remnants of a hierarchical view of the MNC, where headquarters are vested with the role, power and ability to maintain overall organizational rationality. A case in point is the paper's suggestions on how rent-seeking behaviour of subsidiary managers may be curbed by headquarters. In this regard, Mudambi and Navarra (2004) discuss the role of appropriate control structures, such as the centralized M-form, as well as motivators for subsidiary managers. The latter involves participatory management practices that serve to create subsidiary manager orientations beyond a mere opportunistic subsidiary focus with the effect of upholding the overall organizational rationality.

In a similar vein, the conceptualization of politics falls between a generic and aspectual perspective. While politics, power and conflict are seen as everyday occurrences, reflecting a generic politics perspective, the mainly negative connotation of subsidiary power is more reflective of an aspectual view of politics. In this view, subsidiary power leads to unwanted aberrations from overall organizational rationality and proper organizational life.

The extent of rent-seeking and consequent resource misallocation is dependent upon the extent to which bargaining power can be influenced by subsidiary actions. As internal bargaining power considerations become more important, resources devoted to firm-focused support of other units of the MNC fall. (Mudambi and Navarra 2004: 393)

Hence, while the paper also adopts elements of a natural-system perspective, its overriding conceptualization of MNCs as rational systems and its aspectual view of politics, places the paper clearly within the ambit of a rationalistic-managerialist perspective.

In terms of theory, the paper builds on a combination of a differentiated network perspective, principle agent theory and implicitly on resource-dependence theory. While power assumes a key role in the paper, no specific theorization of organizational power is offered. The implicit concept of power is episodic and based on a resource-dependence perspective. Although power is not defined, the paper develops elaborate hypotheses with respect to determinants of subsidiary power. Mudambi and Navarra (2004) see knowledge assets (research and development [R&D] intangibles mainly) as the key sources of subsidiary power. Specifically, the paper theorizes and confirms that the greater the total knowledge output of a unit, the greater its knowledge outflows to other units within the MNC, the greater the knowledge outflow to its location and the greater the level of process control exercised by a given subsidiary, the greater its bargaining power within the MNC. In sum, subsidiary power is above all rooted in the knowledge intensity and pattern of knowledge flows.

The actors considered comprise headquarters and subsidiary managers. However, as subsidiary managers' interests are equated with subsidiary interest, the approach is essentially confined to organization-level actors.

Subsidiary managers are stakeholders in the firm, and are driven by both firm-focused and individual objectives (Coff 1999). Their individual objectives are generally more aligned to their subsidiaries than to the firm as a whole. (Mudambi and Navarra 2004: 392)

A main goal of the paper is to develop a theory of subsidiary behaviour within MNCs. It is noted that subsidiaries tend to have their own objectives, which are only partly in alignment with the MNC as a whole. Subsidiaries and their managers' behavioural orientation are seen as driven by two objectives. The first is external, based in 'profit seeking', and involves 'maximizing shareholders' value through market operations aimed at maximising profits' (Mudambi and Navarra 2004: 386). The second, which is the focus of the paper, involves the appropriation of internally distributed rents.

Thus, managers' attempts at serving firm-focused shareholder value maximization objectives (profit seeking) coexist uneasily with their attempts at maximizing their bargaining power within the firm (rent-seeking) (Scharfstein and Stein 2000). (Mudambi and Navarra 2004: 392)

The headquarters' behavioural orientation, in turn, is associated with realizing overall shareholder value. This objective involves curbing the rent-seeking behaviour of subsidiaries. Put simply, while subsidiaries tend to act opportunistically to increase bargaining power with the goal to appropriate corporate rents, the headquarters aim at restricting the opportunistic behaviour of subsidiaries through monitoring and limiting subsidiary autonomy. These behavioural assumptions are reflective of the principle–agent perspective of the paper, with headquarters taking the role of the principle and subsidiaries the role of the agent.

We use the lens of agency theory to view subsidiary managers as agents of headquarters. Within this framework, agents (the subsidiaries) bargain with the principal (headquarters) to maximize their share of MNC-wide rents. (Mudambi and Navarra 2004: 388)

Mudambi and Navarra (2004) do not theorize extensively the contextual constitution of actor or subsidiary behaviour. The actors' behavioural orientations are mainly related to their embeddedness within the MNC. Behavioural orientations of subsidiaries and headquarters are assumed as given, that is, as springing from the principle–agent relationship between subsidiaries and headquarters. This also implies that there is little consideration for variations in the behavioural orientation of different subsidiaries, let alone among different individual actors within MNC subunits. While the paper does not develop a differentiated understanding on the contextual basis of actor interests, it does provide some understanding of the contextual constitution of subsidiary power. Although this includes aspects related to the external environment, most of the contextual conditions considered are internal to the MNC. As explicated above, they mainly relate to the situation of the subsidiary with respect to subsidiary knowledge stock and knowledge outflows. As the paper shows only limited concern with respect to actor-context relations, there is also little consideration for the question if and how actors can shape their environment.

Balancing subsidiary influence in the federative MNC: a
business network view, by Ulf Andersson, Mats Forsgren and
Ulf Holm, published in the *Journal of International Business
Studies* in 2007

Empirical focus

Similar to the paper by Mudambi and Navarra (2004), Andersson
et al. (2007) are interested in how the outcome of subsidiaries' rent-
seeking efforts in MNCs is affected by their bargaining power. This
includes asking what determines subsidiary bargaining power. The
subsidiaries' rent-seeking efforts are conceptualized as their efforts to
influence strategic decisions or, more specifically, to influence strategic
investments in MNCs.

The paper by Andersson *et al.* (2007) focuses on intraorganizational power in MNCs and its sources. The paper pays particular
attention to the question to what extent varying subsidiary influence
can be explained by the subsidiary's embeddedness within an external
business network. The paper finds that the strength and influence of
the subsidiary's external business networks only matter for subsidiary
power if the subsidiary provides technology to other units within the
MNC. In other words, a strong external subsidiary network only provides a subsidiary with an influence in the MNC, if the subsidiary
contributes to the internal network. Andersson *et al.* (2007) also find
that headquarters' knowledge about the subsidiary's external business
networks has a moderating effect on subsidiary influence. Put differently, the authors focus on subsidiary influence in MNCs as an explanandum and see different bases of power, primarily networks and
derived resource-dependency situations, as their explanans.

Theoretical focus

The paper falls half way between a rational and natural system perspective of MNCs. On the one hand, the paper gives up the idea of an
MNC as a hierarchically coordinated and controlled entity that is able
to fully maintain a centrally defined and overarching organizational
rationality. On the other hand, the paper still falls into a rationalistic-
managerialist stream as it sees headquarters and subsidiaries or their
management as rational actors furthering the strategic interests of their

units by employing sources of power towards the units' own ends or interests.

In comparison to Mudambi and Navarra (2004), however, Andersson *et al.* (2007) move further away from an aspectual view of politics and are closer to adopting a generic politics perspective. In this view, politics, power and conflict are defining elements of organizational life in MNCs. A further expression of the natural-system perspective and the related generic politics perspectives is seeing organizational life in MNCs as marked by both conflict and tension but also by collaboration and coalition.

It must be pointed out, though, that our model does not imply that conflicts and market-like power struggles are the only features of organisational life in MNCs. There is also room for a strong sense of collaboration and mutualism, and even a 'social welfare' mentality in the sense of the support or charters given to subunits experiencing difficulties (Galunic and Eisenhardt, 1996). We posit, though, that an intra-company competition for influence, based on the control of critical resources, is a necessary ingredient in a model that intends to capture the strategic behaviour of MNCs. (Andersson *et al.* 2007: 816)

Andersson *et al.* understand MNCs as federative entities that are constituted by multiple actors and 'dispersed structures of power'. Such a perspective implies that 'the headquarters is perceived as one player among others' (Andersson *et al.* 2007: 808) in the corporate bargaining processes. The actors considered are at the organizational level and comprise subsidiaries and headquarters. Their main behavioural orientation is geared towards influencing strategic decisions in MNCs in their interest. This also implies that units tend to have different interests based on their role and embeddedness within and outside the MNC. Although headquarters are seen as one player among others, Andersson *et al.* (2007) still hold on to seeing headquarters' behaviour as geared towards the MNC as a whole.

While an individual subsidiary will be partial to its own interest, rooted in its local business, the headquarters needs to consider initiatives and suggestions from all subsidiaries, and not only those that are considered important for others within the MNC. The headquarters must make sure that a certain amount of future investment will be placed in sub-units other than the most important ones, probably often in opposition from the latter. (Andersson *et al.* 2007: 808)

In the corporate bargaining processes, actors differ in their ability to influence strategic decisions. This points to differences in power among actors which are related to their divergent bases of power. In this sense, the contribution contests a simple rationalistic-managerialist perspective of hierarchical power in which top management oversees, controls and governs the MNC in line with clearly defined organizational goals (c.f. Mudambi and Navarra 2004 who are more optimistic about headquarters' ability to maintain overall organizational rationality of the MNC).

The paper builds on an episodic understanding of power where actors employ available power bases to pursue their interests in instances of organizational politics. In terms of theoretical roots, the paper combines network, intraorganizational power and resource-dependency perspectives. The conceptualization of power builds primarily on a Weberian definition of organizational power as adopted by Dahl (1957) and Emerson (1962). Andersson *et al.* (2007) concede that concepts of power are context specific. In the context of understanding subsidiary power and influence, they find power 'to be strongly associated with the ability to "win" political fights: that is, it is the ability of the headquarters and the subsidiaries to get things done, regardless of the motivation of and resistance from others within the MNC' (Andersson *et al.* 2007: 805). Moreover, to identify bases of power within a federative MNC, they draw on a resource-dependence perspective-based understanding of power (e.g. Pfeffer and Salancik 1978). Specifically, 'a subunit's access to resources that are critical for other subunits in the federative MNC is the primary base of power, rather than personal traits like reputation or charisma' (Andersson *et al.* 2007: 805). A subunit's access to resources, in turn, is constituted by the relationship the unit has with its business network. Moreover, drawing on Krackhardt (1990), Andersson *et al.* (2007) argue that power may not only be based on the network centrality but also on the network knowledge of a subunit. In this view, subunit power can also be rooted in an accurate perception of the network, irrespective of a unit's own network position. In summary, network embeddedness and network knowledge are theorized as key sources of power in MNCs. Following this perspective, key sources of subsidiary power are the degree of subsidiary embeddedness in its local business context. However, the latter only serves as a source of power if a subsidiary is important for the competence development of other units in the MNC. The authors also argue that subsidiary influence can only be properly understood if we consider the balancing power or counter-forces of the headquarters. The headquarters' power for its part includes its formal authority, but goes beyond it, as it crucially rests on headquarters' knowledge of subsidiary external networks based on monitoring these networks.

In comparison to Mudambi and Navarra (2004), Andersson *et al.* (2007) pay more attention to the contextual constitution of both actor interests and resources. Andersson *et al.* (2007) very explicitly relate the actors' behavioural orientations, that is, the interests and power of organizational units, to their embeddedness inside and outside the MNC. The embeddedness or actor-context relationship is conceptualized as relationships between actors that are tied to each other through resource exchanges. While the internal embeddedness involves the question of to what extent a subunit contributes to the competence development of other units, the external environment relates to subunit's external business network embeddedness. The perspective takes a particular close look at how the local environment constitutes a power base of subsidiaries. It emphasizes that the 'effectiveness of a subsidiary's linkages with its local environment as a power base can vary... depending on the characteristics of these linkages, including with whom the subsidiary has linkages' (Andersson *et al.* 2007: 803). So the paper accentuates specific relationships with key customers and suppliers. Although the internal and external environments are important to understand the behavioural orientation of different organizational actors in MNCs, the paper does not theorize much on the ability of organizational units to shape and structure their environments. Nevertheless, there is some implicit understanding that just as headquarters can develop a better knowledge of subsidiary external networks, so subsidiaries can develop their external business networks over time. In this sense, subunits as actors in MNCs are not viewed as fully determined by their environment but rather as agents who can proactively develop their environment.

Managing power in the multinational corporation: how low power actors gain influence, by Cyril Bouquet and Julian Birkinshaw, published in the *Journal of Management* in 2008

Empirical focus

At the core of this conceptual paper lies the question of how low-power actors in MNCs gain influence. Bouquet and Birkinshaw (2008) look at subsidiary units in low-power status positions within the MNC. In focusing on this question, the paper is quite distinct from the two previous ones. First, it does not look primarily at the powerful actors and their sources of power but rather at the variety of political strategies that low-power actors can employ to gain influence. Influence is seen as the achievement of three types of strategic objectives, which are achieving legitimacy, controlling resources upon which others depend and gaining centrality in the intraorganizational network. Second, the paper emphasizes agency and degrees of freedom of low-power actors and, thereby, challenges politics and power perspectives that see actors and their behavioural orientation as determined by structural or contextual embeddedness. Third, the paper shifts from a static perspective to a more dynamic perspective of politics in MNCs. It does so by discussing a wide range of political games that can serve to challenge and change the status quo of the power balance within the MNC. Bouquet and Birkinshaw (2008) summarize their approach as follows:

Most of the international management literature takes a top-down approach to understanding how MNCs can exert their power, or it examines in a purely descriptive sense the way that power and influence are distributed across an interorganizational network. But such approaches underplay or ignore the important role of managerial agency on the part of the subsidiary unit, or other subordinate entity, in changing the power balance in the system. By focusing in this study on the strategies low-power actors can take to increase their degrees of freedom, we provide an important point of view on the dynamics of change in MNCs. (Bouquet and Birkinshaw 2008: 478)

Politics and power are at the very core of this paper. Political games are the explanans for the shifting power and influence of low-power subsidiaries in MNCs (explanandum).

Theoretical focus

In our trilogy of rationalistic-managerialist papers, the paper by Bouquet and Birkinshaw (2008) moves closest to a natural system perspective of organizations. In comparison to Andersson *et al.* (2007), organizational life in MNCs becomes even messier. While low-power subsidiaries are assumed to behave rationally in their interest, that is, trying to gain more power and influence, there is no guarantee that they will succeed with the alternative strategies they resort to. This is because political dynamics are too complex to make straightforward predictions about possible outcomes. In this context, Bouquet and Birkinshaw (2008) also speak of a 'cacophony' of competing initiatives, where actors at different levels pursue their strategic interests. In this sense, Bouquet and Birkinshaw (2008) move very close to seeing MNCs as natural systems.

Similarly, the politics perspective adopted can be understood as generic, as MNCs are seen as 'highly political arenas' in which 'factions, coalitions, and cliques are continuously trying to influence one another to advance the interests of their members' (Bouquet and Birkinshaw 2008: 492). As organizational life is constituted by political games and micropolitics, the organizational behaviour of MNCs is largely a reflection of political interests. It is evident that this perspective challenges the idea of MNCs as hierarchically coordinated and controlled entities that follows a centrally defined and overarching organizational rationality.

The paper relates politics and power closely to each other in a causal means–ends relationship. In this view, politics, or rather political games, are the means to change the power balance and to gain influence. While this understanding is indicative of an episodic view of power where power games are used to pursue recognized interests in instances of organizational politics, the paper's power perspective also shades into a systemic perspective because it addresses the question how low-power actors can challenge an extant structure of domination in the MNC.

As in the previous papers, the actors considered are primarily organizational units within the MNC. Even though there is some mentioning of subsidiary managers, their behavioural orientation is equated with that of the subsidiary. The focal actors in this contribution are the subsidiaries who are understood as semiautonomous actors. The conceptualization of subsidiary actors as semiautonomous stresses that while subsidiaries are hierarchically dependent on their corporate parents they tend to have substantial degrees of freedoms and powers to influence the organizational behaviour in MNCs.

To develop a comprehensive understanding of the behavioural orientation of actors, or more specifically of the low-power actors, the paper synthesizes three theoretical lenses on power and influence in MNCs. Specifically, to understand the interests of low-power actors in MNCs, the paper draws on new institutionalist (e.g. DiMaggio and Powell

1983; Scott 1987), resource-dependency (e.g. Bacharach and Lawler 1980; Pfeffer 1981, 1992; Pfeffer and Salancik 1978) and social network perspectives (e.g. Hickson *et al.* 1971). Bouquet and Birkinshaw (2008) argue that low-power actors follow three 'strategic objectives' to gain influence. They comprise, in correspondence with the theories mentioned, the objective of increasing legitimacy, the objective of controlling critical resources and the objective of gaining centrality in corporate and external networks. It is assumed that these three objectives are crucial for gaining power and influence within the MNC. Importantly, these three objectives, legitimacy, resource dependency and network centrality, are seen as interrelated. While resources are the means that contribute to power and influence, resources without an actor's legitimacy or centrality may not be effective in influencing upper or central actors within the MNC (Bouquet and Birkinshaw 2008: 489).

Bouquet and Birkenshaw (2008) argue that low-power actors can resort to two broad approaches to reach their objectives. The first involves adopting 'creative strategies' that are geared to challenging the status quo in the MNC. The second involves playing political games with the aim of establishing an agenda in the existing 'circuits of power'. Regarding the first option of challenging the status quo Bouquet and Birkenshaw (2008) discuss three different approaches:

The first approach involves proactive initiative taking to build and develop the subsidiary, perhaps by developing new products or by bidding for new corporate investments. The second approach, profile building, consists of strategies aimed at building stronger relationships with other parts of the global company, with a view to enhancing the reputation of a subsidiary so that it can better develop in the future. The third approach, like the first, is the most radical in nature and involves low power subsidiaries attempting to 'break the rules of the game'. (Markides 2000)

Breaking rules involves particularly high levels of risk as it implies that subsidiaries are working around or outside the corporate system to change their position and power. Cases in point are subsidiaries teaming up with local governments to leverage external resources or external legitimacy, to enhance their internal standing and reputation.

Bouquet and Birkenshaw (2008) distinguish six types of power game based on whether strategies rest on individual or collective efforts (modes of action) and whether they involve addressing simple, complicated or complex problems (problem resolution). These different games are discussed at some length including the question of how readily available and risky they are. Bouquet and Birkinshaw (2008) also elaborate that these games do not equally benefit the different objectives as there are different trade-offs to consider. Finally, they allude to the condition that power games are highly intertwined which adds to their complexity and a need for holistic perspectives when playing them.

Bouquet and Birkinshaw (2008) only partially relate actors and their behavioural orientation to their contextual and external environmental embeddedness. On the one hand, the fact that some subsidiaries are at a given point in time low-power actors is directly related to their contextual situation (low legitimacy, low resources and low network centrality) within and outside the MNC. In a similar vein, subsidiary objectives of overcoming their weak position in the MNC are also informed by their internal and external situation. On the other hand, the authors stress that overcoming this situation is not entirely constrained or determined by the current contextual embeddedness of the subsidiary. After all, the main message of the paper is that even weak or low-power actors have a substantial scope for agency, even if their legitimacy, resources and network centrality is low. The authors are, however, ambivalent with respect to how much scope for agency there really is. In other words, the degrees of freedom of low-power actors in choosing their means or strategies are not entirely independent of the current structural situation of subsidiaries. Bouquet and Birkinshaw (2008) illustrate, for instance, that the strategy of 'breaking the rules' may rely on leveraging the influence of strong actors or institutions in their local environment. Similarly, political games based on 'coalition building' depend to some degree on shared interests as well as on more or less established relations with other units. Moreover, the game of comopetition is only available to units that have already built up some legitimacy and hold some critical resource base or network position.

Nevertheless, the main message of the contribution is that low-power actors are not held hostage by their structural constraints but have always some scope for agency. Agency implies, in turn, that actors can turn the tables by changing their internal and external situation. In this sense, the paper sees the environment as malleable, conceptualizing the actor-context relation as a recursive one.

Conclusion

The three contributions discussed all fall within the rationalistic-managerialist stream (see Table 4.2 for a summary). They do so because organizational behaviour in MNCs is still connected to some organizational rationality if only at the level of the subsidiary. At the same time, these papers increasingly question the existence of an overall organizational rationality. Specifically, while Mudambi and Navarra (2004) still hold on to the possibility of MNCs keeping in check the political behaviour of subsidiaries in favour of an overall organizational rationality, Andersson *et al.* (2007) and Bouquet and Birkinshaw (2008) see organizational life and behaviour as constituted by politics and interest divergence. Hence, we see in the contributions an increasing shift towards natural-system perspectives, in combination with a full adoption of a generic politics perspective of the MNC. In terms of the conceptualization of power, all three perspectives adopt an episodic perspective, as they are all concerned with subsidiary power and the bases of such power. Only the contribution of Bouquet and Birkinshaw (2008) moves somewhat beyond such a perspective in that it looks at low-power actors and suggests that their political games might ultimately change the current power balance, that is, a given structure of domination. While all three contributions adopt a political perspective on the organizational behaviour of MNCs, none of them adopt a micropolitical perspective. Even where individual actors are mentioned, their behavioural orientation is largely equated with that of the unit into which they are embedded. Needless to say, that actor diversity and interest diversity below the organizational level find no consideration in these contributions. Accordingly, the main behavioural orientation of the actors is improving the position and influence of the subsidiary within the MNC by drawing on different sources of power or engaging in political games. Both behavioural goals and means or strategies to pursue them, spring from the internal and/or external network embeddedness of the subsidiary and the resources that can be leveraged through such relationships. It is important to note, however, that the contribution by Bouquet and Birkinshaw (2008) departs from structural determinism in that it discusses how low-power actors can improve their situation through political games even when they are not in a structurally favourable position.

Table 4.2 *Overview of seminal contributions of the rationalistic-managerialist school*

Contribution analytical dimensions	Mudambi and Navarra (2004)	Andersson *et al.* (2007)	Bouquet and Birkinshaw (2008)
Empirical focus	Extent of subsidiary rent appropriation within the MNC based on its bargaining power	Understanding subsidiary influence on strategic investments in MNCs	How low-power actors in MNCs can gain influence
Centrality of politics, power and conflict	High centrality of power concept Subsidiary bargaining power in MNCs as both explanans and explanandum in the model	High centrality of power concept Subsidiary power in MNCs as explanandum and different bases of power as explanans	High centrality of politics and power concept Strategies and political games as means (explanans) to gain power and influence (explanandum)
Theoretical focus	Combines principle agent theory network and resource-dependence perspectives	Combines network, intraorganizational power and resource-dependence perspectives	Combines new institutionalism, resource-dependence and social network perspectives
Concept of MNC	Between hierarchical rational-system perspective and natural-system perspective of MNCs	Gives up rational-system perspective at overall MNC level and moves close to natural-system perspective of MNCs	Natural system perspective of MNCs

Table 4.2 *(cont.)*

Contribution analytical dimensions	Mudambi and Navarra (2004)	Andersson *et al.* (2007)	Bouquet and Birkinshaw (2008)
Concept of politics, power and conflict	Between aspectual and generic understanding of politics Episodic understanding of power (No definition) Power based on knowledge assets and dependency of other units on those assets Conflict perspective present but not developed	Shift from aspectual to generic understanding of politics Mainly episodic understanding of power (based on Dahl 1957 and Emerson 1962) Power derives from network embeddedness, resource dependencies and network knowledge Conflict perspective present but not developed	Generic understanding of politics Emerging systemic understanding of power drawing on different theory traditions (e.g. DiMaggio and Powell 1983; Pfeffer and Salancik 1978; Hickson *et al.* 1971) Political games are the means to change the power balance and to gain influence Conflict perspective present but not developed
Concept of actors and behavioural orientation	Essentially organization level actors considered Subsidiary managers act opportunistically on behalf of the subsidiary	Organization-level actors considered All organizational units in MNC aim at influencing strategic decisions in MNC in their interest	Organization level actors considered Low power units employ different strategies and games to gain power and influence in MNC

(cont.)

Table 4.2 *(cont.)*

Contribution analytical dimensions	Mudambi and Navarra (2004)	Andersson *et al.* (2007)	Bouquet and Birkinshaw (2008)
	Headquarters monitor and seek to restrict opportunistic subsidiary behaviour		
Concept of actor-context relation	Actor interest derives from the role as principle or agent Power derives from the knowledge related positon of the subsidiary, mainly within the MNC	Actor interest and power constituted by internal and external network embeddedness (position)	Low-power actor situation and objectives constituted by internal/ external network situation Ability to overcome low-power situations Structurally influenced but not determined as degrees of freedom and scope for agency exist

Finally, we would like to address the question of what the contributions of the rationalistic-managerialist school have to offer to the conceptualization of micropolitics in MNCs? As discussed above there are important variations in the perspectives presented. However, despite all variation, a common trait of the contributions is that the constitution of actors and their behavioural orientation can only be properly understood if we consider both their internal and external embeddedness. Hence, if we wish to understand the interests and sources of power of different actors, we cannot ignore their specific situation, position, roles and relationships within and outside the MNC. Despite all the recognition of actor and interest diversity that challenge the MNC's overall organizational rationality, rationalistic-managerialist contributions remind us that MNCs are not organizational anarchies. Instead, they are organization entities in which hierarchy, managerial intentionality and goal orientation as well as organizational structures and strategies (while subject to politics themselves) have an influence or a structuring effect on the politics, power and conflict that unfolds within them.

References

Andersson, U., Forsgren, M. and Holm, U. 2007. Balancing subsidiary influence in the federative MNC: a business network view. *Journal of International Business Studies*, 38(5): 802–818.

Bacharach, S. B. and Lawler, E. J. 1980. *Power and Politics in Organizations*. San Francisco, CA: Jossey-Bass.

Bouquet, C. and Birkinshaw, J. 2008. Managing power in the multinational corporation: how low-power actors gain influence. *Journal of Management*, 34(3): 477–508.

Dahl, R. A. 1957. The concept of power. *Behavioral Science* 2(3): 210–215.

DiMaggio, P. J. and Powell, W. W. 1983. The iron cage revisited: institutional isomorphism and collective rationality in organizational fields. *American Sociological Review*, 48(2): 147–160.

Emerson, R. M. 1962. Power-dependence relations. *American Sociological Review*, 27(1): 31–40.

Hickson, D. J., Hinings, C. R., Lee, C. A., Schneck, R. E. and Pennings, J. M. 1971. Strategic contingencies theory of intraorganizational power. *Administrative Science Quarterly*, 16(2): 216–229.

Krackhardt, D. 1990. Assessing the political landscape: structure, cognition, and power in organizations. *Administrative Science Quarterly*, 35(2): 342–369.

Mudambi, R. and Navarra, P. 2004. Is knowledge power? Knowledge flows, subsidiary power and rent-seeking within MNCs. *Journal of International Business Studies*, 35(5): 385–406.

Pfeffer, J. 1981. *Power in Organizations*. Marshfield, MA: Pitman.

1992. *Managing with Power: Politics and Influence in Organizations.* Boston, MA: Harvard Business.

Pfeffer, J. and Salancik, G. R. 1978. *The External Control of Organizations.* New York: Harper & Row.

Scott, W. R. 1987. *Organizations: Rational, Natural and Open Systems* (2nd edn). Englewood Cliffs, NJ: Prentice-Hall.

5 | Seminal contributions of the institutionalist and micropolitics schools

MIKE GEPPERT AND KAREN WILLIAMS

The contested space of multinationals: varieties of capitalism, varieties of institutionalism, by Glenn Morgan and Peer-Hull Kristensen, published in *Human Relations* in 2006

Empirical focus

Morgan and Kristensen's (2006) conceptual paper starts with the puzzle of 'institutional duality' related to the question of how multinational corporations (MNCs) deal with home and host country specific pressures and 'pulls' (Westney 1993). However, in contrast to mainstream institutionalist studies where the question of 'pulling' is mainly discussed in rather neutral and passive terms, as home and/or host country effects, the authors describe the puzzle of 'duality' in political terms by referring to MNCs' 'contested spaces' and thus put powerful key actors within the headquarters and subsidiaries in the driving seat. Accordingly, it is stressed that the transfer of knowledge and resources from headquarters to subsidiaries 'makes micropolitics essential to an understanding of multinationals' (Morgan and Kristensen 2006: 1469). The central empirical question from a micropolitical angle, it is stressed further, is how far key actors within the subsidiaries are able to participate in negotiations with key actors within the headquarters when it comes to cross-national transfers of 'processes, people and resources' (ibid.).

The paper starts with a critique of the rationalistic-managerialist perspective of MNCs by arguing that institutional analysis has helped to correct some of the shortcomings of the economic models of the MNC. It is further argued that institutionalists have rightly pointed to diverse contextual rationalities constituting the 'transnational social spaces' of MNCs (e.g. Morgan 2001), but their chief empirical focus on external institutional pressures made it difficult to capture the dynamic aspects

141

and the micropolitical nature of the institutional duality of MNCs. In order to capture the micropolitical nature of institutional diversity it is therefore suggested that we study MNCs as:

a highly complex configuration of ongoing micropolitical power conflicts at different levels in which strategizing social actors/groups inside and outside the firm interact with each other and create temporary balances of power that shape how formal organizational relationships and processes actually work in practice. (Morgan and Kristensen 2006: 1473)

From such a perspective the empirical focus is on the variety of political contests and conflicts emerging between key actors associated either with the headquarters and/or local subsidiaries, which are based on often quite contrary interests and identity differences. To put it differently, when micropolitics move into the centre stage of the study of MNCs, actors are still seen as being co-constituted by institutions. The latter, however, do not just constrain political strategizing inside and outside MNCs, but also enable certain forms of political activities, ranging from straight complaints to aggressive forms of political bargaining at the subsidiary level. Similar to Clark and Geppert's (2011) ideas about political sensemaking, powerful key actors are not just understood as being rule-takers when making sense within the contested space of the MNC but also as rule- and sense-givers, who actively take part in on-going local institution-building processes.

To sum up, different types of micropolitics within MNCs, played between key actors in headquarters and the subsidiaries, are the empirical focus of this article. Different types of micropolitics are the explanandum, which are triggered by various processes of knowledge and resource transfer, usually initiated by the headquarters in order to create coherency of organizational structures and processes, because of and despite institutional differences. The explanans (the ingredients) for different types of micropolitics are the strategic resources which local key actors are able/unable to make use of when trying to resist HQ-imposed transfers of 'processes, people and resources'.

Theoretical focus

The paper falls into the natural perspective of organizations. Interest and identity differences and related conflicts between key actors within the headquarters and local subsidiaries are at the centre of the analysis. Compared to rationalistic perspectives, actors' political strategizing approaches and related interest differences between key actors are not only explained with reference to internal MNC power relations and hierarchical structures but are seen as co-constituted with reference to home and host country specific institutional differences.

The theoretical roots of the paper are very much in the tradition of comparative institutionalism. Clear references are made to theories of varieties of capitalism (Hall and Soskice 2001) and divergent capitalism (Whitley 1999) and, to some extent, also to new institutionalism, especially to research by Kostova *et al.* (2008). However, in contrast to these rather structuralist explanations of how external institutional pressures determine the internal organizational behaviour of MNCs, the authors apply an actor-centred institutionalist perspective, which concentrates on the internal micropolitical dynamics and actors involved. Based on the ideas of Crozier (1964) they highlight that a core question is about how micropolitical contests about accounting and performance 'numbers' (Morgan and Kristensen 2006: 1746) are locally interpreted and socially mediated between powerful actors. Transfer processes, it is stressed further, are often initiated by the headquarters to improve the performance of the MNC as a whole and of individual subsidiaries. Consequently, micropolitical contests are triggered by different uses and interpretations of 'numbers' which are a core problem of justifying and locally legitimizing cross-national transfers from headquarters.

MNCs are thus conceptualized as 'contested spaces' and four ideal-typical forms of micropolitics are distinguished. The latter are triggered by two distinct strategic transfer approaches of the HQ plus two distinct forms of local resistance. The two headquarters-initiated transfer approaches are typified as: (i) 'transfer to subsidiaries of practices, processes, policies and work systems within a framework of benchmarking and "coercive comparisons"'; and (ii) 'transfer to subsidiaries of financial capital (for new investment), knowledge capital (to become research and development [R&D] centres) and reputational capital (to become exemplar of a process)' (Morgan and Kristensen 2006: 1475). The two local modes of resistance are characterized as: (iii) 'high resistance' to headquarters, which is related to cohesive subsidiaries, which are highly locally embedded; and (iv) 'low resistance', which is related to lack of cohesion of subsidiaries and low local embeddedness (ibid.). The four ideal-typical forms of micropolitics discussed in the article are described as a mixture of these two-by-two approaches but are also discussed in the context of wider global societal institutional processes, i.e. the increased dominance of capital markets on the political behaviour of and within contemporary MNCs. This is seen as a key reason for the rise of quantified subsidiary performance measures via benchmarking and 'coercive comparisons'. Accordingly, it is shown that micropolitics will show higher degrees of resistance when subsidiaries are highly locally embedded. This form of micropolitics, which can mainly be found in coordinated market economy contexts, is compared with subsidiaries in liberal market economies, which often have weak local network support and resources. In short, local actors here can draw on only limited 'toolkits' to organize effective forms of local resistance (see also Williams and Geppert 2011). Accordingly, the concept of power is mainly applied in an episodic manner when distinguishing different forms of micropolitics. However, they also make references to systemic power when headquarters' transfer strategies are seen as closely intertwined with wider societal features of dominant international financial capital market influences on organizational behaviour within MNCs.

The study highlights that 'coercive comparisons' of subsidiary performance might lead to a further weakening of the power sources of subsidiaries which are already weak in terms of coherence and of local resource. This will hinder them from organizing forceful resistance to headquarters' demands. This problem is seen as a typical scenario for micropolitics of subsidiaries operating in liberal market economies. Here it is stressed that local actors and especially managers are keen to prove that they can play 'the numbers game' and manage their subsidiaries according to central benchmarks set by the headquarters not least because industrial relations systems are weak and the 'power of organizations over employees is strong' (ibid.: 1477). Micropolitical approaches of subsidiaries operating in coordinated market economies, however, are seen as better equipped to organize potent local resistance because of the high degree of local embeddedness often based on more supportive industrial relations systems:

Locally embedded managers are more likely to be found where institutions are strong, networks between local firms and local associations and local government are supportive and where support for the development of employee skills and employee representation is also important. Actors feel more deeply embedded in the local context and are less dependent on the MNC. (Morgan and Kristensen 2006: 1478)

The role of local key actors and how they try to win competitive micropolitical games triggered by headquarters' distribution and rewarding of strategic resources to subsidiaries is addressed by Morgan and Kristensen (2006: 1479–1482) with reference to research by Delany (1998). Consequently, the authors distinguish between 'boy scout' and 'subversive' strategies of local actors when discussing the question of whether and how both strategic approaches are able to influence the distribution and reward decisions of headquarters' management. It is highlighted that 'boy scouts' are more likely to follow the demands of the headquarters because these actors are more likely to be interested in developing their individual careers and moving up within the hierarchy of the MNC. This limits not just their interests in mobilizing local resources to influence and resist certain global standardization and benchmarking strategies, but also local institution building because the increase of the subsidiary mandate and leadership in R&D is not part of their often narrow individualistic agendas. 'Subversive' local strategizing, however, is described as a continuous focus on enlarging and improving subsidiary mandates. The latter is supported by the deep embeddedness of subsidiaries in local innovation and supplier networks. This also means that these actors' micropolitical strategizing is likely to be more resistant against headquarters' global standardization approaches that undermine local power sources and institution-building (ibid.). It is concluded that increased benchmarking and 'coercive comparisons' will trigger two quite opposite forms of micropolitics:

Whilst Boy Scouts cooperate with the undermining of their own subsidiary (a prospect that divides the workforce between the managers, for whom the locality is a temporary step on a path to steps up the internal or external labour market, and the workers, most of whom are likely to be locked into the local labour market), subversive strategists work to coordinate local cooperative responses to such pressures. (Morgan and Kristensen 2006: 1483)

In short, the conceptualization of actors is seen as contextually determined: headquarters and subsidiary key actors are described as being strategically oriented, on the one hand. On the other hand, both headquarters management transfer approaches as well as local forms of resistance are also conceptualized as highly situational rational.

Actors' interests and local contexts in intrafirm conflict: the 2004 GM and Opel crisis, by Susanne Blazejewski, published in *Competition and Change* in 2009

Empirical focus

The aim of this paper is a move away from the focus on aggregate concepts and dominant actor groups, which have been the main foci of industrial relations explanations of conflict. In contrast, Blazejewski (2009) investigates a particular conflict between a multinational company headquarters and its subsidiaries in Germany from a micropolitical perspective by highlighting the views and actions of a marginalized group in the German system of industrial relations and in multinational companies more generally, shop stewards.

An in-depth investigation is conducted into the 2004 strike at General Motors (GM) Opel in Germany based on reports and interviews in published material on the conflict process. The conflict was ostensibly about multinational restructuring plans and job losses, although further investigation revealed 'multiple, competing interests and internal conflict lines as key driving forces behind the 2004 Opel crisis' (Blazejewski 2009: 244). These went beyond the immediate restructuring and proposed job cuts to conflicts within the workforce about how to respond to this within the wider context of the assignment of production charters by GM and their European brand strategy using a calculation and allocation of losses which was seen as unfair by GM subsidiary management. Thus, although the focus of the research is on a specific conflict episode, this conflict takes place within wider conflicts in MNCs as part of the process of globalization, which involve a range of actor groups, both management and workers, across Germany, Europe and globally.

The explanandum in the article are the different responses of the local actors involved in the GM conflict, where there were competing rationalities in play in the workforce, particularly between the shop stewards and the formal workforce representative body, the works council. The explanans are based on the importance of local contexts, traditions and identities to local actors like shop stewards rather than on the formal industrial relations institutions in Germany. This helped to explain the very different responses from the workforce representative groups across the different GM sites in Germany, including within the Bochum plant itself. Intranational and intrafirm differences are thus highlighted by the article rather than any convergence based on the national system of formal industrial relations institutions and the multinational company and subsidiaries as homogenous units.

Theoretical focus

The article provides an overview and a critique of a number of prominent research fields focusing on multinational companies and actor interests. Institutionalist research streams, for example, focus on home and host country influences on actors in multinational companies and their subsidiaries but investigation tends to be limited to the effects of national level institutions on formal industrial relations actors, not on different local contexts and more micro-level actors (Almond and Ferner 2006). Often a deterministic perspective is also adopted in understanding how national contexts influence actor behaviour.

Blazejewski's (2009) article, in contrast, focuses on the ambiguities of national institutions and how they are subject to different interpretations by actors depending on different actor interests. Based on Giddens' (1984) concept of duality, actors are also able to influence institutions and help shape their operation through their reinterpretation and selective application of practices and rules. The study makes use of two key research streams to focus attention on actors and their micropolitical behaviour: micro-organizational/politics literature and the concept of the 'situation' as well as recent work in varieties of capitalism and labour process theory on intranational heterogeneity. The article further develops the concepts of actor interests, motivations and conflict of interests, whereby institutions are, for example, seen as repertoires from which actors can select based on their interpretation of interests. The concept of 'situation' or 'interest-based contextual constitutions' (Blazejewski 2009: 233) is used to illustrate the fact that institutions may or may not feed into the actors' definitions of a situation depending on whether they are seen as important for pursuing their interests. Thus the combination of actor interests plus situation is used to explain the different responses of the workplace actors in the GM conflict.

The focus of the article is an explanation of the two very different rationales of the workforce in GM Opel's Bochum plant, where shop stewards and the works council each interpreted the contextual framework they were working in very differently; each group made use of different elements of the context depending on the perception of their interests. For example, the shop stewards emphasized the local environment as key and made use of a strong local identity of fighting for workers' rights against large multinational companies and wide community support in a local situation where there were high levels of local unemployment. In their view, the formal problem-solving route of negotiations between works council and management had failed as they had not been able to prevent job losses as part of the restructuring programme so they now took recourse to unofficial strike action against the company. The works council, in contrast, continued to emphasize their formal legitimation as legal actors in the workplace and established procedures based on negotiation as the only means of dealing with the conflict issues. The article investigates the process by which the works council was eventually successful in bringing the unofficial strike action led by the shop stewards back within the ambit of the official framework of cooperation with management. Situational changes, in the form of works council-union (IG Metal) cooperation to take control of the unofficial action and GM's offer of a generous compensation scheme for workers made redundant, led to a change in the dynamics from unofficial strike action led by the shop stewards to formal negotiation led by works council members.

In line with Morgan and Kristensen (2006), Blazejewski (2009) views the multinational company as a contested social space within which a wide range of different actor groups with different interests draw on their different contextual situations in different ways to defend their interests. The focus on underrepresented groups such as shop stewards is of particular note in this study, highlighting as it does the very different intrafirm interests of different groups in the workforce even in the same plant. The ways in which the shop stewards draw on elements of the local context in their interpretation of worker interests in contrast to the works council which draws on its formal rights in the national system of employment relations illustrate the importance of taking subnational contexts into account in any investigation of conflict processes in multinational companies.

An organizational politics perspective on intrafirm competition in multinational corporations, by Florian Becker-Ritterspach and Christoph Dörrenbächer, published in *Management International Review* in 2011

Empirical focus

The starting point of the article by Becker-Ritterspach and Dörren-bächer (2011) is that mainstream research on intrafirm competition and subsidiary mandate change in the international business (IB) literature has paid little attention to the political dimensions of competition within MNCs. A core interest of this conceptual paper is therefore to develop an alternative actor-centred framework, based on the concept of organizational micropolitics. The authors aim to shed some light on the questions of: (i) who the key actors are; (ii) what their behavioural rationales are; and (iii) what the contextual conditions of micropolitics are. Taken together these questions lead to a micropolitical agenda for the study of intrafirm competition in MNCs.

The paper identifies a clear research gap in the IB literature, which emerges because of the limited conceptual understanding of dominant rationalistic-managerialist and contingency theory approaches on intrafirm competition within MNCs. Moreover, IB research on subsidiary mandate development and innovation tends to concentrate on political bargaining between HQ and subsidiaries, where both subunits are largely conceptualized as relatively homogenous collective actors. Different political strategizing approaches of and between individual actors within a certain subunit, such as within a particular local subsidiary, are often overlooked. Instead it is assumed that the political interests of local key actors are in line with the overall strategic approach of the organizational subunit and/or the MNC as a whole.

In contrast to these views Becker-Ritterspach and Dörrenbächer (2011) emphasize the important role of diverse interests and of conflicting political goals between powerful key actors at local subsidiary level, because these might lead to suboptimal bargaining approaches for the subsidiary as a whole, especially when own political interests harm local resource- and institution-building processes (see also Clark and Geppert 2011). Consequently, it is suggested that the empirical analysis of the micropolitics of intrafirm competition in MNCs needs to start bottom-up, from the individual level of subsidiary managers:

their ability to mobilize resources (based on their resource exchange relationships) within and outside the multinational corporation (MNC) and
their willingness to employ these in favour of the subsidiary (based on
their strategic orientation) form an important strategic asset in intra-firm
competition. (Becker-Ritterspach and Dörrenbächer 2011: 534)

To put it differently, the abilities and willingness of all subsidiary managers to get involved in political strategizing in order to mobilize local
resources for upgrading or against downgrading initiatives of the headquarters are not seen as similar or as driven towards the achievement of common individual goals. Thus, the key empirical focus of
the article is on the diversity of individual interests of powerful key
actors within a local subsidiary which are explained in terms of differences in their career paths, career aspirations and positions within
the hierarchy of the MNC. The authors' key empirical question is:
how do these different individual characteristics of subsidiary managers inform their micropolitical strategizing approaches in intrafirm
competition for scarce resources and negotiations about headquarters-
initiated mandate changes? Different resource mobilizing strategies of
subsidiary managers are the explanandum. Differences in the individual strategic orientations of key actors in terms of career interests and
the availability of resources within and outside the situational context
of the MNC are the explanans.

Theoretical focus

The paper contributes to a natural perspective of organizations by
focusing on multiple and conflicting interests of key actors within
MNCs. In line with Morgan and Kristensen (2006), MNCs are seen
as being 'contested' social spaces where intrafirm competition for
resources, influence and reputation triggers micropolitical struggles
between key actors in the headquarters and subsidiaries. In comparison to Morgan and Kristensen (2006), however, the focus is clearly
on the individual actors and their strategic orientations, which make
use of contextually situated resources in the micropolitical games they
play in the light of intrafirm competition.

   The theoretical roots of the paper are clearly in organization theory. In line with Weber's (1947) and Pfeffer's (1981) seminal research,
power is defined 'as the ability of actors to influence the process of

intrafirm competition in their interest' (Becker-Ritterspach and Dörrenbächer 2011: 542). It is further argued that power is not a property
of certain actors but 'relational', based on the exchange of resources
(see also Clegg *et al.* 2006). Related to the latter, the authors stress that
'both the availability of resources and the ability to engage in *resource
exchange relationships* in organizations' (ibid.: 542) constitute political strategizing in MNCs.

When conceptualizing the 'abilities' of subunits within organizations
the authors refer to theories about intraorganizational politics and
here especially to the work of Astley and Zajac (1990, 1991). At the
centre of the discussion are questions about which resources the power
of subunits is based on, the role of strategic orientations of subunits and
their contextual situatedness. It is, however, also highlighted that the
role of individual actors has been neglected by this stream of literature
and that individual actors' strategizing approaches might be quite different and even contradictory to the approaches followed by a specific
subunit or the organization as a whole. That is why a micropolitical
approach of intrafirm competition is adopted. In their conceptualization of micropolitics, the authors draw on the seminal work of Crozier
and Friedberg (1980) and thus an episodic understanding of organizational power relations is at the focus of analysis.

It is emphasized that all individual actors' political approaches rely
on established resource exchange relations (means) which can be developed into effective 'toolkits' by successful micropolitical players (see
also Williams and Geppert 2011) when they seek to change the rules
of the game (ends) in order to gain influence, e.g. for bargaining about
upgrading mandates or resisting HQ strategies of mandate downgrading. In line with Crozier and Friedberg (1980), power relations are
understood as being highly context-specific and based on 'uncertainty
zones', from which sources of power for individual actors emerge.
These are: (i) special skills and functional specialization; (ii) relations
between an organization and its environments; (iii) control of communication and information; and (iv) the existence of general organizational rules (Becker-Ritterspach and Dörrenbächer 2011: 544). The
willingness of actors to make use of these sources when playing micropolitical games, however, is seen as intertwined with the geographical, hierarchical and functional positions of individual subsidiary managers, all of which strongly influence their future interest in following
certain career paths and aspirations or their desire for either 'going

local' (Loveridge 2006) or moving up in the organizational hierarchy. So, how are the above building blocks of the micropolitical framework for the study of intrafirm competition applied in the context of the MNC?

The paper develops nine prepositions to explore whether subsidiary managers might act in favour of their subsidiaries, e.g. in negotiations about mandates, and whether they are willing to resist unreasonable demands from HQ which would limit the power base of the subsidiary as a whole in intrafirm competition. To put it differently, when addressing one of the key questions of the article, whether subsidiary managers will turn into 'assets' or 'liabilities' for their local subsidiaries when engaging in the micropolitics of intrafirm competition (outlined in prepositions 7–9), a first set of prepositions (1–3) around the question of how current career paths and hierarchical positioning of the local managers are linked to the actors' abilities to mobilize resources is important. Consequently, it is proposed that:

Subsidiary managers whose career path involved multiple prolonged stays in different local subsidiary contexts combined with regular prolonged stays in the headquarters context command the strongest and most diverse resource exchange relationships. (Becker-Ritterspach and Dörrenbächer 2011: 541)

It is assumed that power episodes leading to mandate gains are related to proactive actors who are highly locally embedded. Thus proactive micropolitical strategizing is recursively linked with key actors' strong interests in local career paths and positions. The opposite is proposed for subsidiary managers who have limited abilities to mobilize resources when engaging in local resource-building initiatives. They are described as passive political strategists because of their limited local engagement and limited interest in local affairs, career paths and positions.

The second set of prepositions (4–6) is focused on the question of the strategic orientation of local key actors, especially about their career aspirations of either remaining or moving on to another subsidiary or to the HQ. Therefore, it is proposed that:

Subsidiary managers with career aspirations within their local subsidiary will show a high strategic orientation towards that subsidiary. (Becker-Ritterspach and Dörrenbächer 2011: 551)

Moreover, the opposite is proposed for subsidiary managers who move a lot within the multinational group and have career aspirations beyond the local subsidiary. They are less likely to see the local subsidiary as an 'asset' and thus micropolitical engagement for building local resources is quite restricted.

In conclusion, the paper provides a strong conceptual framework for the analysis of episodic power and for capturing highly context-specific forms of micropolitical strategizing of subsidiary managers related to their career paths, position and aspirations. The article does not, however, go into much detail about the underlying elements of the systematic power in comparison to the conceptualization of micropolitics in Morgan and Kristensen's approach (2006), which strongly linked micropolitical game-playing with the dominant role of capital markets and the financialization of contemporary MNCs.

Subsidiary integration as identity construction and institution building: a political sensemaking approach, by Ed Clark and Mike Geppert, published in *Journal of Management Studies* in 2011

Empirical focus

This article focuses on the sensemaking roles played by powerful social actors in the post-acquisition integration process of constructing a new relationship between the MNC and the acquired subsidiary. The actors investigated include the senior decision makers in the post-acquisition transition management team, both headquarters and local subsidiary managers. Multinational enterprises are seen as highly politicized organizations with conflicting relations between different actors, in this case between headquarters and subsidiary managers. Since the focus of the study is Western multinational companies which have purchased brownfield sites in post-socialist countries, conflict relations are expected to be all the more marked due to the very different Western and post-socialist manager viewpoints, interests and institutions. Contexts are important and 'expressed in political actions of powerful actors' (Clark and Geppert 2011: 396). The political sensemaking approach emphasizes the importance of identity construction and institution building work, which is central to the process of integrating two different organizations from two different contexts. In this process, to achieve their political interests, social actors draw on a variety of power sources, some structural but also informal and emergent forms (Clark and Geppert 2011: 397).

Theoretical focus

Key theories drawn on in the article are organizational identity theory (Clemens and Cook 1999) and institutional views of MNCs (Kostova 1999). Subsidiary identity formation is seen as a political process reflecting different actor interests through a process of sensemaking and sensegiving (Clark and Geppert 2011: 399). This takes place against a background of different institutional contexts which influence the actors' views on the organized practices of the MNC. A high level of institutional distance between HQ and the subsidiary, for example, will influence the levels of dissent between local and HQ managers (Clark and Geppert 2011: 396).

The authors focus in the article on disputes about the acquired site's identity or central characteristics and its institutions (its main organizational practices). In the authors' view this 'construction of subsidiary identity and institutions is a political accomplishment of powerful actors who engage in sensemaking to interpret each other's political interests and stances and sensemaking to enforce their own preferences on the subsidiary' (Clark and Geppert 2011: 396).

Their approach to relations between the MNC and the subsidiary in the post-acquisition integration stage is processual, political and actor-centred. The process of confronting and resolving conflicts over the nature of the subsidiary, its meaning and the legitimacy of its structures (Clark and Geppert 2011: 397) is the explanadum. The explanans are based on the political interests of the key actors involved who draw on a range of power sources to promote their viewpoints in a process of political sensemaking (Clark and Geppert 2011: 397). The potential for conflict in this process is seen as great, particularly in the cases investigated of Western MNCs and their post-socialist brownfield subsidiaries.

The context in which this process of sensemaking by the key actors takes place is multilevel: local, corporate and global. Whilst headquarters' actors draw on the global and corporate levels in their understanding of the subsidiary's pre-acquisition status and its initial strategic assignment (Clark and Geppert 2011: 399), subsidiary actors will focus more on the local context. These different context rationalities are seen as reflected in the actors' meanings and interests expressed in the process of political sensemaking, whereby they seek to realize their subsidiary identity and institutional preferences in the post-acquisition process dynamic. A variety of potential outcomes of this process are possible: organizational order, organizational impasse, conflict or change (Clark and Geppert 2011: 400).

Four different post-acquisition scenarios are conceptualized in Clark and Geppert's (2011) paper based on the different headquarters and subsidiary views of subsidiary identity. From the headquarters actors' point of view, the subsidiary can be viewed either as a 'strategic dependant' with limited autonomy or as a 'strategic partner' with a more creative mandate. From the post-socialist subsidiary manager point of view, subsidiary identity can be either that of a 'local patriot', locally embedded with local interests at the centre, or as a 'cosmopolitan player', more open to learning from the MNC.

The processes involved in sensemaking by the actors using these different perspectives produce a number of different scenarios ranging from consensual sensemaking of both sides (a strategic partner and cosmopolitan player combination), defensive sensemaking (with strategic partner and local patriot combinations), dominated sensemaking (strategic dependant and cosmopolitan identities) and, finally, oppositional sensemaking with contested adoption and institutional crisis in the post-acquisition process (a combination of a strategic dependant and a local patriot identity). Thus the process patterns of integration post-acquisition can be accumulating, adaptive, non-adaptive and deteriorating depending on the sensemaking approaches used by the two sets of actors involved.

The article distances itself from the rational-functional international business perspective of the post-acquisition process and emphasizes rather the importance of intracorporate power and contestation in MNCs (Clark and Geppert 2011: 410). Thus organizational plurality, processes and politics are seen as significant factors in any explanations of MNC construction.

The approach adopted in the paper is open to further development such as an expansion of the range of actors included in an assessment of the post-acquisition process and an extension of the variety of different subsidiary identities since the research on which the article is based focused on brownfield sites in countries with very different institutional histories to the MNCs themselves.

Power, institutions and the cross-national transfer of employment practices in multinationals, by Anthony Ferner, Tony Edwards and Anne Tempel, published in *Human Relations* in 2012

Empirical focus

The focus of this article is the incorporation of power and interests into the analysis of the cross-border transfer of MNC practices. Power is understood in terms of the power capabilities of different multinational company actors, both in headquarters and the subsidiaries, to influence the institutional environment inside and outside the MNC in order to shape the transfer process in their own interests. MNCs are seen as political actors and the power of the actors is linked to the institutional context in which it is being exercised; thus the power capabilities of actors are shaped by the institutional context in which they operate.

The authors investigate the transfer of human resource and employment practices in the article since MNC headquarters actors often view them as important objects of transfer to protect corporate competitive capabilities, yet they are also strongly subject to host country influences. Power and interests are viewed as integral to relations between employers and employees in MNCs because the relationship between them is one of 'structured antagonism' (Ferner *et al.* 2012: 165).

The explanandum of the article are the outcomes of the process of transferring human resource and employment practices in MNCs, while the explanans are the different power capabilities and interests of the actors involved in this process. It is a conceptual paper which draws on examples of empirical findings in the literature about transfer processes to develop a framework which includes a range of different processes and the reasons behind them. The conceptual model developed comprises five scenarios, all with different outcomes: functional hybridization (high transfer), resistive hybridization (low transfer), failed transfer, ceremonial or ritual compliance and reverse transfer (from the subsidiary to MNC headquarters).

Theoretical focus

The paper reviews the neo-institutionalist approach to transfer of practices in MNCs, which focuses on rival isomorphic pressures from home and host countries in the MNC as well as the effects of institutional distance (Kostova 1999). However, Kostovian approaches fail to investigate the effects of power, coalitions, interests and competing value systems. Actors, the paper argues, are not only influenced by institutions as per the neo-institutionalist approach, but can also influence them in line with their power capabilities and interests.

The authors adopt both a systemic and episodic view of power. The global dynamics of capitalism are referred to in the paper and these are based on the exercise of agency by powerful actors in the economic and technological realm. As a result of this, organizations are susceptible to contestation. Certain MNCs play a more dominant role in this power process and exert influence across a range of dimensions including global, national, subnational and sector levels as well as within their own organizations. Thus MNCs can be rule makers as well as rule takers and are able to influence institutions in both the home and host countries in which they operate, exploiting gaps in institutional frameworks, for example, to assert their interests (Ferner *et al.* 2012: 169). In terms of the episodic perspective, the paper investigates instances of actual transfer of HR and employment practices in specific MNCs found in the academic literature. This is then used to develop a broad conceptual framework, which incorporates the power capabilities of different actors and the outcomes of this in terms of the actual transfer of practices in MNCs. Although the study focuses on key HQ and subsidiary actors, not marginalized actors as in the case of Blazejewski (2009), these two sets of actors are not viewed as monolithic blocks and it is assumed that other actor groups may also be involved in influencing the transfer processes in practice.

In the authors' view, the use of institutional profiles in assessing home and host country influences, as well as the institutional distance assessments found in Kostovian neo-institutionalist analyses, are too blunt an instrument to be able to accurately assess transfer processes and they suggest that researchers may need to look at a wider range of subnational levels in practice, which may be quite different to the overall national country profiles.

The power concept used in the paper is based on a Lukesian three dimensions of power perspective (Lukes 1975, 2005) and Hardy's (1996) application of these dimensions to business issues. The three power dimensions used are: the power of resources, i.e. ability to control scarce resources, the power of processes, i.e. the power to control organizational processes and the power of meaning, i.e. which relates to power relations in the economic and technological realms. The power capabilities of headquarters- and subsidiary-level actors are then investigated as the key actors in transfer processes. While headquarters' power is viewed as transcending context and therefore the greater, subsidiary actors have a lower contextual range of power, being dependent on the resources of the specific institutional setting of their subsidiary. However, although headquarters does usually have the key power resources, there is still scope for subsidiary challenges to this and a lot of contestation is possible in transfer processes.

Although the current paper is based on headquarters and subsidiary management actors in the transfer process, the authors suggest that further research may need to look at different groups within these two broad groupings, such as management and workforce actors in the subsidiary or, within subsidiary management, the operations and human resources (HR) managers. Skilled and unskilled workers may also have different interests and power resources which are brought into play during the transfer process with some actor groups supporting transfer whilst others resist it. Actor perception of their interests and the perceived 'criticality' to their interests of the practices being transferred will also influence the levels of resistance to or acceptance of change (Ferner *et al.* 2012: 177).

The conceptual model developed includes different constellations of institutional distance or modified institutional distance (mID) depending on the relative power of the MNC compared to the subsidiary and the different macro- and micro-level power capabilities and interests of the different actor groups involved in transfer as reflected in the three dimensions of power outlined earlier. Five typical scenarios based on the factors above are then investigated. These lead to five different outcomes in the transfer process between MNC headquarters and the subsidiaries: functional hybridization, where there is a successful transfer of practices from headquarters to the subsidiary, resistive hybridization, where there is low internalization of the practice being transferred, a failed transfer process, a ceremonial or ritual compliance and a reverse transfer process, where the headquarters adopts practices from the subsidiary itself.

The article provides a modification of the Kostovian approach to practice transfer processes in MNCs. While the proposed model includes familiar elements found in neo-institutionalist approaches to assessing transfer of practices in MNCs, such as institutional distance and macro- and microinstitutional factors, it also incorporates the interests and power capabilities of the different actors involved to explain the contestation which occurs in many instances. Interests and power can be both episodic and limited to the one instance of transfer, or systemic involving long-term durable interests such as survival of the organization for both HQ and subsidiary actors. The conceptual ideas developed, it is argued, now need to be further explored via in-depth case-studies of actual transfer processes between MNC headquarters and subsidiaries to assess the viability of the variables included in the model.

Conclusion

All five contributions in the institutionalist and micropolitics school of thought section adopt an open-systems approach (see summary Table 5.1). This reflects on the important role played by home and host country contexts as well as headquarters and subnational levels where, as Blazejewski (2009) has shown, very different rationalities can come into play between different subsidiaries in the same country and workplace actors within the same subsidiary. Morgan and Kristensen (2006) also draw on the coordinated and liberal market economy national context differences in their explanation of the different levels of contestation by subsidiary managers. In all the studies, context has an influence on factors such as sensemaking, the power resources of different actors, levels of contestation and the extent of micropolitical activity of both management and workforce representatives.

The studies also reflect a move away from the IB preoccupation with rational organizational systems in MNCs to natural systems comprising a wide range of different actors with different interests. The focus of the papers is on the type of interests promoted, the reasons behind these and how interests are contested in the MNC setting. The foci of the contestation vary: Morgan and Kristensen (2006), for example, focus on micropolitics about headquarters' numbers in

Table 5.1 *Overview of seminal contributions of the institutionalist and micropolitics schools*

Contribution analytical dimensions	Morgan and Kristensen (2006)	Blazejewski (2009)	Becker-Ritterspach and Dörrenbächer (2011)	Clark and Geppert (2011)	Ferner et al. (2012)
Empirical focus	How far are subsidiary key actors able to participate in negotiations with headquarters actors when it comes to cross-national transfers of processes, people and resources?	Why do local actors in multinational companies respond to headquarters decisions in different ways within the same national context?	How are the individual resource exchange relationships of subsidiary managers informed by their career path, position and aspirations?	The post-acquisition process in MNEs based on the identity construction and institution-building activities of the key actors involved in Western MNE acquisitions in post socialist economies	The factors influencing the outcomes of MNC transfer of human resource and employment practices to subsidiaries
Centrality of politics, power and conflict	MNC power relations as a means (explanans) and outcome (explanandum) of micropolitics triggered by both headquarters transfer strategies and local resistance strategies	The focus is on different actor interests, their power resources and conflict behaviour in the case of headquarters restructuring involving job losses	Local actors political strategizing (means) is at the centre and how it influences managers' interests in seeing their subsidiary as an asset or liability for institutional resource building (ends)	Different outcomes in the post-acquisition process (explanandum). The explanans is based on key actor political sensemaking, which is seen as a politicized, power-based process, which may lead to conflict outcomes	Main factors investigated are the interests and power capabilities of key actors such as HQ and subsidiary managers involved in the transfer process
Theoretical focus	Combines actor-centred comparative institutionalist and micropolitical approaches	Draws on institutional entrepreneurship and micropolitics literature and the interaction between actors and	Combines organizational theory approaches on power, intraorganizational politics and micropolitics	Combines organizational identity theory and institutional theory together with sensemaking by the key actors	Combines neo-institutionalist and power-based theory to investigate the power capabilities of key actors

Concept of MNC	MNCs are contested social spaces which are constituted through a variety of interconnected micropolitical games played between HQ and subsidiaries	MNCs are contested social spaces with a wide range of actor groups pursuing different interests. Micropolitical games draw on different contextual situations	MNCs are contested social spaces which are constituted through micropolitics triggered by intrafirm competition for scarce resources	A politicized arena with organizational plurality where key actors draw on different contexts to develop their sensemaking approaches to subsidiary identity and institutions	MNCs are organizations subject to contestation within a wider global order shaped by dominant actors, which is itself subject to contestation.
Concept of politics, power and conflict	Strong focus on episodic power: political games are the means and ends to explain changes in power relations. Systemic power comes into play via capital market pressure and financialization	The focus is on a case of episodic power: the conflict between GM Opel and workforce actors in 2004. This is placed within a wider conflict field which includes disputed HQ restructuring, allocation of production mandates and the calculation and allocation of losses between subsidiaries	Micropolitics is based on differences in availability of local resources and in the interests of local key actors to mobilize these resources in favour of the local subsidiary	Social construction of the strategic identities of subsidiaries is in the hands of powerful actors, which may lead to conflicts in the post-acquisition process	Actor responses in the transfer process are shaped by interests and power capabilities (episodic power) within the wider context of a global, national and subnational order, which is itself shaped by power and interests of dominant groups (systemic power)

(cont.)

Table 5.1 (cont.)

Contribution analytical dimensions	Morgan and Kristensen (2006)	Blazejewski (2009)	Becker-Ritterspach and Dörrenbächer (2011)	Clark and Geppert (2011)	Ferner et al. (2012)
Concept of actors and behavioural orientation (BO)	Actors: powerful key actors in headquarters and subsidiaries BO: combination of different political strategizing approaches of headquarters and subsidiaries lead either to a strengthening or weakening of local institution building	Actors: marginalized local actors – shop stewards in subsidiaries in Germany BO: combination of interests and use of local contextual framework	Actors: powerful local key actors' strategic orientations are informed by career paths, aspirations and position BO: combination of availability of local resources and differences in the strategic orientations of subsidiary managers explains their passive or proactive resource building	Actors: powerful key actors in headquarters and the subsidiaries BO: actors are involved in sensemaking in different contexts at local, corporate and global levels. This helps to shape the outcomes of the post-acquisition process in MNEs	Actors: powerful headquarters and local actors are involved in transfer processes in MNCs BO: combination of key actor group interests and power capabilities shape the outcomes of practice transfer processes in MNCs
Concept of actor-context relation	Actors' interests are constituted by high/low degrees of local embeddedness and whether local resources are available and used to resist 'comparative comparisons' from MNC headquarters	Local (workforce) actor interests draw on their interpretations of the local context to shape their responses to headquarters decisions	Local actors interests are constituted by local resource availability and their strategic orientations which are informed by their career paths, aspirations and positions in the MNC hierarchy	Key actors draw on different aspects of the wider context in which they operate in developing their sensemaking approaches to subsidiary identity and institutions in the post-acquisition process	Important influence of microinstitutional (MNC) and macroinstitutional (host country) contexts in shaping the interests and power capabilities of different actor groups in the transfer process

accounting and performance, which have been influenced by financialization and global capital markets. Blazejewski also alludes to this in her references to disputes about GM's European brand strategy using a calculation and allocation of losses which was seen as unfair by GM subsidiary management in Europe. The main focus of her paper, however, is on micropolitics about restructuring and job losses in GM subsidiaries and the divisions, even among workforce actors, about how to respond to MNC decisions. Becker-Ritterspach and Dörrenbächer (2011) focus on the micropolitics of subsidiary management around subsidiary mandate changes and how different manager career paths, aspirations and positions within the MNC all affect the mobilization strategies of managers to contest or accept MNC decisions. Clark and Geppert (2011), on the other hand, focus on the micropolitics of disputes between key actors about subsidiary identity and institutions in the post-acquisition process and the factors influencing the different sensemaking strategies employed by headquarters and subsidiary managers. Finally Ferner *et al.* (2012) focus on the micropolitics involved in the transfer of HR and employment practices from HQ to subsidiaries in MNCs.

References

Almond, P. and Ferner, A. (eds.) 2006. *American Multinationals in Europe.* Oxford University Press.

Astley, W. G. and Zajac, E. J. 1990. Beyond dyadic exchange: functional interdependence and subunit power. *Organisation Studies*, 11(4): 481–501.

1991. Intraorganizational power and organizational design: reconciling rational and coalitional models of organization. *Organization Science*, 2(4): 399–411.

Becker-Ritterspach, F. and Dörrenbächer, C. 2011. An organizational politics perspective on intra-firm competition in multinational corporations. *Management International Review*, 51: 533–559.

Blazejewski, S. 2009. Actors' interests and local contexts in intrafirm conflict: the 2004 GM and Opel crisis. *Competition and Change*, 13(3): 229–250.

Clark, E. and Geppert, M. 2011. Subsidiary integration as identity construction and institution building: a political sensemaking approach. *Journal of Management Studies*, 48(2): 395–416.

Clegg, S. R., Courpasson, D. and Phillips, N. 2006. *Power and Organizations.* London: Sage.

Clemens, E. S. and Cook, J. M. 1999. Politics and institutionalism: explaining durability and change. *Annual Review of Sociology*, 25: 441–466.

Crozier, M. 1964. *The Bureaucratic Phenomenon*. University of Chicago Press.

Crozier, M. and Friedberg, E. 1980. *Actors and Systems: the Politics of Collective Action*. University of Chicago Press.

Delany, E. 1998. Strategic development of multinational subsidiaries in Ireland. In J. Birkinshaw and N. Hood (eds.), *Multinational Corporate Evolution and Subsidiary Development*. London: Macmillan, 239–267.

Ferner, A., Edwards, T. and Tempel, A. 2012. Power, institutions and the cross-national transfer of employment practices in multinationals. *Human Relations*, 65(2): 163–187.

Giddens, A. 1984. *The Constitution of Society. Outline of the Theory of Structuration*. Cambridge: Polity.

Hall, P. A. and Soskice, D. (eds.) 2001. *Varieties of Capitalism. The Institutional Foundations of Comparative Advantages*. Oxford University Press.

Hardy, C. 1996. Understanding power: bringing about strategic change. *British Journal of Management*, 7(suppl. 1): 3–16.

Kostova, T. 1999. Transnational transfer of strategic organizational practices: a contextual perspective. *Academy of Management Review*, 24: 308–324.

Kostova, T., Roth, K. and Dacin, T. M. 2008. Institutional theory in the study of multinational corporations: a critique and new directions. *Academy of Management Review*, 33(4): 994–1006.

Loveridge, R. 2006. Embedding the multinational enterprise: The microprocesses of institutionalization in developing economies. In M. Geppert and M. Mayer (eds.), *Global, National and Local Practices in Multinational Companies*. Houndsmill: Palgrave-Macmillan, 189–220.

Lukes, S. 1975. *Power: A Radical View*. London: Palgrave-Macmillan.

2005. *Power: A Radical View* (2nd edn). London: Palgrave-Macmillan.

Morgan, G. 2001. The multinational firm: organizing across national and institutional divides. In G. Morgan, P.-H. Kristensen and R. Whitley (eds.), *The Multinational Firm. Organizing Across Institutional and National Divides*. Oxford University Press, 1–24.

Morgan, G. and Kristensen, P.-H. 2006. The contested space of multinationals: varieties of institutionalism, varieties of capitalism. *Human Relations*, 59(11): 1467–1490.

Pfeffer, J. 1981. *Power in Organizations*. New York: Harper Business.

Weber, M. 1947. *The Theory of Social and Economic Organization*. New York: Free Press.

Westney, E. 1993. Institutionalization theory and the multinational corporation. In S. Ghoshal and E. Westney (eds.), *Organization Theory and the Multinational Corporation*. Basingstoke: Macmillan: 53–76.

Whitley, R. 1999. *Divergent Capitalisms. The Social Structuring and Change of Business Systems*. Oxford University Press.

Williams. K. and Geppert, M. 2011. Bargained globalization: employment relations providing robust 'tool kits' for socio-political strategizing in MNCs in Germany. In C. Dörrenbächer and M. Geppert (eds.), *Politics and Power in the Multinational Corporation: the Role of Interests, Identities, and Institution*. Cambridge University Press, 72–100.

6 Seminal contributions of the critical management school

CHRISTOPH DÖRRENBÄCHER AND
JOANNE ROBERTS

Language and the circuits of power in a merging multinational corporation, by E. Vaara, J. Tienari, R. Piekkari and R. Säntti, published in *Journal of Management Studies* in 2005

Empirical focus

The paper by Vaara *et al.* (2005) is concerned with the role of power in language policy choices in multinational corporations (MNCs) that undergo a merger. While language has been a topic in organizational studies since the 1970s, the role of language in MNCs, i.e. the dominant organizational form for international business, has received very little attention. The study of language policy choices and the role of power therein is a relevant gap in research. Multiple languages (similar to multiple cultures or nationalities) inherently create tensions, especially in situations of cross-border mergers that juxtapose and confront parties that have different natural languages, while at the same time a need for a common corporate language emerges in order to safeguard the effective functioning of the merged company.

The paper empirically draws on a single revelatory case, that is the 1997 merger of the Finnish Merita Bank with the Swedish Nordbanken, the first case of a cross border merger of retail banks in Europe. Based on rich ethnographic material the focus of the study is on the selection of Swedish as the official corporate language and the 'deeper level meaning' (Vaara *et al.* 2005: 601) of this decision for actor power, power structures and conflict in the merged company. Power, politics and conflict are seen as central to explain language policy choices in merging MNCs and are an explanans to the organizational effects of such a choice.

Theoretical focus

The paper is rooted in post-colonial theory and its more recent application outside immediate colonial debates:

Particularly relevant for our analyses, 'post colonial' researchers have examined the relationship between colonizing and colonized people from a power/domination perspective...This approach has lately inspired many postmodernist researchers outside the immediate colonial debates to try to understand the social forces behind marginalization and exclusion. (Vaara *et al.* 2005: 599)

Conceptually the paper draws on Clegg's (1989) 'circuits of power' framework in order to provide an integrated view on power, politics and conflict involved in language policy choices and forces of marginalization and exclusion triggered by language policy choices in MNCs. In line with Clegg's 'circuits of power' approach Vaara *et al.* (2005) engage in three distinct levels of investigation in order to 'illustrate the complex power implications of language policies' (ibid.: 605). At the level of *observable social interaction* the paper details how language skills are empowering and disempowering resources that nationally confined groups of actors hold in the merger. At the level of *identity and subjectivity construction* the paper describes how the language policy decision is (re)constructing the identity and subjectivity of actor groups. At a final level the paper explores the *reification of structures of domination* through the language policy choice.

Underlying this analysis is an understanding of the multinational corporation as a natural system which however does not foreclose a certain functional rationality in decision making, as the authors argue:

Language policies should *not merely* be treated as practical means to solve inevitable communication problems; rather they should be viewed as exercise of power. (Vaara *et al.* 2005: 596; emphasis added)

This links up to the generic concept of politics applied by Vaara *et al.* (2005), who are explicitly stressing the 'inherently political nature of multinational corporations' (ibid.: 621). Even though the paper deals with a particular episodic instance where actors apply available power resources to pursue their recognized interest, the overall concept of power applied is systemic as the authors rigorously trace structural antecedents for deeper level effects of the language policy choice (e.g. that this choice vitalizes historically constructed conceptions of superiority and inferiority and reifies structures of domination). The fact that, based on colonial history, Finns learn Swedish as their first language in school strongly informed the choice of Swedish as the corporate language of the merged company. This in itself then led to an exclusion of Finnish managers from certain positions, to a disempowering of their professional resources and to a feeling of professional incompetence. While hardly elaborating on the conflict dimension, the paper nevertheless discussed resistance strategies of Finnish managers such as: deliberately switching to English in official meetings, looking for career options in parts of the merged bank where Swedish was of no or of minor importance, or leaving the firm.

The paper is fairly differentiated when considering the actors involved and affected by the language policy choice in the case company. Restricted to managerial actors, the paper distinguishes several groups and subgroups of managers (e.g. Finnish and Swedish managers, top and middle manager, bilingual and Finnish managers with a weak command of Swedish, etc.) and discusses how the language policy choice affected their interests and power positions. This also informs the level of alignment between the organizational decision for Swedish as the corporate language and particular goals that can be found among several actors and groups. For instance, alignment to the decision for Swedish as corporate language was high with Swedish managers, but low for Finnish managers with a weak command of Swedish. As indicated above when discussing the different resistance strategies, actors are conceptualized as autonomous in their reactions to the language policy choice but they are seen as informed by their particular interests and contextual conditions. Here Vaara *et al.* (2005) report a rich array of national, hierarchical, organizational, suborganizational and individual biographical contexts that inform the Swedish proficiency of managers, which is seen as indicative for the way the individuals are affected by the language policy choice. By the same token Swedish language proficiency is considered to be a basic means. Actors' means–ends orientations, however, are not studied systematically.

The multinational corporation as a third space: rethinking international management discourse on knowledge transfer through Homi Bhabha, by M. Frenkel, published in *Academy of Management Review* in 2008

Empirical focus

Frenkel's (2008) paper focuses on the cross-border transfer of knowledge and practice within MNCs and the way this is discussed in the mainstream international management discourse. The paper in particular refers to transfers between the first world and third world. Given the fact that the majority of large MNCs are from the first world, and a growing number of their foreign affiliates are located in the developing (third) world, the paper assumes that "the transfer and management of knowledge and practices is increasingly a matter of relations between dominating and dominated societies" (Frenkel 2008: 925).

Consequently the knowledge transfer process is seen as embodying the unequal power relations between the dominating and the dominated forces in the contemporary world order 'whether in relation to the colonial empires of the eighteenth and nineteenth centuries or in relation to today's superpowers and economic empires' (Frenkel 2008: 925). This makes geopolitical power relations into a central element (explanans) to explain political maneuvering and conflict associated with knowledge transfer processes (explanandum).

Theoretical focus

The paper draws heavily on post-colonial theory both as a critique to the mainstream management discourse on knowledge transfer in MNCs and as a source for a new multilevel research programme that overcomes the aforementioned critique.

Following Frenkel (2008), a post-colonial reading of the mainstream management discourse on knowledge transfer in MNCs uncovers that mainstream contributions: (i) are excluding and silencing organizational knowledge from the third world; (ii) are representing the third world in an over simplistic way; and (iii) falsely link transfer failures to the third world affiliates' missing cultural and institutional capacities (Frenkel 2008: 925, 930). Drawing on Homi Bhabha's (1994) epistemology of 'mimicry, hybridity, and the third space', the paper presents an alternative understanding and a new multilevel approach to study knowledge transfer in terms of forces. 'Mimicry' is understood as a control practice in which the colonizer (the first world MNC) forces the colonized to mimic the colonizers knowledge. This is accompanied by a discourse that mimicry is for the colonized's own good as the knowledge from the colonizer is superior. 'Hybridity' refers to the impact that knowledge and practice transfers have on the reformulation of national identities and cultural beliefs in recipient countries. This not only includes colonizers' domination but also resistance of the colonized. What emerges is a 'third space of in-between' in which the 'cutting edge of translation and negotiation' (Bhabha 1994, cited according to Frenkel 2008: 928) occurs between the colonizer and the colonized.

In Frenkel's (2008) view, MNCs are concrete examples of such a 'third space of in-between'. Here 'politicize[d] knowledge production' (ibid.: 937) takes place through a contested and power-laden process in which the colonizers and the colonized interact and mix with one another. It is here where mutual perceptions as well as the manner by which perception shapes the process of knowledge transfer and implementation surface. This clearly highlights Frenkel's (2008) – respectively Bhabha's – understanding that MNCs are natural systems, in which political maneuvering is generic and constitutive to organizational life. The power of MNC actors in such a politicized knowledge production is systemically confined by unequal geopolitical power relations and associated conceptions/perceptions of nationhood and culture, that tend to be reproduced though the content of knowledge that is transferred in MNCs, i.e. knowledge from the first world (Frenkel 2008: 929). Although the paper does not delve into the issue of conflict, the paper maintains that the transfer of knowledge and practices in MNCs needs to be seen 'as a process occurring in a conflict-ridden context' (Frenkel 2008: 937) where conflict emerges when subaltern actors resist imposed knowledge and practices (Frenkel 2008: 927, 936).

According to Frenkel (2008) subaltern actors in processes of knowledge and practice transfers are managers and workers in third world affiliates of MNCs, as well as third world affiliates of MNCs as such. The MNC headquarters is considered to be the dominating actor, whose objective or subjective understanding of the MNC's needs defines what is to be transferred, and thereby incorporates and perpetuates the foreign units' dependence on the headquarters (Frenkel 2008: 929, 931). Actors are typically characterized as contextually determined, with the geopolitical position of the country they stem from (either from the first or the third world) framing their behaviour. Bounded rationality is assumed for all actors, but in particular elaborated for local subsidiary managers whose behaviour might vary according to: (i) their identification with the local unit; (ii) previous training in the headquarters; and (iii) situational political circumstances (Frenkel 2008: 936). The paper does not explicitly discuss sources of actor power. As it transpires from the paper, however, headquarters' power is largely conceptualized as hierarchical power, the power to shape discourses on superiority and inferiority of knowledge and practices and as the power to influence the reformulation of national identities and cultural beliefs through the transfer of knowledge and practices. Local actors' sources of power are only broadly characterized by their potential to resist such transfers. Actors are seen as actively enacting their contextual conditions (be they national, individual, and/or discursive) thereby having an influence both on the sedimentation or the alleviation of unequal relationships within the MNC and beyond.

Infra-political dimensions of resistance to international business: a neo-Gramscian approach, by S. Böhm, A. Spicer and P. Fleming, published in *Scandinavian Journal of Management* in 2008

Empirical focus

The paper by Böhm *et al.* (2008) is concerned with a better understanding of how international business is resisted. In particular, it zooms in on what has been labelled by Scott (1990) as 'infra-politics', i.e. the informal and clandestine ways to challenge international business that have so far been largely neglected in academic debates. This encompasses a large number of practices including workplace misbehaviour, guerrilla action and direct action protests (Böhm *et al.* 2008: 174).

In addition to further elucidating these decentralized, non-hierarchical, grassroots resistance activities, Böhm *et al.* (2008) strike a link between informal and formal forms of resistance, with the latter including state, union and non-governmental organization (NGO) resistance to international business. Here the paper goes beyond describing and classifying different forms of resistance by taking a conceptually informed account of how different types of resistance combine and interconnect in order to articulate counter-hegemonic discourses (Böhm *et al.* 2008: 170).

Theoretical focus

Theoretically the paper builds on Gramsci's (1971) concept of hegemony. This concept highlights that the domination of one social group over another not only occurs in one social sphere such as the economy but also in the other social spheres including the state and civil society. Thereby a hegemonic regime is vitally dependent on the construction of consent structures throughout the spheres, with resistance to hegemony then leading to latent or manifest conflicts in all spheres. Following Böhm *et al.* (2008) multinational companies today dominate all spheres and generically provoke resistance as they are embedded in multiple antagonistic power relations. Hence Böhm *et al.* (2008) conceptualize multinational companies as natural systems that are internally shaped by the capital–labour divide and externally by antagonistic relationships with state and civil society actors. In line with Gramsci's concept of hegemony, the paper further assumes that power is systemic, with MNCs seen as trying to forge their hegemony in cultural and institutional norms. As an example the paper here refers to MNCs' billboard and TV advertisements as well as movie production that aim to control 'signs, signification and meaning' (Böhm *et al.* 2008: 174).

Overall the paper takes a rather comprehensive actor perspective with all actors being described as trying to proactively shape their environments. Within the MNC, the paper conceptualizes the capital side as a unified rational actor (with no differences between the owner and managers) that aims to safeguard profitability and hegemony, whereas workers and trade unions are seen as bounded in their rationality as their resistance is largely seen as confined by the MNC strategies and their negative outcomes such as bad working conditions, environmental pollution, low pay, weak labour representation, etc. Actors outside the MNC considered encompass governmental and civil society actors that similarly are assumed to resist MNC strategies when they conflict with their particular interests or worldviews.

The paper highlights that those actors resisting MNC strategies use formal and informal modes of protest, with 'formal resistance strategies...always accompanied and supplemented by informal, infra-political forms of resistance'(Böhm *et al.* 2008: 175). This is seen as opening up opportunities to overcome 'egoistical acts' of resistance (Böhm *et al.* 2008: 179) by individual power holders and to actively engineer counter-hegemonic discourses that enhance the power of the resisting actors. Within MNCs, formal resistance extends to traditional trade union activities such as 'strikes, go-slows or demands for increased salaries' (Böhm *et al.* 2008: 175). This is supplemented by informal means to resist and undermine managerial practices such as 'sabotage, theft, cynicism and absenteeism' (ibid.: 175). Formal state resistance to MNC strategies includes the creation of a regulatory framework that governs MNCs' activities as well as nationalization policies (in some cases). Informal state resistance refers to the policies of 'non-bureaucratized political groups or networks that try to influence state policy (e.g. the Zapatista movement in Mexico). Finally, formal means of civil society resistance extend to bureaucratized NGOs' strategies to watch and to politicize the more problematic practices of MNCs such as human rights violations with the aim of creating public consciousness. Informal means mentioned here are swiftly organized direct actions by social movements such as the activities of the anti-globalization movement in response to World Trade Organization (WTO) or International Monetary Fund (IMF) meetings.

Overall, actors' resistance behaviour seems to be driven by actors' goals as well as by the particular power position of the actor and the means that are available in the actor context. The most relevant context for resisting actors following Böhm *et al.* (2008) is the sphere an actor is located in (economy/firm, state or civil society) as well the organizational form actors have taken on (formal vs. informal organizations).

Rollerball and the spirit of capitalism: competitive dynamics within the global context, the challenge to labour transnationalism, and the emergence of ironic outcomes, by N. Lillie and M. Martínez Lucio, published in *Critical Perspectives on International Business* in 2012

In this review paper Lillie and Martínez Lucio (2012) take transnational capitalism as the context in which the relations between MNCs and their global workforces occur. Neo-liberal globalization is presented as the dominant narrative, which results in an economic system wherein economic progress is dependent on global competition. The authors argue that recognition of the socially constructed nature of globalization offers hope for the construction of alternative narratives. Yet, the hegemony of transnational capital works to undermine the emergence of such alternatives from national sources of resistance.

Transnational capital takes the form of transnational corporations (TNCs) or MNCs, which compete in global markets and draw resources from across the globe according to their potential to contribute to profitable production. Hence, nationally based workers, localities and states compete for the investments of MNCs, while MNCs present themselves as highly mobile organizations that are subject to the drivers of global competition. This perspective presents power as unevenly distributed between, on the one hand, dominant mobile capital, and, on the other hand, geographically fixed ineffectual labour and states. While national firms are subject to state regulation and must take account of the bargaining power of national trade unions, MNCs are not constrained by such considerations. Because MNCs operate at a global level, they gain power through the ability to play off against one another geographically dispersed nationally based actors. According to the authors, because trade unions have developed in national economic and political contexts they are limited in their ability to organize effectively at a transnational level to resist MNCs and their global production strategies.

Empirical focus

The empirical focus of this paper is the relationship between transnational capital and national and transnational labour unionism in the context of a capitalist neo-liberal conceptualization of globalization. The authors draw primarily on European examples of transnational unionism 'because the EU has the most developed regulatory spaces and processes of transnational union regulation' (Lillie and Martínez Lucio 2012: 75). Transnational capital is embodied in TNCs or MNCs: transnational labour organizations include the International Confederation of Free Trade Unions (ICFTU) and the industry-defined Global Union Federations (GUFs). At a European level these are replicated by the European Trade Union Confederation (ETUC) and European Industry Federations (EIFs).

Such transnational labour organizations are based on national structures of representation with most activity occurring through informal networks of cooperation between independent organizations. Hence:

Trans- and inter- national union strategies can only be understood in the context of the interaction between unions' embeddedness in national regulation, and globalizing production, resulting in transnational unionism consisting of a set of relationships between competing national players with competing visions of the 'global' within global production structures. (Lillie and Martínez Lucio 2012: 75)

It is argued that the mobility of capital, or indeed the mere threat of such mobility, undermines the bargaining power of national trade unions and states. Although transnational labour unionism offers potential to redress the balance between capital and labour, 'the network structure of transnational labour unionism, in formal and informal terms, is in itself an ineffective response to capitalist globalization, and the narrative of global competition' (Lillie and Martínez Lucio 2012: 75).

Transnational trade union organizations, formed through networks, have much less scope for formal centralized control than their nationally based counterparts. They are unable to adopt the same hierarchical control structures as those employed by MNCs. Consequently the ability of transnational trade union organizations to facilitate unified resistance to transnational capital is weak and remains dependent on loose networks in which diverse interests are prone to undermine united action.

In this paper power is placed centre stage as a systemic feature of the socio-economic conditions of contemporary capitalism. The dominant narrative of globalization which promotes competition as the driving force for economic progress (explanans) explains the power exercised by transnational capital over nationally based labour unions and states (explanandum). Following on from this, the mobility of capital together with the geographical fragmentation of labour (explanans) explains the inadequacy of organized labour to counterbalance capital at a transnational level (explanandum).

Theoretical focus

This paper is firmly embedded in the Marxist tradition of class conflict. For instance, Lillie and Martínez Lucio (2012) argue that:

The shift in the geographic scale of capitalist production and accumulation to the transnational level is a part of this ongoing process of segmentation and class conflict (Gough 2004), as firms seek cost and operational advantages within their pursuit of profitability and expansion. Like the division of labour in factories, transnational production allows capital greater control over the production process, and helps to obscure the relations of production in such a way as to make it more difficult for workers to recover a share of the extracted surplus value. (Lillie and Martínez Lucio 2012: 76)

The authors draw on literature from international industrial relations to support their argument that if labour organizations are to resist transnational capital they require more systematic and structured transnational trade unions or new forms of networking as well as the construction of a convincing counter narrative to that of global competition.

Lillie and Martínez Lucio (2012) point to the irony of transnational capital's exploitation of globalization, through, for instance, forcing concessions from labour, depending on the continued construction of difference. Hence, globalization does not lead to homogenization but rather it creates difference so that local actors and spaces can be played off against each other.

Transnational capital is viewed as a rational united actor driven by the search for profit. In contrast, labour is seen as context dependent, with its rationality bounded by the dominant capitalist narrative of global competition. The hegemony of capital, though resisted at national levels by trade unions and national regulatory frameworks, is free from serious contestation at the global level where the mobility of transnational capital undermines efforts to provide unified transnational labour resistance.

Lillie and Martínez Lucio (2012) suggest that the relationship between transnational capital and labour is much the same as the relationship between TNCs and the masses depicted in the 1975 film *Rollerball*, directed by Norman Jewison. In the dystopian future portrayed in this film, TNCs rule the world and promote the violent game of 'rollerball' to create the illusion of competition and maintain difference in loyalties among the masses.

Conclusion

The four articles considered in this chapter illustrate the critical management school, which brings together scholars concerned with the socio-economic structures that create and perpetuate unequal power relations in the contemporary world (see Table 6.1 for a summary). Drawing on various roots such as labour process, post-structuralist and critical theory, the critical management school developed in the 1990s and diversified into several functional subdiscourses such as critical accounting, critical organization theory or critical international business (Alvesson and Deetz 2000; Fournier and Grey 2000). Critical international business, that is of particular concern when studying micropolitics in MNCs, is engaged in a radical discussion on the nature of globalization and international business with the aim to uncover hegemonic structures both in MNCs as well as in the world economy and to counter the prevalent mangerialist logic (Cairns and Roberts 2005). As we have seen above, this imprint makes the topics of power, politics and conflict central and generic themes of critical management scholars' accounts of micropolitics in MNCs. While the first two papers showed how power, politics and conflict unfold with regard to particular important issues in MNCs, that is the choice of a corporate language (Vaara *et al.* 2005) and the cross-border transfers of knowledge in MNCs (Frenkel 2008). The two other papers focused on various forms of resistance to managerial strategies of MNCs, with the paper of Böhm *et al.* (2008) concentrating on informal resistance strategies (e.g. by civil society actors) whereas the paper by Lillie and Martínez Lucio (2012) deals with trade union actors' strategies.

But what does critical management offer to the conceptualization of micropolitics in MNCs in a more theoretical perspective? As Vaara *et al.* (2005) and Frenkel (2008) reveal, unequal power relations are evident in the language used in the subsidiaries of MNCs and the knowledge transferred between them. What Böhm *et al.* (2008) and Lillie and Martínez Lucio (2012) show is that resistance to such micropolitical conditions in MNCs is subject to resistance at micro, meso and macro levels, through the actions of trade unions, NGOs, civil society, states and transnational labour organizations. The papers provide evidence to support the existence of unequal power relations arising from the activities of MNCs at various levels of analysis and expressed in a variety of forms. Moreover, efforts to resist these unequal power relations come from both actors in the micro context as well as organizations and institutions operating at a macro level.

Although the critical management school offers insights into micropolitics in MNCs, research in this field focuses largely on the plight of

Table 6.1 *Overview of seminal contributions of the critical management school*

Contribution analytical dimensions	Vaara *et al.* (2005)	Frenkel (2008)	Böhm *et al.* (2008)	Lillie and Martínez Lucio (2012)
Empirical focus	Language policy choice in merged MNCs	Knowledge and practice transfers in MNCs	Formal and informal forms of resistance to MNC strategies	Trade union network-based transnational cooperation and its inadequacy as a counterbalance to transnational capital
Centrality of politics, power and conflict	High centrality of power, politics and conflict as an explanans of the organizational effects of the language policy choice	High centrality of power: unequal power relations between first and third world actors in MNCs to explain domination, conflict and political manoeuvrings associated with knowledge and practice transfers in MNCs	High centrality of power and conflict in MNCs through focusing on different forms of resistance that are triggered by unequal power relations (explanandum) and lead to latent and manifest conflicts (explanans)	Dominant narrative of globalization and competition (explanans) explains the power exercised by transnational capital over nationally based labour and states (explanandum). Mobility of capital and the geographical fragmentation of labour (explanans) explains the failure of organized labour to counterbalance capital at a transnational level (explanandum)
Theoretical focus	Post-colonial theory; applying Clegg's (1989) circuits of power approach	Post-colonial theory; applying Homi Bhabha's (1994) epistemology of 'mimicry, hybridity, and the third space'	Gramsci's (1971) concept of hegemony	Marxist tradition of class conflict. Transnational capital extracts surplus value from workers. Labour resistance through trade unions is undermined by the differential geographic levels of operation between MNCs and labour

Concept of MNC	MNCs are seen as inherently political systems	MNCs are seen as inherently political systems ('third space of in-between' home and host country)	MNCs are seen as inherently political systems in which the capital's side attempts for hegemony create resistance and conflict	As part of transnational capital, MNCs are seen as inherently political. MNCs seek to extract surplus value from labour
Concept of politics, power and conflict	Generic and systemic understanding of power and politics	Generic and systemic understanding of power and politics	Generic and systemic understanding of power	Generic and systemic understanding of power
Concept of actors and behavioural orientation	Restricted to managerial actors; they are seen as partly autonomous in their reactions to language policy choice. Language proficiency as basic actor means that informs behaviour	Subaltern and dominating actors; managerial actors and workers, are seen as contextually bound in their behaviour with subsidiary managers being subject to multiple contextual realities	The MNC's capital side is conceptualized as unified rational actor (with no differences between the owner and managers) aiming at profit and hegemony. Resisting actors are seen as bounded in their rationality as their resistance is largely seen as confined by the MNC strategies and their negative outcomes.	As part of transnational capital MNCs are seen as rational actors seeking profit and hegemony. Resisting actors are seen as contextually determined and bounded in their rationality which is confined by the dominant capitalist narrative of globalization and the necessity of competition.
Concept of actor-context relation	Historical/national, hierarchical, organizational, suborganizational and individual biographical contexts influence actors means, interests and behaviours	Actors actively enact their contextual conditions and have an influence on the sedimentation or alleviation of unequal relationships in MNCs and beyond	Actors are shaped by the sphere in which it is located (economy/firm, state or civic society) as well by the organizational form (formal vs informal organizations). Actors are proactively trying to shape their contexts	The hegemony of transnational capital provides the contextual conditions for labour. Though proactive at a national level, labour's efforts to unite at a transnational level are undermined by transnational capital's mobility and subsequent ability to fragment transnational labour coalitions.

labour and its resistance to MNCs as an embodiment of capital. There is little effort to explore the strategies of MNCs from the perspective of capital. While this might seem counterintuitive from the position of a critical management scholar, there may be important insights to be gained from deepening the appreciation of capital through the lens of critical management studies. In addition, the theoretical approaches adopted by critical management scholars tend to overlook the nuanced experiences of individuals, which are generally presented as an aggregate group of labour or managers. Furthermore, as most of the papers considered in this chapter reveal, there is a tendency to view actors as bound by their context. Vaara *et al.* (2005) are alone in presenting actors as having a degree of autonomy.

References

Alvesson, M. and Deetz, S. 2000. *Doing Critical Management Research*. London: Sage.
Bhabha, H. K. (ed.) 1994. *The Location of Culture*. London and New York: Routledge.
Böhm, S., Spicer, A. and Fleming, P. 2008. Infra-political dimensions of resistance to international business: a neo-Gramscian approach. *Scandinavian Journal of Management*, 24(13): 169–182.
Cairns, G. and Roberts, J. 2005. Introduction from the editors. *Critical Perspectives on International Business*, 1(1): 4–6.
Clegg, S. R. 1989. *Frameworks of Power*. London: Sage.
Fournier, V. and Grey, C. 2000. At the critical moment: conditions and prospects for critical management studies. *Human Relations*, 53: 7–32.
Frenkel, M. 2008. The multinational corporation as a third space: rethinking international management discourse on knowledge transfer through Homi Bhabha. *Academy of Management Review*, 33: 924–942.
Gough, J. 2004. Changing scale as changing class relations: variety and contradiction in the politics of scale. *Political Geography*, 23(2): 185–211.
Gramsci, A. 1971. *Selection from Prison Notebooks*. London: Lawrence and Wishart.
Lillie, N. and Martínez Lucio, M. 2012. Rollerball and the spirit of capitalism: competitive dynamics within the global context, the challenge to labour transnationalism, and the emergence of ironic outcomes. *Critical Perspectives on International Business*, 8(1): 74–92.

Scott, J. C. 1990. *Domination and the Hidden Arts of Resistance: Hidden Transcripts*. New Haven, CN: Yale University Press.
Vaara, E., Tienari, J., Piekkari, R. and Säntti, R. 2005. Language and the circuits of power in a merging multinational corporation. *Journal of Management Studies*, 42(3): 595–623.

PART III

Analytical tools and applications

Introduction

This section seeks to give some hands-on advice to researchers who want to use the micropolitical framework developed in this book to conduct their own empirical research projects. Chapter 7 presents a stratified analytical framework that develops a step-by-step approach to researching politics and power in the multinational corporation (MNC): the authors suggest that a critical political event, where processes of (agentic) power are manifest and visible, is usually a good starting point for the research process. From there researchers might decide to expand their research perspective in two directions: a socio-spatial dimension and a temporal dimension. Whereas the socio-spatial dimension leads to a research process that integrates more and more contextual layers around the critical event in focus (the local context, the organizational context, the national context, etc.) in order to understand the systemic embeddedness of the political act, the temporal dimension helps to reconstruct the paths and events that lead up to the critical event. It thus allows taking account of the impact of past events, traditions, routines or prior experiences on the current political processes and also draws attention to the effects of foreshadowing (e.g. actor expectations) that might influence current political activities. While it is evident that both dimensions are essential to develop a full picture of power and politics in the MNC, the stepwise extension of perspectives should help researchers to structure their empirical work and to keep the research process somewhat manageable.

Chapter 8 looks at the research process as a political process in itself. The authors first show that the standard literature on business and management research still only rarely addresses the political dimension of researching and the political role of the researcher. Whereas researchers are often in an unfavourable position regarding access to the research context and data gathering, depending on powerful support, e.g. by top management, data analysis often brings the researcher into a powerful position – selecting and interpreting 'relevant' data – which, again, might be withdrawn by the company under research when management feels threatened by unexpected and unwanted results, as in the introductory example of the chapter. The authors then painstakingly work through all steps of a conventional research project (defining the research questions, negotiating access, etc.) and identify moments and elements of politics and power inside the research process. The chapter thus helps researchers in the field to reflect on the political dimension of researching on politics and power in the MNC and to systematically include a self-reflective, critical (and thus, again, political) stance into their research design and reporting.

7 | Understanding organizational behaviour in multinational corporations (MNCs) from a micropolitical perspective: a stratified analytical framework

FLORIAN A. A. BECKER-RITTERSPACH
AND SUSANNE BLAZEJEWSKI

Introduction

A deeper concern with politics, power and conflict in MNCs is not merely an academic exercise for its own sake. It is our contention that organizational life in MNCs is political and that organizational behaviour, that is, organizational decisions and outcomes, are the result of political processes. In this sense, our starting point is seeing MNCs as open natural systems, that is: collectives whose participants are pursuing multiple and often conflicting interests and whose interests and means or sources to pursue their interests can only be understood with reference to actors that are relevant to and involved in a political event. In this generic politics perspective organizational events or episodes such as market selection and entry mode choices, charter changes or subsidiary evolution, reorganizations or site closures, intrafirm competition, knowledge flows and resistance, are underwritten and constituted by politics.

We would like to add that a generic politics perspective does not only explain episodes and events that mark contested changes, but also inaction, maintenance of a situation and stability, that is, helping to explain why certain choices are not even considered and why certain organizational conditions remain unquestioned and untouched.

While we adopt a generic political perspective, it is our second main contention that understanding organizational-level episodes and events requires not simply a political but a micropolitical agency perspective. We see organizational-level processes and outcomes as

Table 7.1 *The GM/Opel wildcat strike*

On October 14, 2004 the General Motors headquarters in Detroit announced its intention to cut 12,000 jobs in its European plants by 2005 and reduce annual costs by €500 million. At that time, the GM/Opel plant in Bochum was one of the oldest plants of GM in Europe, with three production sites (site I: assembly, site II: gears and axle production, site III: parts support) and approx. 11,000 employees, strongly embedded in the local community and industry culture. Between 1992 and 2004 Opel Bochum had been forced to shed 10,000 jobs, despite major workers' concessions. Right after the announcement of GM headquarters, workers from site II staged a six-day unofficial ('wildcat') strike although the union (IG Metall) and the majority of the Bochum works council opposed the walkout. Because the Bochum plant holds a central position in GM's European production network, operations at GM Antwerp (Belgium), Ellesmere Port (UK) and Rüsselsheim (Germany) were forced to stop after four days. On October 20, 2004 an employee meeting in Bochum voted for a return to work. In 2015 GM closed down site I and II completely. Car production in Bochum thus came to a final stop after fifty-two years.

produced by individual actors or sets of individual actors who interact politically at the micro-level. Here our work coincides with recent developments in strategy and international business research that calls for a better understanding of the microfoundations of organizational events, outcomes and processes in MNCs (Becker-Ritterspach 2006; Felin and Foss 2005; Foss 2011). For instance, within the context of knowledge transfer in MNCs, Foss and Pedersen (2004) note the 'absence of micro-foundations' and call for more disciplined attention to individual behaviour. Clearly, such a persistent bias towards organizational-level constructs and aggregate concepts without an understanding of the underlying patterns of human agency and social interaction can be extended to most research domains within the field of international business and management.

In this chapter, we would like to move beyond a theoretical discussion of literature on politics and power in MNCs and suggest some practical implications of adopting a micropolitical perspective to organizational analysis in MNCs.

We believe that the most obvious starting point for a micropolitical analysis will be a specific episode or event that manifests itself as rather overtly political in the sense that it involves contentious/contested

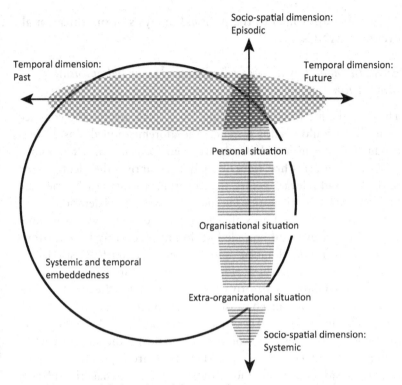

Figure 7.1 A stratified analytical framework

organizational decisions and outcomes in MNCs. To exemplify our approach we will draw on a specific example, that is, the closure of General Motors' (GM) Opel production site in Bochum, Germany (Blazejewski 2009: see case description Table 7.1). The case marks a rather obvious political event and episode in that it has been accompanied by a hefty political battle that ended in 2015 when the production site was finally shut down.

Further, we suggest that depending on the time and other resources available to the researcher a more or less embedded analysis of such political events or episodes should be adopted. This embeddedness comprises both an extended temporal analysis as well as an extended socio-spatial analysis of the agency that constitutes the event. Hence, in the following section, we would like to suggest a stratified model of political analysis to be extended to increasing levels of temporal and socio-spatial analysis (see Figure 7.1).

A stratified approach to the political analysis of organizational events in MNCs

Episodic level: key actors, relations and their behavioural orientation

The episodic level involves focusing on a single temporally confined event. This could be, for instance, the aforementioned closure of a production site in an MNC. Apart from focusing on a temporally confined event, this first level of analysis comprises the identification of the key and relevant actors, their relations towards each other and their behavioural orientations in the event under consideration.

Relevant actors are for us all actors that are in one way or another affected by an event or episode but do not necessarily have a strong influence on its development and outcome (Becker-Ritterspach and Dörrenbächer 2011). These would be regular employees or workers but also their families or private social networks affected by a site closure. *Key actors*, in contrast, are the 'political brokers' (March 1962: 672) in the event. These actors most obviously have the power to influence the development and outcome of the event (Becker-Ritterspach and Dörrenbächer 2011). They are typically executives from the headquarters and the subsidiaries on the managerial side. On the employees' side, these are typically labour representatives within the company. It is important to note, however, that there may also be key actors who are not members of the MNC. We can think of a wide range of extra-organizational stakeholders or societal actors such as union leaders, politicians and media representatives who substantially influence the development and outcome of a political episode or events (Becker-Ritterspach and Dörrenbächer 2009; Bélanger and Edwards 2006; Blazejewski 2009).

Identifying relevant and key actors is the first step in understanding the development and outcome of a political episode. The second step is to consider the *relations* among the actors identified. The questions to be posed here are: which key actors oppose or support each other by forming, for instance, a coalition? Who is the constituency of key actors, that is, which relevant actors do the respective key actors represent? Where do relationships to third parties provide access to power bases the focus actor her/himself does not hold?

In political episodes such as a site closure we will often find that subsidiary executives and employee representatives are in an antagonistic relation to each other. In this scenario, regular employees (relevant actors) are in a relationship of support with their labour representative (key actor) who acts on their behalf. Similarly, subsidiary executives may be key political brokers acting on behalf of corporate headquarters. Yet, as we shall see in the specific example below, we should be careful about making *a priori* assumptions about key actors and actor relations in political events as we might find highly idiosyncratic actor sets and relations of support and opposition that are more complex and cut across a simple management–labour opposition (Blazejewski 2009).

Relations among key and relevant actors in political events typically form around the (common) interests and related power sources, that is, *behavioural orientations* of different actors and actor groups in a given political episode. By behavioural orientation, we mean the interplay of actor interest (motivation) and actor sources of power (ability) that in conjunction influence the development and outcome of an event in a certain direction.

Actor *interests* are a key concept of the different politics and power perspectives (Bacharach and Lawler 1980; Dlugos *et al.* 1993; Fischer 2005). In the literature interests are alternatively defined as preferences (Fischer 2005), needs, desires and concerns (Fisher *et al.* 2011) of individual or collective actors. They may be confined to material and economic interests as in the work by Allen (2004) and Rothman and Friedman (2001) but we may also extend them to other interests such as political, personal and career interests. We understand actor *interests* here as the desired course and outcomes of an event as perceived and articulated by relevant and key actors (see Chapter 2). Simply speaking, in a shutdown of a production plant we will find key actors who strive to avert the site closure. These key actors will act in the interest of a larger group of relevant actors. We will find these actors in opposition to other actors whose behavioural orientation is to close the site. These are likely senior subsidiary managers, who act in the interest of headquarter managers and ultimately shareholders.

Identifying relations and the interests embedded in them is only one side of the coin of understanding the behavioural orientation of actors. The other half involves asking about the *power of actors*. We follow Pfeffer (1981) who suggests that power is a highly 'context specific' concept, requiring a context of application. In keeping with this suggestion, we define the power of actors surrounding a temporally confined event as their ability to influence the course and the outcome of the event in their interests (Giddens 1984). Qualifying this power further calls for an understanding of the sources of power available through and employable in the different social relations among actors. Regarding the *sources of power*, the organizational power literature offers different typologies. Among the first and probably best known is the typology suggested by French and Raven (1960). They distinguish positional power, referent power, expert power, information power, reward power and coercive power. Etzioni (1964), who distinguishes three organizational sources of power, presents a similar typology: coercive, utilitarian and normative power. Crozier and Friedberg (1980) for their part identify four principle zones of uncertainty that define sources of power. These are sources which derive from special skills and from functional specialization, from relations between an organization and its environments, from the control of communication and information, and from the existence of general organizational rules. We shun away from defining a specific set or kinds of power sources. While keeping in mind the different sources discussed, we would like to suggest an empirical openness for the different kinds of power that actors may mobilize and employ. For instance, in the case of the site shutdown subsidiary managers can refer to formal authority and ownership-based decision-making rights to shut down the site. Labour representatives for their part may resort to other rules such as their right to strike or make normative-ethical appeals to social responsibility.

It should also be noted at this point that the above power perspectives have been criticized for seeing power as a property of actors, disregarding that power could only be mobilized through and materialized in social relationships (Clegg *et al.* 2006). While we concur that social relations or exchange relations are a *sine qua non* for mobilizing and enacting power (the concept of resources as a source of power is useless when these resources are socially irrelevant, i.e. they cannot at least potentially be exchanged with other actors), we also recognize that the sources of power that can be mobilized and enacted in social relations may be of different kinds and are unequally or asymmetrically distributed among actors (some actors may have *more* contextually relevant resources that can be traded). Actors are positioned in different contextual fields and situations and are embedded in diverse social relations, which structure the episodic availability and employability of different kinds of resources.

Application

Returning to our example, we may identify that among the relevant actors in the Bochum plant shutdown are all employees and managers who will be affected by the closure of the production site. Affectedness could mean, in this specific case, job losses for workers or for senior managers having to move to another place and organizational unit. Clearly not all actors are affected by the event equally, which has a bearing on their interest in the event. What is more, as not all actors affected by a development can also influence the event, it is crucial to identify those actors that have the power to influence the development in their interest. In the case of the closure of the Opel site, we may therefore investigate the different actors that were directly involved in the negotiations that resulted in the site closure. For instance, the actors that were involved in the last episode of site shut down were the members of the German Opel works council, local shop stewards at the Bochum site and top management at the Bochum site, Opel Germany, GM Europe and GM Detroit respectively. Once key actors are identified, we inquire about their different behavioural orientations in the development of the event. In this case, the works council as well as management in Germany pursued established paths or rituals to voice their objections against the impending job cuts (Blazejewski 2009). Their shared perspective was based on formal authorities and competences and a long-standing cooperative stance between workers' representatives and local/national managers at Opel. They therefore mainly pursued a strategy of negotiations with the MNC headquarters in Detroit. In turn, the shop stewards in Bochum who did not have access to the negotiations or other formally legitimated ways of protest but had strong personal ties to the workers on the shop floor, used this social power base to persuade the shop floor to stage an illegal wild-cat strike at Opel Bochum.

Limitations

The first level of basic micropolitical analysis involves understanding how the developments and outcomes of a specific temporally confined organizational event are connected to specific sets of key and relevant actors, their behavioural orientations and relations. It involves, in particular, asking about the interests as articulated by actors and identifying the different sources of power employed in and available through their relations. Such an analysis serves to explain why certain actors are able or unable to realize their interests. While this perspective allows us to develop a fine-grained understanding of a specific temporally confined event, it falls short of explaining how the development and the outcome of a given event is enabled and constrained by its wider temporal and contextual conditions. These contextual conditions become salient when we want to understand why similar organizational events across time and space result in very different trajectories and outcomes. For instance, our above analysis does not explain why shops stewards in Bochum pursued a strongly divergent path of protest vis-à-vis the members of the Opel works council – albeit they are 'partners in arms' in that both groups represent the workers' interests, are members of the same union (in this case IG Metall) and are strongly embedded in the German industrial relations system. Also, limiting our analysis to the episodic level, we are unable to explain why the wild-cat strike took hold in some of the three Opel plants in Bochum but not in others. Answering these questions requires a deeper understanding of how socio-spatial conditions or their change over time constitute key and relevant actors, their behavioural orientations and their relations.

The socio-spatial and temporal constitution of behavioural orientations

The second level of analysis involves a deeper understanding of how the socio-spatial and temporal embeddedness constitutes actors, their behavioural orientations and relations and, thereby, the development and outcome of an event. It involves essentially shifting from a mere episodic perspective of an event to its wider systemic embeddedness and conditioning. By socio-spatial embeddedness or systemic embeddedness we mean the embeddedness of actors in a particular social position. We draw here on the work of Schütz and Luckmann (1973) and Giddens (1984). Schütz and Luckmann (1973) suggest that the situation defines an actor's position with respect to their contextual conditions. Schütz argues that a situation is defined relative to and dependant on an actor's standpoint. This standpoint or position corresponds with certain interests, stocks of knowledge and experiences. In this view the standpoint also corresponds with the access to specific sets of resources (Blazejewski 2009). Giddens (1984) theorizes actor 'situatedness' or 'positioning' in three respects, that is, chronological (position in daily life, within a lifespan, within a historical period), spatial (physical place or location) and social positioning (with respect to a network of social relations). Similar to Schütz (Schütz and Luckmann 1973), Giddens (1984) sees positioning closely related to the behavioural orientation of actors (Becker-Ritterspach 2006). Drawing on Schütz and Giddens, we suggest that analysing the situation or position of actors in context helps us to understand both actor interests as well as the actor's access and employability of resources in and through social relations or social capital (Becker-Ritterspach and Dörrenbächer 2011).

Giddens (1984) maintains that actors' positioning entails many very different contextual dimensions. This is also a key reason as to why structurally determistic models of actor behaviour are misplaced. For actors have through their multiple social positioning (e.g. in a family, a community, a firm or other organization, a region or a country), a wide range of different contextual reference points (e.g. local/firm, regional or national institutions) the relevance of which is subject to the specific situation of actors in time and social space. What is more, actors may not only draw on different contextual reference points based on their specific social position, but they may also come to vastly different usages and interpretations of the very same reference points. In this view, actor behaviour in micropolitics reflects a creative search of useful contextual reference points as well as a creative interpretation and employment of those contextual reference points selected (Blazejewski 2009; Karnøe and Nygaard 1999; Whittington 1992).

As a starting point for a socio-spatial analysis, we consider the positioning of actors in context as multidimensional and comprising different levels of analysis. This leads us to ask the question about the key dimensions of social embeddedness in a micropolitical analysis. We suggest that the firm (or focal organizational) embeddedness of actors is the most crucial dimension to understand the behavioural orientation of actors in MNC-focused micropolitics. However, as the behavioural orientation is probably never solely structured by an actors' position within the organization we have to inquire about the actors' embeddedness outside the focal organization, that is, his or her broader societal embeddedness. Such extra-organizational embeddedness includes, for instance, an individual's embeddedness in a family, a community, a firm or other organization, a region or a country, etc. As we will discuss in more detail below, these organizational and extra-organizational dimensions can be looked at different levels of analysis, that is, the micro-, meso- and macro-levels. In a last step, we will then introduce the relevance of temporality to a micropolitical analysis.

Organizational position

The most obvious context for understanding the micropolitics in an organization is probably the divergent organizational positioning of actors within the very same organization. After all, it is the very nature and intention of formal organizational design to align organizational positions with specific behavioural orientations, in other words, to allocate organizational goals and sources of power to organizational positions. And even if we disregard formal structures and position and turn to informal structures and positions of actors, it is clear that an individual actors' position in the organization informs the interests and sources of power, hence, the behavioural orientation in a micropolitical event.

Now, considering the position or situation of actors in the organization involves different analytical levels. Moving from macro to micro, we can see actors located at a certain kind of macro-organizational unit. What we have in mind here is organization-level embeddedness such as subsidiary or headquarters-level embeddedness. Inquiring about how this level of embeddedness structures the behavioural orientation of actors we can ask to what extent actors align with the interest of a certain site and can draw on sources of power that are related to this level of embeddedness. Actors may, for instance, fight for the survival of their production site and may draw on a specific source of power that is related to their centrality in the corporate network. Identifying sources of power at this level encompasses the question about the site's formal authority within the MNC, its position, centrality and importance in the global value chain, corporate division of labour or strategic importance with regard to crucial input and output markets (see related dimensions as developed in strategic contingency frameworks as presented by Hickson *et al.* (1971)). For instance, key actors who are located downstream in the value chain in a strategically important subsidiary with high network centrality may be able to draw on a substantial set of relations and resources to defend or expand their position.

Moving on to the next level of embeddedness, we have to consider that actors are positioned in organizational units, departments or work teams. Here we have to ask about the position of actors within a specific organizational entity in terms of his or her functional, professional and hierarchical work role. For example, knowing whether an individual works in a research and development (R&D) or production department, as an unskilled worker or a master craftsman with a rare production skill, as a worker with a labour representative function or senior manager, gives us an indication why some actors are key actors and why they follow one behavioural orientation rather than another. The organizational position of an individual actor or actor groups impacts actor interests as well as access to power bases such as social relations, important networks or organizational resources.

Application

So applying the relevance of the organizational context to our example of the Bochum plant, we may inquire how the different actors' situation or position structures their interest and available sources of power vis-à-vis the threatened closure of the production site. Specific questions may be: do the actors differ in their interests depending on site location, hierarchical or functional position? Answering these questions gives us a strong indication about the interests of the actors involved as well as the sources of power available to them. In the Opel case, the three Opel sites were assigned diverging positions in the Opel production system in Europe (Blazejewski 2009). Whereas site I was at that time an assembly site working at full capacity and site III was largely a support unit shipping out parts to repair shops in Germany, site II produced gearboxes and axles for all other GM Europe production plants. Due to its central and essential position in the production system, workers at site II had not only a strong interest in the strike in order to fight for their jobs, they also had the means at hand to deal a strong blow at GM management by blocking the entire European car production for six days. So, depending on the site, workers were well placed to use their central position in the production system as an effective power base. Or they perceived their position to be rather weak and peripheral and also as largely unthreatened by the impending job cuts, so they withdrew from the increasingly heated struggle.

Apart from the site structure, the international dimension is also crucial for understanding the political episodes at Opel Bochum in 2004. On the one hand, as part of the European production system Opel Bochum was at that time competing against other sites in Belgium and Poland for the assignment of the new Delta production platform – it would ensure important investments into the successful site and provide a perspective for employment there. This situation made it more difficult for management and labour representatives at Opel Bochum to openly counteract decisions from the Detroit headquarters so as not to endanger the assignment of the platform. On the other hand, the Opel sites in Antwerp and Gliwice hosted an active labour force that on the international day of labour solidarity sent workers from Belgium and Poland to Bochum in order to support the local opposition against the impending job cuts. Consequently, an analysis of the contextual embeddedness of the wildcat strike at Opel Bochum discloses that there were opposing forces (competition and solidarity) at play at the same time – thus undermining a unanimous strategy in response to the headquarters' restructuring plans.

Limitation

The key limitation of the organizational-level analysis is to reduce actor behaviour in micropolitics to their organizational embeddedness. Actors are not solely embedded in organizational contexts. Organizations are embedded in extra-organizational and societal contexts and so are the actors in them. Both the societal embeddedness of organizations and actors inform the behavioural orientation of actors within organizations. Such perspectives become relevant in two ways. They explain, for instance, how macro-level institutions at the national level structure the behavioural orientations of actors in rather similar organizational positions differently across countries. Moving to the micro-level of societal embeddedness, such as analysing for instance the family situation of actors or their position within a local community, may also explain why actors in a similar position even within the same unit may come to show quite different behavioural orientations. Hence, moving beyond a mere organizational positioning perspective calls for a societal embeddedness analysis at different analytical levels.

Extra-organizational context/situation

Although important, the actors' position within the organizational context is not the only relevant context. The wider societal context or extra-organizational context, be it at the macro-, meso- or micro-level, shade into and inform the actors' behavioural orientation in micropolitical organizational events. Extra-organizational contexts provide additional power bases such as private or public social networks, access to discourses that can serve to sustain arguments and positions inside the organization as well as resources that can be brought into the political arena. Importantly, not only do extra-organizational contexts inform the behavioural orientation within organizations but they constitute a wider set of key actors outside the organization with a stake in and a potential influence on the micropolitical developments within the MNC.

The relevance of societal context in terms of organizational and actor embeddedness can be theorized in a number of ways. While many more perspectives are thinkable, we restrict ourselves to two major theoretical strands, that is, new and comparative institutionalism, as both of them have been connected to micropolitical processes in MNCs in the literature.

Scholars from comparative capitalism emphasize the structuring effect of macroinstitutions that differs across countries (Almond and Ferner 2006; Ferner *et al.* 2005; Kristensen and Zeitlin 2005; Morgan and Kristensen 2006; see also Chapter 3). Focusing on the macro-systemic level, these approaches have often discussed the structuring role of national institutions in micropolitical processes. A typical example is how the actors' embeddedness in a specific industrial relations system or the vocational training system informs their actors' behavioural orientations (Edwards *et al.* 1999). For instance, unlike American top managers, German top managers would probably see a site closure and related lay-offs only as a last resort due to stringent labour legislation and the related cost of plant closure in Germany.

Workers for their part may see a chance of saving their site based on an industrial relations framework which provides them with specific sources of power. In this view, national institutions provide actors with resources that can be effectively employed in micropolitical battles (Edwards *et al.* 2006). While comparative institutionalists have mainly considered the influence of national institutional systems such an analysis can easily be extended to the regional or local level (Morgan and Kristensen 2006). For instance, comparing different states or regions in the US, we would probably find that legal frameworks and institutions differ from state to state.

New institutional analysis opens up further ways of seeing the structuring effects of society on micropolitics (Blazejewski 2009). New institutionalists emphasize institutional or isomorphic pressures in organizational fields, which contribute to organizational homogenization of organizational structures, forms or practices (DiMaggio and Powell 1983). The probably most widely adopted concept of institutions within new institutionalism stems from Scott (1995), who sees institutions as consisting of normative, cognitive and regulatory pillars. As we suggest below, seeing organizations as embedded in and influenced by other organizations in the organizational field, as well as seeing normative, cognitive and regulatory elements of institutions at different levels of societal analysis, can inform a micropolitical analysis that takes into consideration the impact of the wider societal environment.

Clearly, other organizations, be they located at the national, regional local level, such as media, unions or governments, often introduce further (relevant and key) actors into the micropolitical arena and, thereby, influence the development and outcomes of micropolitical events. In a similar vein, other business organizations or business networks of suppliers and clients have a stake in strategic decisions and may try to influence the process and have an influence on the behavioural orientations of key and relevant actors within the MNC.

From a slightly different angle, but also from a new institutionalist perspective, we can explore how regulative, normative and cultural-cognitive elements of institutions at different levels inform actors' behavioural orientation. Again, we could identify such institutional elements at the national, regional or local level. For instance, actors situated in a certain country, region, local community or organization may differ in their behavioural orientation from other actors. For instance, actors from a certain region may be renowned for their norms of resistance or revolutionary stances in industrial conflicts surrounding plant closures.

Lastly, the societal analysis at the micro-level calls for the specific understanding of the micro-level situation or social situation of individual actors. For instance, a key actor's possible allegiance to and position in a specific educational, professional, ethnic or religious community, as well as an individual's position in his or her family, can be quite crucial to understanding his or her behavioural orientations. Individual actors, even when holding the same organizational role or position and even when embedded in the same macro- and meso-societal context, may differ substantially in their behavioural orientation in organizational events. For instance, the question of how much an actor is affected by the job loss of a site closure also depends on the question of whether he or she has to sustain a family or has strong/weak local or regional roots. For example, top managers or other key actors who started their career as workers at the local production site and gradually moved into top management positions at the local site may have a different behavioural orientation vis-à-vis the site compared to managers who were sent from a foreign corporate headquarters. Hence, differences in the societal embeddedness of key actors can have a strong bearing on their behavioural orientations in micropolitical events.

Application

In the Opel case, the legal framework governing industrial relations in Germany was a key contextual element on the macro-/societal level. On the one hand, it limited the possibilities for strategic action of the works council, e.g. by expounding the conditions under which strikes are legally possible in Germany. On the other hand, it provided the basis for a dual system of worker representation inside the firm: the works council (codified in the Betriebsverfassungsgesetz) as the employer representation at the organizational level *and* the union-affiliated shop stewards (Vertrauensleute) at the shop floor level who were protected by the German Constitution (Grundgesetz) and industry-wide collective labour agreements (Tarifverträge). In the Opel case, both groups drew on the respective legal frameworks and associated resources as bases of power and in legitimating their respective paths of action – albeit according to highly differing interpretations of the formal regulations.

Another important contextual element in the Opel case was the local identity and the culture of solidarity in Bochum and the Ruhr region at large. Rooted in a history of harsh labour conditions in the mining and steel industry and the joint fight for worker rights in the nineteenth century, as well as the shared experience of the industrial decline in the second half of the twentieth century, particularly in Bochum, workers and their families saw themselves as 'fighters', even 'radicals', who were strongly committed to the region and local solidarity. This extra-organizational identity construction provided a considerable resource during the fight for jobs at Opel in 2004.

Limitation

Integrating the societal and communal level in a micropolitical analysis only makes sense when connected to an organizational level analysis. In other words, a societal embeddedness analysis as such will probably never suffice to understand the behavioural orientation of actors in a specific focal organization. Only when combined with the organizational embeddedness of actors do we understand the relevance of the wider societal context. The societal analysis also shares a limitation with a mere organizational-embeddedness-based analysis. Both types of analysis make it rather difficult to understand how temporal effects play into micropolitical events. For instance, we learn in these cross-sectional perspectives little about how past events inform current events. By the same token, we may find it difficult to understand how a current political episode structures future political scenarios.

Socio-temporal extensions

In this last step, we introduce the relevance of temporality to micropolitical analysis. The effect of temporality on micropolitics has to be looked at in conjunction with the social spatial embeddedness. In other words, a concern with temporality entails asking how the contextual embeddedness of actors has changed over time and how this affects their behavioural orientation and thereby the development and outcome of a micropolitical event. We hold that temporality is relevant for the analysis in two ways that are intertwined but shall be kept separate for analytical reasons. These are organizational and societal changes on the one hand and positional changes of actors over time on the other hand.

The first aspect entails a closer look at how organizations and societies change over time. This implies that actors who have not changed their social position face different contextual conditions over time. It also implies that contextual and organizational changes go along with different key and relevant actor-sets. An example for an organizational change would be mergers and acquisition by an MNC (e.g. possible devaluation of exclusive sources of power held before). Another example would be the effect of a plant closure (withdrawal of certain actors) on the chance of survival for other corporate sites. Here we look at how contextual changes over time and past micropolitical events in the organization inform current micropolitical events.

An example for a societal change would be changes in national legislation such as changes in labour law or the introduction of a minimum wage. We can easily imagine that the acquisition of another production site in a low-wage country with weak labour protection could potentially undermine the bargaining position of actors embedded in a production site of a high-wage and high-labour-protection country. A temporal analysis may also involve considering potential future events as they may inform current events. A planned change in corporate strategy may inform the behavioural orientations of key actors. Hence, embedding a micropolitical analysis in temporal terms involves asking how past and potential future events inform the behavioural orientations in current events as well as how contextual changes explain different dynamics and outcomes of events at different points in time.

Organizational and societal changes are only one effect of temporality on micropolitics, however. The other relevance of temporality lies in the changes of actors' social positions across time and space. Such trajectories are typically captured in the actors' biographies but should also include a closer look at their socio-positional aspirations for the future, that is, in organizational (career) and societal terms (intent to emigrate etc.) (Becker-Ritterspach and Dörrenbächer 2011).

The analytical relevance of such an actor-focused change perspective over time has again two aspects to it. First, we can ask how an actor's biography (past societal and organizational positions held) and future aspiration feed into behavioural orientations in current events. We can ask, for instance, whether a subsidiary manager who is on a foreign assignment has had a past career in corporate headquarters and wishes to return to corporate headquarters in his or her home country in the future. Answering this question is likely to give a strong indication as to why he or she supported the plant closure or resisted it, and what kind of sources of power were mobilized in the event. In a second and related perspective, this type of temporal analysis may help us to understand why the same key actors display contrasting behavioural orientations in similar events and under similar contextual conditions across time.

Application

Going back to our example, we find that Opel Bochum was faced with repeated rounds of job cuts and threats of closure in the past that had so far been put off successfully through e.g. workers' concessions regarding employee benefits and the cooperative relationship between the works council and the German management, which buffered German interests in the negotiations with the US headquarters of GM. This shared experience of numerous rounds of impending closure and negotiations influenced the political behaviour of both works council and management in the 2004 episode which – as in the past – relied on negotiations and concession making as the only option to cope with the current threat.

Regarding the temporal effects of the current episode on the future, the Opel case provides another interesting example: as a result of the 2004 wildcat strike, GM rearranged its European production system and established a multiple-site strategy regarding its parts production. In effect, since 2005 the Bochum plant site II was no longer the only site producing gearboxes and axles for the European assembly plants. It thus lost its central and unique position in the European production system, thereby forfeiting important bases of power and strategic leverage for its political agenda.

Introducing a temporal dimension we are thus able to uncover how the organizational and societal context changes over time and how these changes constitute shifts in the behavioural orientations of actors and their chances to realize their desired ends in current and future episodes.

Limitation

Limitations regarding the temporal extension of the political perspective mainly result from methodological challenges. When we start our research process on politics in the MNC with an episodic perspective as recommended here, the primary focus tends to be on the current political situation in the MNC. Often, interviews with actors involved in the current episode are the main source of data at this stage. If we use these same data to sustain the temporal extension of the political perspective, the information available regarding past influences on current political events is necessarily retrospective in kind. In retrospect, past events tend to be (unconsciously) rearranged, re-evaluated and modified as subjective constructions rather than unbiased reports of the past. It is therefore imminent to take account of and present data on temporal developments of political situations as retrospectively constructed and also seek to understand *why* actors reconstruct their past in this particular way. Constructing one's past (as well as one's future) as such is therefore a political act and a worthy subject of political analysis in itself. Apart from interview data, historical accounts of the past events under consideration – when they are available in public reports (journal articles, newspapers) or company archives – can be a productive source of information and help us to understand how and why actors in current political episodes actively construct and make use of temporal developments as they might serve their present and/or future interests.

Conclusion

In order to account for processes of power and politics in MNCs and to understand how strategic action in the MNC interacts with the structures, rules and norms in and around the MNC, researchers need to look at all three perspectives delineated above: the episodic perspective discloses when and how an actor has a stake in the current political events in the MNC, and how actors understand and make use of their own positions and interests in the political struggle. The spatial embeddedness discloses how actors, interests and resources are constituted by local, organizational, regional, national or transnational contexts. Through the temporal embeddedness we come to understand how political action in the MNC is linked to past events and future prospects. For instance, the temporal extension of the politics perspective helps us to recognize how interests and identities relevant in the current political episode have come about through processes of socialization, internalization and institutionalization over time. In this way, the stratified analytical framework presented here enables us to close the loop between episodic and systemic circuits of power and politics (Clegg 1989) and thus to overcome the dominant but limited agentic perspective of early research on politics in the MNC (see Chapter 3). When employing the stratified analytical framework, however, we need to take care of two restrictions which are associated with the stepwise extension from episodic to systemic dimensions: first, while the iterative addition of political complexity in the stratified framework makes the research process and data analysis manageable, it remains somewhat artificial since it suggests that we can analytically separate between the episode and its contextual embeddedness. The dilemma to account for and present this 'paradox of embeddedness', where agency contributes to the construction of structure while at the same time being constituted by structures, is familiar, particularly in the institutional entrepreneurship literature or in research based on Giddens' duality perspective on structure and agency. There is no easy way out; authors should, however, explicitly discuss this dilemma in their work and at the same time continue to seek new ways of presenting data so that episodic and systemic dimensions of power and politics become visible in their own logic without forfeiting their fundamental interactionality. Second, in extending the political perspective beyond the current episode to the contextual constitution of political episodes in the MNC, researchers need to take into account that actors involved in the political episode will construct potentially divergent contexts, i.e. the constitution of contexts is in itself a political process. In particular, in interviews – the dominant data collection method in this field – actors will (re)construct and report on *their* respective contexts, i.e. their potentially idiosyncratic perceptions and interpretations of norms, identities and structures. In the Opel case, for instance, the interpretations of the German labour law differed substantially among actors – even among labour representative bodies – and thus also led to highly diverging behavioural strategies. We should therefore ensure in data collection and data analysis that we not only pay attention to the multiple interests of actors involved in political episodes but also to potentially multiple and diverging constructions of contexts which serve as reference points, identity anchors and/or sources of subjectively legitimate discourses in the political episodes under way. Contradictions or variations between actor-specific contextual constitutions might offer important insights into the interaction between the embedding structures and norms and the irreducible margin of human agency and perspectivity fundamental to our perspective on processes of power and politics in MNCs.

References

Allen, M. 2004. The varieties of capitalism paradigm: not enough variety? *Socio-Economic Review*, 2(1): 87–108.

Almond, P. and Ferner, A. 2006. *American Multinationals in Europe: Managing Employment Relations across National Borders*. Oxford University Press.

Bacharach, S. B. and Lawler, E. J. 1980. *Power and Politics in Organizations*. San Francisco, CA: Jossey-Bass.

Becker-Ritterspach, F. 2006. The social constitution of knowledge integration in MNEs: a theoretical framework. *Journal of International Management*, 12(3): 358–377.

Becker-Ritterspach, F. and Dörrenbächer, C. 2009. Intrafirm competition in multinational corporations: towards a political framework. *Competition and Change*, 13(3): 199–213.

2011. An organizational politics perspective on intra-firm competition in multinational corporations. *Management International Review*, 51(4): 1–27.

Bélanger, J. and Edwards, P. 2006. Towards a political economy framework: TNCs as national and global players. In A. Ferner, J. Quintanilla and C. Sànchez-Runde (eds.), *Multinationals, Institutions and the Construction of Transnational Practices*. Basingstoke: Palgrave Macmillan, 24–52.

Blazejewski, S. 2009. Actors' interests and local contexts in intrafirm conflict: the 2004 GM and Opel crisis. *Competition and Change*, 13(3): 229–250.

Clegg, S. R. 1989. *Frameworks of Power*. London: Sage.

Clegg, S. R., Courpasson, D. and Phillips, N. 2006. *Power and Organizations*. London: Sage.

Crozier, M. and Friedberg, E. 1980. *Actors and Systems. The Politics of Collective Action*. Chicago University Press.

DiMaggio, P. and Powell, W. 1983. The iron cage revisited: institutional iso-morphism and collective rationality in organizational fields. *American Sociological Review*, 48(2): 147–160.

Dlugos, G., Dorow, W. and Farrell, D. 1993. *Organizational Politics*. Wiesbaden: Gabler.

Edwards, T., Coller, X., Ortiz, L., Rees, C. and Wortmann, M. 2006. National industrial relations systems and cross-border restructuring: evidence from a merger in the pharmaceuticals sector. *European Journal of Industrial Relations*, 12(1): 69–87.

Edwards, T., Rees, C. and Coller, X. 1999. Structure, politics, and the dif-fusion of employment practices in multinationals. *European Journal of Industrial Relations*, 5(3): 286–306.

Etzioni, A. 1964. *Modern Organizations*. Englewood Cliffs, NJ: Prentice-Hall.

Felin, T. and Foss, N. J. 2005. Strategic organization: a field in search of micro-foundations. *Strategic Organization*, 3(4): 441–455.

Ferner, A., Almond, P. and Colling, T. 2005. Institutional theory and the cross-national transfer of employment policy: the case of 'workforce diversity' in US multinationals. *Journal of International Business Studies*, 36(3): 304–321.

Fischer, F. 2005. Revisiting organizational politics: the postempiricist chal-lenge. *Policy and Society*, (June): 1–23.

Fisher, R., Ury, W. L. and Patton, B. 2011. *Getting to Yes: Negotiating Agreement without Giving In*. New York: Penguin.

Foss, N. J. 2011. Invited editorial: why micro-foundations for resource-based theory are needed and what they may look like. *Journal of Management*, 37(5): 1413–1428.

Foss, N. J. and Pedersen, T. 2004. Organizing knowledge processes in the multinational corporation: an introduction. *Journal of International Business Studies*, 35(5): 340–349.

French, J. R. P. and Raven, B. 1960. The bases of social power. In D. Cartwright and A. Zander (eds.), *Group Dynamics: Research and Theory* (2nd edn). Evanston, IL: Row, Peterson and Company, 607–623.

Giddens, A. 1984. *The Constitution of Society*. Berkeley, CA: University of California Press.

Hickson, D. J., Hinings, C. R., Lee, C. A., Schneck, R. E. and Pennings, J. M. 1971. A strategic contingencies' theory of intraorganizational power. *Administrative Science Quarterly*, 16(2): 216–229.

Karnøe, P. and Nygaard, C. 1999. Bringing social action and situated ra-tionality back in. *International Studies of Management and Organization*, 29(2): 78–93.

Kristensen, P. H. and Zeitlin, J. 2005. *Local Players in Global Games. The Strategic Constitution of a Multinational Corporation.* Oxford University Press.

March, J. G. 1962. The business firm as a political coalition. *Journal of Politics,* 24(4): 662–678.

Morgan, G. and Kristensen, P. H. 2006. The contested space of multinationals: varieties of capitalism, varieties of institutionalism. *Human Relations,* 59(11): 1467–1490.

Pfeffer, J. 1981. *Power in Organizations.* Marshfield, MA: Pitman.

Rothman, J. and Friedman, V. J. 2001. Identity, conflict and organizational learning. In M. Dierkes, A. Berthoin Antal, J. Child and I. Nonaka (eds.), *The Handbook of Organizational Learning and Knowledge.* Oxford University Press, 582–597.

Schütz, A. and Luckmann, T. 1973. *The Structures of the Life-World (Strukturen der Lebenswelt).* Evanston, IL: Northwestern University Press.

Scott, W. R. 1995. *Institutions and Organizations.* Thousand Oaks, CA: Sage.

Whittington, R. 1992. Putting Giddens into action: social systems and managerial agency. *Journal of Management Studies,* 29(6): 693–712.

8 Doing research on power and politics in multinational corporations (MNCs): a methodological perspective

REBECCA PIEKKARI AND SUSANNE TIETZE

Introduction

That morning the view from the chief executive officer (CEO)'s office on the top floor of a European MNC headquarters was particularly beautiful. The sun was shining brightly over the harbour and the city centre was full of life because of the rush hour. Despite his busy schedule the CEO had personally called to set up a meeting with me and my PhD student, Peter. Together with Peter, I had co-authored an essay on managerial politics which was to be published as part of his dissertation. As a gesture of politeness, we had sent the entire dissertation to the CEO prior to publication as he was the main sponsor of the research project and had granted Peter the access needed to undertake the study. But the CEO did not want to waste time on small talk:

'So you are approaching the final stages of your PhD project, Peter?', he said.

'Yes, it has taken me more than four years to finish the study and it feels great to be at this stage', Peter replied with a big smile.

'Let me be very frank with both of you', the CEO said looking directly at me, 'as we have known each other for many years. I really don't like the way you use the term "politics" and even "lying" in your essay. I know for sure that there is no room for political behaviour under my leadership – politics simply do not exist in my company! I want you to remove the word "politics" from the manuscript,' he ended with anger in his voice.

As the senior researcher, I had to step in and defend our work: 'But this is our interpretation of the many interviews that Peter has conducted over the years with your people! It is common practice in qualitative research that key informants are asked to confirm the facts but it is up to the researcher to draw the conclusions and provide the theoretical framing.'

Peter looked shattered by the CEO's outburst. Things got worse when the CEO gave me the manuscript in which he had crossed out all the words relating to 'politics' in their various forms. He also advised us to retitle the paper, which was based on a play on words alluding to conflict and tension in headquarters–subsidiary relationships. In order to understand the CEO's reaction, however, it must be said that Peter did not set out to study power and politics at the start of the research project but 'stumbled across them' only after completing the data collection and disengaging from the field. In fact, it was the exposure to a critical body of literature that offered him an alternative reading of the findings – one for which the CEO was not prepared.

We put together the above example following Watson's (2000) suggestions on how to write up ethnographic fiction science. Such an approach allows one to construct a compound example by mixing data and observations from a particular research project with experiences that go beyond it. It anonymizes the key informants but also protects the researcher from the potential negative reactions of corporate élites if they were to identify themselves in the text. Our example suggests that talking about power in public is difficult because of our ambivalent attitudes towards it. We tend to approve of power when we use it ourselves, but dislike it once others start using it against us (Pfeffer 1992). Such attitudes reveal a double moral standard towards power which defines when, where and with whom it is appropriate to make references to power and political 'self-interest and aggrandizement' (Burns 1961: 260). From a researcher's perspective, this may mean having to engage in tactical maneuvering, pretence and cunning to collect data on power and politics and get them published.

In this chapter, we focus on the politics of the *research process* rather than on the contents or themes of research projects that study politics in organizations. We do so because political considerations can have a significant impact on the management and execution of a research project from its very beginning to the final stages of the publication process. Nevertheless, many methodological textbooks neglect process-related political aspects apart from providing guidance about gaining access to research settings or developing solid research instruments. We want to draw attention to these political aspects; in our opinion they are as important as the choice of topic and research questions.

It could be argued that researching power and politics in the context of the MNC is no different from studying these processes in domestic or 'non-MNC' settings because aspects of power and politics figure in all management and business research. They are an intrinsic part of the entire research process, although they are not always directly visible or noticeable. Aspects of power and politics start from posing research questions, gaining access, building relationships with research participants and among research collaborators, collecting and analysing data in empirical projects and publishing research accounts (Easterby-Smith *et al.* 2012). None of these activities associated with the research process are neutral or result in objective knowledge. In business and management research in particular, interacting with powerful members of society such as corporate élites is beset by problems as the opening vignette suggests (Welch *et al.* 2002).

In this chapter, we adopt the position that researching power and politics in an MNC setting means dealing with additional complexities, all of which inform the research process. It involves issues such as gaining access to multiple units, locating research activity in diverse historical, political, cultural and linguistic contexts, considering internal power hierarchies between headquarters and foreign subsidiaries and among the subsidiaries themselves. It requires researchers to focus attention on the external power games in global value chains as well. In such rich and manifold research settings, questions emerge in terms of how and where to locate oneself as a researcher and how to make sense of the layers of networked relationships. An additional issue stems from the use of different languages, including English, as a way to control knowledge and as a source of power. These aspects differentiate research in and around MNCs from research on companies operating solely in the domestic market (see also Roth and Kostova 2003 on the MNC as a research context).

This chapter is written from a particular perspective on the MNC, which also affects how we conceptualize power and politics. We see the MNC as constituted of on-going processes of negotiations and constructions between situated agents. Our understanding resonates with Anselm Strauss' (1978) notion of organizations as 'negotiated orders'. This suggests that organizations are viewed as created by individuals and collectives who negotiate and interact with each other on a regular basis in changing contexts. These negotiations take place in project-based multilingual teams (Hinds *et al.* 2014; Tenzer *et al.* 2014) or in times of change, cross-border mergers and acquisitions (Vaara *et al.* 2005). Negotiations are informed by collective and individual interests, perspectives and positions, and are based on assumptions of co-existing pluralities and differences between MNC actors. Judged from this perspective, MNCs should be treated as contested, negotiated terrain and not as unitary entities (Blazejewski 2006; Collinson and Morgan 2009), or even a battlefield (Kristensen and Zeitlin 2001) where struggles over resources, identities and influence are played out in multiple and sometimes conflicting discourses and narratives (Dörrenbächer and Geppert 2011). We view this as a normal rather than a dysfunctional aspect of MNCs.

Set against this view of the MNC, we adopt a more sociological understanding of power and politics than often assumed in functionalist studies (Dörrenbächer and Geppert 2011). We agree with Dörrenbächer and Geppert (2011: 27), who argue that power relations are 'interactively and discursively constituted by actors with specific identities and interests' (see also Geppert and Dörrenbächer, Chapter 9 in this volume). In this regard, we see power and politics as a communicative process where political activities involve both resistance and negotiations. This view of power and politics is actor-centred and dynamic and propelled from the bottom of the organization. It emphasizes individual agency in power games because individuals may resist and destabilize established institutions in the MNC.

Our methodological discussion of power and politics is organized chronologically along the research process. While we acknowledge that the research process is seldom a linear one that flows logically from the objectives of the study to the outcome (Easterby-Smith *et al.* 2012) – instead it is 'a package deal' (Buchanan and Bryman 2007: 495) influenced by many factors – a chronological portrayal makes the discussion more accessible. We start from the philosophical underpinnings of the study and proceed with an analysis of how power and politics enter negotiations regarding access, data collection and analysis, exiting the field, engagement with theory, and writing-up and publishing. The final section evaluates the quality of studies on power and politics in MNCs, self-reflexivity, ethics and translation. Each of these steps in the research process is scrutinized as to its hidden political aspects.

It is worth noting that the chapter does not adopt a prescriptive approach on how to do fieldwork on power and politics in the MNC and aims instead to raise awareness of these issues through reflective questions. Nor does it offer an exhaustive review of research methods for studying power and politics in the MNC. We would also like to point out that the specific methodological literature on researching the political MNC is still in its infancy. Wherever possible, we provide examples of researchers' experiences – our own or those of others – who have engaged with the complexities of doing research in MNC settings and incorporated or reflected upon issues of power and power imbalances in their published research accounts. As authors, both of us espouse interpretative approaches to research which often give voice to meanings, individuals and groups that are less visible and silenced. In our experience, different stages of the research project – whether located at the topic selection stage, the data collection stage or the publication stage – are imbued with political assumptions and perspectives. This means that empirical research is in fact a value-laden process that is neither neutral nor objective. We believe this to be the case for all research, regardless of the paradigmatic preferences of the researchers.

Philosophical assumptions when studying power and politics

Instead of drawing on the traditional division between quantitative and qualitative research, we find the distinction by Evered and Louis (1981) between 'inquiry from the inside' and 'inquiry from the outside' as the end points of a continuum useful for our purposes (see also Michailova *et al.* 2014). Evered and Louis argue that when inquiring from the inside, researchers immerse themselves in the field, and their fieldwork is likely to be intimate, open-ended and holistic. Inquiring from the outside, on the other hand, tends to be less intimate, closed-ended and more transactional. While qualitative researchers are often more immersed in the field and engaged in the inquiry from inside than quantitative researchers, qualitative researchers may also analyse secondary data such as media texts or documents. Our approach is therefore applicable to both research paradigms.

In the inquiry from the inside, the researcher needs to cultivate and manage relationships with informants in the field. They vary between the two extremes of highly hierarchical and highly egalitarian power relationships with informants (Karnieli-Miller *et al.* 2009). In business and management research, fieldwork often involves interaction with gatekeepers and corporate élites in the organizational hierarchy who have the power to alter and influence the direction of the study. As Easterby-Smith *et al.* (2012: 96) point out, 'when research is conducted in companies, it is the researcher who is often the least powerful party' in the transaction. A related aspect is the extent to which this relationship can be characterized as a partnership; this is also reflected in the vocabulary used to refer to research participants (e.g. collaborator, informant, co-participant or respondent; Karnieli-Miller *et al.* 2009: 281). In partnerships, company informants may start theorizing and co-producing knowledge together with the researcher and the roles between them get blurred (Karnieli-Miller *et al.* 2009; Michailova *et al.* 2014). This suggests that fieldwork is a social process rather than a technical exercise (Macdonald and Hellgren 2004).

On the other hand, in the inquiry from the outside, the roles of the researcher and the informant are more distinct and differentiated: typically the researcher contributes to the thinking that goes into the project, while the informants provide the data. Rather than being co-constructed, the 'data are transferred to the researcher', who then processes and interprets them 'without significant active participant input' (Karnieli-Miller *et al.* 2009: 284). In this approach, scientific rigour is seen to replace partnership with informants and the researcher plays the role of a neutral and detached observer who objectively examines the phenomena from a distance (Karnieli-Miller *et al.* 2009).

This chapter advocates inquiry from the inside as an approach to study power and politics in MNCs. We locate the researcher in the immediate organizational context rather than discuss how to conduct inquiries through more detached means. This is because aspects of power and politics may remain invisible from outside. Research projects from inside often set out to explore both 'episodic theories of power (the direct exercise of power) and systemic forms of influence (power that is congealed into more enduring institutional structures)' (Fleming and Spicer 2014: 240). Hence, as we will discuss later, the researcher needs to gain access and insight into the inner workings of the MNC in order to appreciate such aspects of power and political behaviour.

Despite the emphasis of this chapter on bottom-up, actor-centred approaches, we acknowledge that inquiries into power and politics can be studied from the outside based on realist ontology and positivist epistemology. For example, contributions by Ferris and colleagues (Ferris and Kacmar 1992; Ferris *et al.* 2007) have drawn attention to the existence of political aspects in organizational behaviour. In their later work, the authors develop a measurable construct of political skills that includes dimensions such as social astuteness, interpersonal influence, networking ability and apparent sincerity. These are valuable approaches for gaining an understanding of individual behaviours from a political perspective because they emphasize the importance of exercising political skills or 'savvy' to advance one's career. Likewise, this stream of research contributes to construct development and the establishment of validity across contexts (Kacmar and Ferris 1991). What is less obvious in these studies is how and in which contexts 'savvy' behaviour is exercised, activated and received or how it may contribute to silencing some voices and making others heard. In this regard, this stream of research reveals less detail about the historical and cultural embeddedness of collective processes played out in multi-cultural and multilingual settings which define the MNC.

Politicizing the researcher, research methods and the research process

MNCs are political systems where 'it is difficult for researchers to respect conventional norms of observer neutrality by avoiding en-tanglement in power and political issues' (Buchanan and Bryman 2007: 489). In business and management research, the myth of researcher neutrality has to some extent given way to 'the inevitable politicization of the organizational researcher's role' (Buchanan and Bryman 2007: 496). In a similar vein, neither are research methods neutral (Macdon-ald and Hellgren 2004; Westwood 2004). As Westwood (2004: 56) states: '[M]ethodology [is] as ineluctably embedded in ontological and epistemological assumptions, as well as in the motivations and values of the researcher. These are in turn enfolded in a historically, institu-tionally and ideologically informed discursive context...We cannot reflect on methodology without reflecting on matters epistemological, ontological and ideological. Research methods are not innocent: they are political.'

In order to gain an understanding of whether and how the researcher, research methods and the research process have been politicized, we undertook a cursory review of thirteen methodological textbooks. Building on the analysis by Michailova *et al.* (2014) we divided them into two broad groups: (i) general methodological textbooks in social sciences (eight textbooks); and (ii) specific methodological textbooks in business, management and organization studies (five textbooks). Our brief review revealed that political aspects of research are rarely discussed in methodological textbooks. Only three books explicitly mention power or politics in the table of contents. Two of them

(O'Leary 2004; Prasad 2005) belong to the general category of textbooks while one (Easterby-Smith *et al.* 2012) falls under the specific category. The limited discussion tends to be about the challenges associated with gaining and negotiating access to research sites or managing relationships with informants in the field. We often found methodological articles (e.g. Buchanan and Bryman 2007; Karnieli-Miller *et al.* 2009) rather than textbooks more insightful when eliciting the political nature of research.

An exception among the textbooks, however, is the recent book by Easterby-Smith *et al.* (2012), who divide the sources of political influence on management research into four groups: (i) experience of the researcher; (ii) subject of the study; (iii) corporate stakeholders; and (iv) academic stakeholders (supervisors and students). We will only briefly cover the personal experience of the researcher and pay more attention to the subject of the study and to the corporate and academic stakeholders later in this chapter. At this stage it is sufficient to define corporate stakeholders as representatives of MNCs, other companies and public organizations who may take on the role of a sponsor in terms of providing access and managerial time or even funding the study, directly or indirectly (Easterby-Smith *et al.* 2012). Academic stakeholders in turn include members of the academic community such as journal editors, referees, supervisors, conference organizers and representatives of funding bodies who exercise influence in various stages of the research project (Easterby-Smith *et al.* 2012). Hence research is no longer an individual scholarly pursuit of knowledge for its own sake.

Buchanan and Bryman (2007: 495) identify four points in time when the researcher is likely to be politically engaged: 'when negotiating research objectives, when obtaining permissions to access, respondents, aligning with stakeholder groups, and when attempting to publish findings'. In a similar vein, Karnieli-Miller *et al.* (2009: 284) discuss power relations during different stages of the research process (initial subject/participant recruitment, data collection, data analysis and production of report, validation, additional publications). They also point out that a research project follows a developmental rather than a linear trajectory because some of the stages can reoccur several times (e.g., doing the analysis during the collection of data which leads to changes in the interview guide and future collection of data). Nevertheless, we will next decipher the political aspects of research chronologically for reasons of accessibility.

Starting the research

In the following, we will examine aspects of power and politics in defining the research question, selecting the appropriate research site and negotiating and renegotiating access to the MNC.

Defining the research question

In 1995, Susanne started her doctoral studies. She needed sponsorship to conduct her research on the experience of non-native speakers of English at workplaces that functioned 'in English only'. Based on a hermeneutic approach, she presented her proposal to the doctoral committee of a university in the UK which rejected it on the grounds that it did not have sufficient academic potential and relevance for business and management studies. In a conversation afterwards, Susanne was advised to select a topic of a 'more strategic nature and business relevance'. In reflecting on this experience, it appears to Susanne today that the very core of her proposal – the assumption that the use of languages informs workplace behaviour – was out of line with the dominant discourses of what constitutes relevant business and management projects. Her project was therefore not deemed fundable. Susanne's experience reveals the hidden hegemony in shaping what is valid knowledge and worthy of a doctoral dissertation.

Easterby-Smith *et al.* (2012: 77) state that 'it is rare for good research ideas to be derived directly from the literature' and Susanne's experience confirms this; the choice of topic was indeed driven by her experience. There are many other factors such as the attitudes and perceptions of one's peers and funding bodies rather than prior research which determine the kind of research questions posed. It is therefore not possible to separate scholarship from the influence and interest of a multitude of stakeholders of which the researcher is but one, and frequently not the most powerful as discussed earlier. Gatekeepers and corporate élites, to whom we will now turn, may also find the research topic too sensitive and hence decide not to grant the researchers access to informants and materials.

Selecting the research site and negotiating access

Gaining access to the research site is probably the stage of the research process which most often has been approached from a political perspective. This is because in the constellation of various stakeholders, the research subjects tend to be more powerful than the researchers themselves who can gain access 'by permission' only (Buckley and Chapman 1996: 239). Corporate élites have the means to undermine access, even if it was granted at the outset of a research project. Given this, one may ask who has control over the research process – the researcher or the research subjects (Karnieli-Miller *et al.* 2009).

While gaining access is challenging in most empirical research, the process can be particularly prolonged and precarious in MNC settings because of the number of stakeholders, their interests and the multiple perspectives involved. Geppert's (2014) cross-national study of Lidl, a European food discounter, is a case in point. Geppert selected Lidl because it represented an 'extreme case' of a firm that shows totalitarian tendencies in managing its stores and that has transferred its business model across the European continent. Since he was interested in exploring sensitive issues of how employee voice was exercised or constrained, gaining access in the traditional way was not possible in some of the countries selected for the study. Instead, he relied, for example, on social media to initiate and conduct interviews. In the Finnish setting access was easier to gain as the local government had exercised more control over Lidl's operations than in some of the other countries included in the study. Critical management scholars often select case companies and research sites that stand out from the norm. They are not interested in 'average' cases but in outliers which are particularly insightful and intriguing targets for research.

In the MNC setting, a gatekeeper located at headquarters may champion the proposed project and grant access to the researcher. However, this does not necessarily imply access to the subsidiary level because local gatekeepers can deny it. The example provided by Marschan-Piekkari *et al.* (2006: 253–254) illustrates this point. Rebecca wanted to undertake a study into a strategic alliance between an MNC and its foreign partner. The research proposal was approved by an executive vice-president at corporate headquarters, but the local manager of the strategic alliance found the topic 'irrelevant and uninteresting' (ibid.: 253). After months of negotiations, some limited access to the local respondents was granted. At the same time, Rebecca used her own networks to gain direct access to the respondents of the strategic alliance. Consequently, the local manager refused to cooperate further and cancelled all the interviews. Work on the project came to a halt. This is an example where the research project itself is subject to tactical maneuvering, negotiations and ultimately rejection.

In the above example, Rebecca entered the MNC through corporate headquarters. This may be interpreted among gatekeepers in foreign subsidiaries to mean that the researcher is an ally of headquarters. Klitmøller (2013) also entered the organization through the executive suite and this is why his informants in subsidiaries attempted to channel the information up to headquarters during the research interviews. Thus, even after having gained formal access, the researcher may have to negotiate and renegotiate informal access lower down in the MNC although this may vary from country to country (Macdonald and Hellgren 2004). Buchanan and Bryman (2007: 490) refer to this process as 'layered permission'.

Michailova (2004) reports on long and contracted negotiations of gaining access in Eastern European Countries (Russia and Bulgaria). Her own background as a Bulgarian researcher, her personal networks and her willingness to work in a reciprocal manner with a CEO, enabled her to access a particular organization. It is important to note that 'reciprocity' is a moral obligation in these countries rather than a superficial and pragmatic exchange of favours. In research on the MNC, it is possible that national research teams have to negotiate access in different cultural and historical contexts where normative assumptions about appropriate behaviour vary. Michailova's (2004) example from Eastern Europe suggests that there are national contexts which are less supportive of academic research and have different ideas and views of what constitutes 'good research' (Easterby-Smith *et al.* 2012: 88).

Relocations of MNC headquarters and cross-border mergers and acquisitions may dramatically change the process of negotiating access. Macdonald and Hellgren (2004: 268) relate their experiences of a Swedish MNC whose headquarters was transferred from Sweden to the UK: '[O]ur research team in Sweden suddenly found itself on the organizational periphery. In negotiating with the new corporate headquarters, our team had to navigate its way past several layers of gatekeepers.' Similarly, cross-border mergers and acquisitions are likely to change 'the traditionally open and receptive attitude' of Swedish firms towards academic research and challenge more generally 'the close, almost symbiotic relationship' between universities and the business world prevailing in the Nordic countries (Macdonald and Hellgren 2004: 268–269).

In sum, the planning and initiating of a research project within an MNC is beset by the same phenomena that are also at the centre of a study on power and politics; the perspectives, interests and voices of multiple stakeholders come to bear on each other and may be in conflict. Moving beyond access to the other stages of the research process we will suggest that they are equally influenced by multiple relationships and the variety of contexts in which research on the MNC is embedded.

Data collection

The majority of qualitative research in management and international business published in prestigious journals is based on case studies (Welch *et al.* 2011). In the field of international business, the typical case study uses interviewing as the data collection technique (Piekkari *et al.* 2009). We will therefore focus on the challenges of interviewing which can be defined as 'talking – usually face to face – with those knowledgeable about what is being studied' (Macdonald and Hellgren 2004: 264). We embrace this definition as it implies questions about 'who is knowledgeable' and 'what is deemed knowledge and why'. In other words, it provides a useful platform to scrutinize a data collection technique from a politically aware perspective.

The challenges of relying on interview data

One of the challenges in collecting data through interviewing is associated with the openness and truthfulness of the informants. Sometimes researchers notice that they are being told half-truths or lies by interviewees who want to portray a particular image of themselves or of the organization they represent (Reeves 2010). Even if respondents in the research project reveal sensitive information about political or tactical behaviours that suit a researcher's agenda, it often comes with the caveat that it must not be used outside the interview context. Macdonald and Hellgren (2004: 271) provide examples of interviewees who shared such information: 'I think at the present time it's the Minister that opposes it. As I understand (and I hope you fillet out this part), he is extremely paranoid about it [sic].' Informants may also deliberately feed 'information into the project, which is likely to support their political agendas' or withhold it because they think it is not important or irrelevant. They may also have genuinely forgotten it (Easterby-Smith *et al.* 2012: 86).

The interview process has been examined in international business research only to a limited extent (Daniels and Cannice 2004; Macdonald and Hellgren 2004; Welch and Piekkari 2006) and even less so in the specific context of the MNC (Marschan-Piekkari *et al.* 2006). These authors clearly see a difference between interview processes in domestic or international settings which relate to the diverse cultural, national and linguistic contexts in which international business research is typically conducted. Questions like how to build rapport to generate meaningful data and maintain engagement during the interview process; how to plan and execute interviews that involve international communication and travel; and what research skills are required (e.g. cultural sensitivity; language skills) to engage in such interviewing in a productive way become central for the researcher who is embarking on a study of power and politics in an MNC. While few methodological contributions to international business research explicitly address issues of power, politics and the hidden agendas of participants and other stakeholders in the research process (cf. Marschan-Piekkari and Welch 2004; Piekkari and Welch 2011), the work by Macdonald and Hellgren (2004) and Welch and Piekkari (2006) does so.

Macdonald and Hellgren (2004) discuss the various political constraints that the international business researcher may face when attempting to exploit information from interviews. These constraints stem from an (over)reliance on top managers as informants in empirical research (Westney and Van Maanen 2011). Macdonald and Hellgren (2004: 265) are highly critical of the assumption 'that the more senior the individual, the more that individual will know about the organization'. Top management may not be aware of what is going on lower down in the organization and the ignorance of corporate headquarters has been previously acknowledged in international business research (Holm *et al.* 1995). Macdonald and Hellgren (2004) warn researchers about falling into the trap of having to please senior managers and surrender critical distance in order to retain access to interview data.

Given the above challenges, critical researchers may want to avoid the use of interview data altogether. For example, media texts provide a viable avenue to circumvent the challenges associated with publishing research accounts that are based on personal interviews with company representatives or observations at the workplace. Vaara and Tienari (2008) used only media texts to understand how a controversial shutdown of a long-standing marine engine factory in Turku, Finland was legitimized by a Finland-based MNC in the Finnish press. They highlight the political consequences for the employees involved.

Multilingual interview data

In international business research, fieldwork is rarely a monolingual experience (Brannen *et al.* 2014). Welch and Piekkari (2006) investigate language and translation issues in cross-cultural interviewing in the context of international business research. Espousing a perspective which views interviewing as the construction of shared meaning, they point out that interviewing practices may create power dynamics as the selected interview language has implications for the interviewee–researcher relationship. Indeed, questions of language choice (which access language, which interview language, which post-interview language, which language to use in the research team) were shown to have an overall effect on the research process and outcome. Although English as the frequently dominant corporate language in MNCs was often used by managers as their lingua franca, they could also use it as a jargon to 'fall back' on when repeating company policy instead of providing individualized responses. It cannot be stated conclusively whether such interview behaviour is expressive of relative language competence or possibly indicative of avoiding sensitive topics (which, of course, are of particular interest to the researcher), but points instead to the invisibility of motivations. Welch and Piekkari (2006) cite an example of a young male researcher who used his language skills as a way to 'level' the power in a situation where his interviewees had hierarchy, status and seniority on their side. The interview language can be used to neutralize identities or emphasize a particular national identity. Building on Ryen (2002), the authors conclude that the 'cross-cultural interview is therefore a series of linguistic interactions and negotiations through which participants actively assemble a localized understanding' (Welch and Piekkari 2006: 431).

Another example of the hegemonic use of language comes from international collaborative research. Two Finnish and two British researchers studied identity construction in management consulting

(Meriläinen *et al.* 2008). Their reflexive piece demonstrates how the co-production of knowledge was problematic as empirical material in English was privileged and therefore resulted in 'othering' the Finnish perspective. Translation of the Finnish data into English – a necessary part of the publication process – decontextualized the Finnish data and thereby rendered the 'local voice' less audible. However, these hegemonic processes were disrupted through the reflexive engagement of the researchers with each other and the research process (Meriläinen *et al.* 2008).

To conclude, the above discussion brings to the fore a set of useful questions for researchers who wish to use interviews to shed light on political processes in MNCs. These include: who do I need to interview and which locations of the MNC need to be represented? Which level of seniority is needed? Is it more beneficial for the research project to interview junior managers, operatives, clerks or middle managers rather than senior managers or CEOs? Who has given me access to interviewees and how have people been included or excluded? Which questions can I prepare beforehand and which may emerge during the interview? How will I respond to requests to remove the really revealing data? Do I need to talk to external stakeholders? To which extent do interviewees present a collective voice or their own perspective only?

Exiting fieldwork

A stage that is often bypassed in methodological writings is exiting fieldwork. Michailova *et al.* (2014: 139) define this critical step as 'a process (rather than a single act) of ending relationships developed with research participants over a period of time, be it longer or shorter'. Exiting is a dual state of being connected and disconnected to the field. This stage in the research process is temporally closer to the data analysis and write-up than data collection.

The political aspects of exiting come into play when scrutinizing the nature of the researcher's relationships with informants in the field. Michailova *et al.* (2014) argue that the researchers' relationships with informants may be so close that they become too deeply absorbed in the world of the research subjects. This 'over-rapport' (Miller 1952) makes it difficult, if not impossible, to maintain a critical distance to the subject at hand. Ethnographers refer to this phenomenon as 'going native' (Paul 1953: 435). In the MNC context, researchers may perceive foreign locations as different, exotic and more exciting, which may make them bond ever more closely. Macdonald and Hellgren (2004) talk about 'the hostage syndrome', suggesting that the researcher is mentally locked in and imprisoned in relationships built during fieldwork. Like hostages who identify with their captors, researchers attempt to generate findings and produce research reports that please the research participants and are sympathetic to their accounts.

Data analysis

The fact that data are often captured in several languages is characteristic of research on the MNC (e.g. through interviews, company material and public documents). While knowledge about MNCs is predominantly disseminated and published in English (in itself this is indicative of hegemonic practices; Tietze 2004; Steyaert and Janssens 2013; Tietze and Dick 2013), many researchers engage in a hidden process of sensemaking and translation when analysing multilingual data sets. Researchers may translate themselves if they have the requisite language skills or rely on professional translators – at least when researchers who are non-native speakers of English reach the stage of publishing in English. The challenge is whether the richness of quotations can survive multiple translations (Macdonald and Hellgren 2004). In a recent article, Chidlow *et al.* (2014) treat translation as a social practice and suggest that it be reframed as a process of intercultural interaction rather than a technical exercise of following the protocols of back translation. So far, the way researchers cross the language boundary in data collection and analysis is rarely documented in published work or discussed in methodological texts (see Chidlow *et al.* 2014; Marschan-Piekkari and Reis 2004; Welch and Piekkari 2006, for exceptions).

In their study of how language diversity affects the work processes of corporate boards, Piekkari *et al.* (2015) explain how translation was part of the data analysis stage. They conducted a total of thirty-two personal interviews with former and current board members, managing directors and executive managers in nine Nordic firms. Out of these interviews, twelve were carried out in English and twenty in various Nordic languages, i.e. Finnish, Swedish, Danish and Norwegian. Thus, the large majority of the interview quotes had to be translated from a local Nordic language into English which was indicated in the article.

The translation process followed several steps. First, in order to share interesting insights and powerful quotations with other members of the research team, Rebecca summarized the interviews in English. The interviews that had been conducted in Finnish, in particular, could not be understood in the original language by the other members of the research teams (see also Meriläinen *et al.* 2008). Second, once the authors had selected the interview quotes for publication they themselves iterated several times between the original and the target language to maintain the intended meaning and the richness of the interviewee's verbatim expressions during the course of the translation. Third, two professional proofreaders, who were native speakers of English, carefully read all the quotes translated by the researchers into English and the specific meanings and nuances of different words and expressions were discussed. Taken together, the translation process itself deeply immersed the researchers in the qualitative data and triggered novel insights and interpretations of the phenomenon at hand (Piekkari *et al.* 2015).

Using and engaging with theory to frame the data analysis

By 2015, the field of international business had changed because sociological approaches (Geppert and Dörrenbächer 2014) and linguistically inspired approaches (Brannen *et al.* 2014) are increasingly employed to investigate typical MNC topics such as knowledge transfer. Recent work highlights socio-political interactions of subsidiary managers (Williams 2011), unequal power relations and identity discourse (Blazejewski 2012; Ybema and Byun 2011) and the contestation of social space (Maclean and Hollinshead 2011). These approaches both expand the plethora of traditional topics on the MNC as well as connect them to theories and concepts from other disciplinary fields.

We understand theory here as a way of seeing and thinking about the world. Using post-colonial and critical discourse perspectives, for example, opens up avenues to understand data in particular ways which include the existence of imbalances of power between different individuals and collectives and also the consequences of these imbalances. The choice of a particular theoretical lens is a decision made by the researcher who has the 'monopoly of the interpretation'

(Karnieli-Miller *et al.* 2009: 283). The researcher decides what the study is 'a case of' (Ragin 1992). While research design and data generation in themselves are also subject to political processes as our previous discussion suggests, it is the selection of a theoretical frame that expresses the researcher's critical position and values most clearly as opposed to more traditional, mainstream research. The selection of the theoretical frame often occurs only after the field has been exited. Hence, critical engagement with the researched phenomena takes place in the stages of data interpretation, analysis and the writing up.

Geppert's (2014) and Geppert *et al.*'s (2015) studies, which we introduced earlier, illustrate this point well. The researchers attempted to study the practices of Lidl within institutionalist frameworks (Geppert 2014) and how its strong centralized globalization strategy had consequences for episodic power (store level), rules of the game (access to influence rules at store level) and both global and local domination (social organizational power). The research project was difficult to carry out for reasons of access but also because traditional institutional theory does not lend itself to a focus on employee voice, actor-driven behaviour or critical analysis. Geppert (2014) turned to the sociological roots of organization studies and used the work of Goffman to conduct comparative analysis of extreme cases and total institutions. In the sister paper, Geppert *et al.* (2015: 14) aligned micro-data at store level within national contexts and corporate strategy to understand how organizational actors in different contexts can influence the 'rules of the game', whereas in other circumstances implementation of decent work and employment practices in stores was likely to depend on personal decisions by managers not to abuse their dominant power positions.

While the above studies must have posed some critical research questions from the very beginning (the overall project focus was on the work and employment relations of European multinational food retailers), critical approaches can also arise from the researcher's engagement with the data at the stage of data analysis and writing of research accounts. Dick and Collings (2014) undertook a critical examination of the strategy discourse of senior managers in US-owned subsidiaries in Ireland. They draw on data from a larger research project exploring human resource practices adoption in the Irish subsidiaries. This project draws on interviews with seventeen employees in the Irish subsidiary as well as company documents and observational data; yet the article itself only uses one key interview and employs critical discourse analysis to interrogate the data about the inherent instability of the strategy discourse as it is used to reconcile contradictory accounts of corporate success and failure.

We suggest that critical discourse analysis, post-colonial theory and the language-based approaches inspired by translation studies lend themselves well to an understanding of organizational politics. For example, critical discourse analysis is often used to frame political aspects of MNCs (Ahonen *et al.* 2011). Such discursive approaches tend to incorporate the national and cultural embeddedness of MNCs and their actors in a discussion of power relations. Vaara (2003) uses a longitudinal research design in his account of a post-acquisition integration process in a Finnish furniture manufacturer which acquired units in Sweden. Importantly, to make sense of the case, Vaara himself acted as a consultant to the company and was thus able to draw on participant observation, written company materials from 1996 to 2000 and thematic interviews with key decision makers from both the acquiring and the acquired units. The location of the researcher afforded him direct access to data, whereby the more hidden side of mergers in all their cultural complexities and shifting and unequal power relationships between key actors could be explored during the post-acquisition phase.

Alongside critical discourse analysis, post-colonial theory offers an alternative ideology to frame research on power and politics in the MNC (Boussebaa *et al.* 2014). Frenkel (2008, see Chapter 6) uses the critical cultural theorist, Homi Bhabha, and his epistemology of cultural mimicry, hybridity and the third space to reinterpret knowledge transfer processes within the MNC. Frenkel develops a post-colonial perspective that locates MNC practices in particular cultural and institutional contexts. Frenkel (2008: 937) calls for an 'interpretive, relational and multilevel/multivocal research design that will treat the transfer of knowledge and practices within the MNC as a process occurring in a conflict-ridden context and not as a finished outcome'. She focuses on 'the contested and power-laden spaces in which colonizers and the colonized interact and mix with one another. In these spaces the way that the various Western and "other" actors perceive themselves and each other is revealed, as is the manner in which perception shapes the process of knowledge transfer and implementation' (Frenkel 2008: 937). Vaara *et al.* (2005, see Chapter 6) integrate some of these 'different spaces' into their study of a merging Nordic bank as they consider the historical, political and national relationships in their analysis. They show that the introduction of Swedish as the common corporate language in the Nordic bank recreated historical structures of domination and reinvented identities of superiority and inferiority in the contemporary financial institution.

A stream of studies has drawn attention to agency-driven microprocesses in MNC settings from a language-sensitive perspective. Conceptually, this stream defines the MNC as multilingual communities (Luo and Shenkar 2006), and focuses on 'language agents' who individually or collectively negotiate between headquarters, foreign subsidiaries and teams. They 'make sense, manipulate, negotiate, and partially construct their institutional environments' (Kostova *et al.* 2008: 1001) through context-sensitive choices about which language to use, when and with whom in conversations and communications with others. Their local actions and choices have been described as 'linguascaping', i.e. an on-going process of negotiations, irrespective of existing corporate language policies or language hierarchies of the MNC (Steyaert *et al.* 2011). Consequently, languages are used to silence or marginalize particular points of views, to hide information from certain constituencies or to assert the local right to exercise voice and resist formal language policies (Hinds *et al.* 2014; Neeley 2013; Piekkari *et al.* 2005; Vaara *et al.* 2005). In global multilingual teams, members may switch languages to render information less accessible to speakers from other language backgrounds, triggering tactical, political and emotional responses (Blazejewski 2012). As an informant in the study by Tenzer *et al.* (2014: 524) notes, '[l]anguage can be used as an instrument of power, a means to ostracize people. If you want to exclude listeners, you just use a language they don't master. In my view, people do this on purpose.' Such code-switching and the use (or non-use) of translation are language-based mechanisms that may lead to conspiracy thinking among global team members. They may also feel threatened when other team members speak better English. Overall, the above studies demonstrate that language use is imbued with emotional subtexts; it is political in character and expressive of power relationships between different language speakers.

Translation studies also offer a rich conceptual trajectory for challenging the notion of equivalence of meaning between languages (Baker 2006; Cunico and Munday 2007; Janssens *et al.* 2004; Venuti 1998). Translation scholars largely agree that meaning gets changed, lost and transformed in the course of the translation process. Agents of translation, who are not always professional translators but ordinary managers and workers, are therefore viewed as important actors in the MNC. They can access meanings coded in different languages and make decisions about which aspects to translate and which not to, and whether to replace foreign (headquarters) meaning with local (subsidiary) meaning (Logemann and Piekkari 2015). This provides language agents with the opportunity to interfere in MNC processes or imposed practices and to resist and challenge them. How and when they do this is barely understood. The transformative nature of meaning poses considerable epistemological challenges for MNC researchers who have embraced constructionist approaches in their research (Chidlow *et al.* 2014; Janssens and Steyaert 2014). Thus, the exploration of situated, on-going and dispersed acts of translation represents an exciting yet underexplored area of research on the political aspects of the MNC.

The above studies use post-colonial analysis, critical discourse analysis, translation studies or other language-based approaches to frame their data theoretically. The authors rarely articulate a political research agenda in terms of the research design itself in the published research accounts. Instead, the political nature of these contributions lies in the treatment of data and in the selected analytical apparatus and the less orthodox critique that are brought to bear on the empirical data (Jack and Westwood 2006; Westwood 2004). What unites the above studies is a context-sensitive and actor-based approach, acknowledgement of the existence of difference and conflict and the use of qualitative methodologies to access and understand political processes in the MNC.

Writing-up for publication

The requirements of multiple audiences often pull researchers in different directions. While academic peers look for the theoretical contribution, managers expect practical recommendations and research participants are primarily concerned with maintaining anonymity.

These expectations can be difficult to align, thereby further challenging the 'text-book connection' between research questions and methods (Buchanan and Bryman 2007: 492).

'Being political' in writing and published accounts can have very serious consequences. O'Connor (1995) studied written accounts of change in a high-technology company. These accounts praised the efforts of the organization development function whose role was presented as pivotal in change initiation and implementation. In her conclusions, however, O'Connor observed how involvement in key decisions was limited to a small group of key managers, how disagreement was treated as resistance and lack of understanding rather than as involvement and how change narratives revolved around a heroic figure and his adversaries. The high-technology company did not welcome O'Connor's interpretation. Her gatekeeper denied her account, described it as shocking, outrageous and unacceptable, and never met with her again. While such candid accounts are unusual, they almost certainly reflect a relatively common experience in fieldwork. A critical research agenda may also prevent a research project from taking place altogether. A colleague of ours confessed the following in an informal conversation: 'How can you ever say anything critical about Goldman Sachs when 50 per cent of your MBA students are sent by them!' Corporate sponsorship in its various forms raises the delicate question of whether the alliance between business schools and companies is unholy, even corrupt, and 'contaminates' research findings.

Evaluating the quality of research

Given that many researchers undertake context-sensitive 'inquiries from the inside' (Evered and Louis 1981) when studying power and politics in the MNC, it is not meaningful to evaluate them as to whether they are generalizable, replicable or objective. In fact, such criteria would be inappropriate for a research project that does not subscribe to positivist ideals. Nevertheless, the use of positivist quality criteria dominates management research (Gibbert *et al.* 2008) and these criteria are often employed as 'commonsense benchmarks' to evaluate qualitative research (Johnson *et al.* 2006: 136), as if one size would fit all.

How to evaluate the quality of qualitative research is a contentious issue, representing a longstanding area of discussion and debate among methodological authorities (Creswell and Miller 2000; Kirk and Miller 1986; Lincoln and Guba 1985; Symon and Cassell 2012). Johnson *et al.* (2006: 133) argue that evaluation criteria are not neutral or 'value-free' but 'constituted by particular philosophical conventions'. They propose a contingent criteriology that 'enables different sets of evaluation criteria to be contingently deployed so that they fit the researcher's mode of engagement' (Johnson *et al.* 2006: 134).

Given the diversity of views of what constitutes appropriate quality criteria, calls have been made for increasing the transparency of qualitative research (Bansal and Corley 2011; Bluhm *et al.* 2011). This requirement does not only cover describing the range of data sources used or the steps taken in data analysis, but also an explanation of how the findings were generated. As Bansal and Corley (2011: 236) state, '[b]ecause discovery can be serendipitous, methodological rigor is conveyed through the authenticity and candor of the text. It is important that researchers be able to describe how they discovered their insight'. Authors may also illuminate why they selected particular theoretical and ideological frames for their projects. In addition, researchers of MNCs may include details about the languages used during the research process (to gain access, in the work of the research team, during data generation with different gatekeepers, translators or interpreters).

Depending on the researcher's philosophical assumptions, reflexivity can be a relevant quality criterion. Reflexivity refers to research that takes into account 'the social production of scientific "facts"' (Hardy *et al.* 2001: 532). 'Whereas objective knowledge claims to be unsituated – true any time and any place – reflexive knowledge is situated and includes a recognition of the multiple translation strategies that bring it into being' (Hardy *et al.* 2001: 554). Johnson and Duberley (2003: 1279) add that reflexivity 'entails noticing, evaluating and being suspicious of the relationship between the researcher and the "objects" of research'. In this regard, researchers could probe the outcomes of their own inquiry in terms of which data 'get translated' in a way that audiences can access them and which data disappear and remain invisible. Moreover, who are the agents of translation/interpretation and how is their work acknowledged and even incorporated into the research outcomes?

Overall, while researchers engage in political actions during various steps of the research process, this is rarely acknowledged in the methodological writings or in journal publications. Easterby-Smith

et al. (2012) encourage researchers to critically reflect on all the political influences on their research, and to make these thoughts available
to their peers. They argue that such reflexivity 'should increase, rather
than decrease, the credibility of the results' (Easterby-Smith *et al.* 2012:
86).

Implications for researchers

In this chapter, we have deliberately not offered a blueprint for conducting research on MNCs from a political perspective or advocated
particular research methods as the best or even appropriate tools to
collect empirical data, because we believe it is not possible to do so.
Instead, we have focused on the research process and rehearsed examples from the MNC literature to demonstrate how researchers have
dealt with political challenges. As we have shown, the entire research
process is political because different stakeholders at different stages of
the research inform and influence the study. This causes some dilemmas
which the researcher has to address.

If one wants to conduct empirical research on micropolitics in MNC
settings one needs access to data. The dilemma a researcher or research
team faces is whether to declare one's political interests to potential funding bodies and research participants up front. We have seen
that it is possible to gain support from funding bodies while pursuing a critical agenda (e.g. the work by Geppert and his colleagues).
Here, being aware of which funding body to target is a necessary
pre-requisite for receiving funding for emancipatory, critical research.
Nevertheless, in MNC settings gaining access to local organizations
can be difficult and can include activation of non-organizational networks. Alternatively, the researcher may decide to use secondary data
such as media texts to address problems of access (e.g. the work by
Vaara and his colleagues), or, like Dick and Collings (2014), bring a
critical mindset to the data only when they began to conceptualize their
findings. These examples show that it is possible to conduct empirical,
critically oriented research in MNC settings, but the process is precarious. Researchers need to reflect on the sources of data, the research
questions they wish to explore, the funding and sponsoring bodies that
support their projects, and to what extent they will make their findings available to which group of stakeholders and at what stage in the
research process.

Our opening vignette has shown that collaborators and gatekeepers do not always take critical research findings favourably. Controversy, conflict and unequal power relations may be accepted as normal, interesting and unavoidable phenomena by academic audiences and many practitioners will agree with this view, too – particularly if it concerns organizations other than their own. However, having organizational politics publicly discussed and analysed is a different matter and may lead to a hostile reaction by influential members of the researched collective.

In our opening vignette, the researchers' critical engagement with the research scene unfolded in the data analysis stage. The senior gatekeeper rejected the findings as 'untruthful' and damaging prior to publication. There are no easy answers in situations like this. Researchers may use their institutional ethical protocols and processes to safeguard themselves and their projects from interventions by MNC representatives, e.g. by adhering to standards of anonymity and confidentiality. However, research that detects malpractices may need to name the MNC participant in order to challenge these behaviours. By drawing on secondary material and using personal or social media networks, access to information may be gained while over-dependence on organizational sponsors is avoided. While these are not infallible prescriptions for managing the political aspects of the research process in MNCs, they do provide some guidance as to how to prepare for their occurrence.

Finally, in some cases it may be appropriate to adjust one's writing strategy beyond the procedures of rendering participants and organizations anonymous and treating sources as confidential. The approach we employed in the opening vignette is advocated by Watson (2000). It relies on a combination of social science writing with fictional elements which enables researchers to disguise people, situations and contexts while drawing on analytical concepts and rigour. Nevertheless, writing and publishing semifictional accounts can also detract from conveying powerful messages about micropolitical behaviour, its ties with wider historical and societal processes and the darker sides of how influential corporate élites exercise power. Also, some academic journals may not accept this approach as suitable for the treatment of empirical data and the furtherance of knowledge.

In sum, we invite researchers interested in studying the MNC from a micropolitical perspective to address a host of questions which are not

only of an academic nature but also fundamental to the implementation of their research projects. In particular, management researchers
whose research is located in MNCs or other international settings meet
with additional complexities that form part of the political backdrop
to all research. Understanding these additional complexities also from
a political perspective is an essential part of the research process from
instigation to execution and publication.

Conclusion

Research instruments, research method, research questions and themes
are products of particular socio-historical conditions. We have depicted
the research process as political at its very core and at all stages, from
design and execution to dissemination of findings and generation of
knowledge. While we have provided some examples and reflections
about how to engage with this political reality, especially in MNC networks – which are diverse, complex, ambiguous and unequal – we cannot offer a clear protocol for dealing with the issue.

To conclude, Howard Becker (1967) urges us as researchers to ask
a fundamental question: Whose side are we on? He argues that this
question is always with us. While some encourage researchers 'not to
take sides, to be neutral and do research that is technically correct and
value free ... [o]thers tell them their work is shallow and useless if it
does not express a deep commitment to a value position' (ibid.: 239).
Becker (1967: 247) does not provide a simple answer to this dilemma,
but suggests the following: 'We take sides as our personal and political
commitments dictate, use our theoretical and technical resources to
avoid the distortions that might introduce into our work, limit our
conclusions carefully, recognize the hierarchy of credibility ... and field
as best we can the accusations and doubts that will surely be our fate'.
We agree with Becker that some side-taking is unavoidable because
knowledge is always produced from a particular standpoint.

References
Ahonen, P., Tienari, J. and Vaara, E. 2011. 'There is no alternative' – or is
there? A critical case study approach for international business research.
In R. Piekkari and C. Welch (eds.), *Rethinking the Case Study in*

International Business and Management Research. Cheltenham: Edward Elgar, 85–106.

Baker, M. 2006. *Translation and Conflict: a Narrative Account*. London and New York: Routledge.

Bansal, P. and Corley, K. 2011. From the editors: the coming of age of qualitative research: embracing the diversity of qualitative methods. *Academy of Management Journal*, 54(2): 233–237.

Becker, H. S. 1967. Whose side are we on? *Social Problems*, 14(3): 239–247.

Blazejewski, S. 2006. Transferring value-infused organizational practices in multinational companies: a conflict perspective. In M. Geppert and M. Mayer (eds.), *Global, National and Local Practices in Multinational Companies*. Houndmills: Palgrave Macmillan, 63–104.

2012. Beyond or betwixt the lines of conflict? Biculturalism as situated identity in multinational corporations. *Critical Perspectives on International Business*, 8(2): 111–135.

Bluhm, D. J., Harman, W., Lee, T. W. and Mitchell, T. R. 2011. Qualitative research in management: a decade of progress. *Journal of Management Studies*, 48(8): 1866–1891.

Boussebaa, M., Sinha, S. and Gabriel, Y. 2014. Englishization in offshore call centres: a postcolonial perspective. *Journal of International Business Studies*, 45(9): 1152–1169.

Brannen, M. Y., Piekkari, R. and Tietze, S. 2014. The multifaceted role of language in international business: unpacking the forms, functions and features of a critical challenge to MNC theory and performance. *Journal of International Business Studies*, 54(3): 77–97.

Buchanan, D. A. and Bryman, A. 2007. Contextualizing methods choice in organizational research. *Organizational Research Methods*, 10(3): 483–501.

Buckley, P. and Chapman, M. 1996. Theory and method in international business research. *International Business Review*, 5(3): 233–245.

Burns, T. 1961. Micropolitics: mechanisms of institutional change. *Administrative Science Quarterly*, 6(3): 257–281.

Chidlow, A., Plakoyiannaki, E. and Welch, C. 2014. Translation in cross-language international business research: beyond equivalence. *Journal of International Business Studies*, 45(5): 562–582.

Collinson, S. and Morgan, G. (eds.) 2009. *Images of the Multinational Firm*. London: Wiley.

Creswell, J. W. and Miller, D. L. 2000. Determining validity in qualitative inquiry. *Theory into Practice*, 39(3): 124–130.

Cunico, S. and Munday, J. 2007. Encounters and clashes: introduction to translation and ideology. *The Translator*, 13(2): 141–149.

Daniels, J. D. and Cannice, M. V. 2004. Interview studies in international business research. In R. Marschan-Piekkari and C. Welch (eds.), *Handbook of Qualitative Research Methods for International Business*. Cheltenham: Edward Elgar, 185–206.

Dick, P. and Collings, D. G. (2014). Discipline and punish? Strategy discourse, senior manager subjectivity and contradictory power effects. *Human Relations*, 67(12): 1513–1536.

Dörrenbächer, C. and Geppert, M. (eds.) 2011. *Politics and Power in the Multinational Corporation. The Role of Institutions, Interest and Identities*. Cambridge University Press.

Easterby-Smith, M., Thorpe, R. and Jackson, P. 2012. *Management Research*. London: Sage.

Evered, R. and Louis, M. R. 1981. Alternative perspectives in the organizational sciences: 'inquiry from the inside' and 'inquiry from the outside'. *Academy of Management Review*, 6(3): 385–395.

Ferris, G. R. and Kacmar, K. M. 1992. Perceptions of organizational politics. *Journal of Management*, 18(1): 93–116.

Ferris, G. R., Treadway, D. C., Perrewe, P. L., Brouer, R., Douglas, C. and Lux, S. 2007. Political skill in organization. *Journal of Management*, 33(3): 290–320.

Fleming, P. and Spicer, A. 2014. Power in management and organization science. *The Academy of Management Annals*, 8(1): 237–298.

Frenkel, M. 2008. The multinational corporation as a third space: rethinking international management discourse on knowledge transfer through Homi Bhabha. *Academy of Management Review*, 33(4): 924–942.

Geppert, M. 2014. Reflections on the methods of how we present and compare the political contents of our research: a prerequisite for critical institutional research. *Journal of Management Inquiry*, 24(1): 100–104.

Geppert, M. and Dörrenbächer, C. 2014. Politics and power within multinational corporations: mainstream studies, emerging critical approaches and suggestions for future research. *International Journal of Management Reviews*, 16(2): 226–244.

Geppert, M., Williams, K. and Wortmann, M. 2015. Micro-political game playing in Lidl: a comparison of store-level employment relations. *European Journal of Industrial Relations*, 21(3): 241–257.

Gibbert, M., Ruigrok, W. and Wicki, B. 2008. What passes as a rigorous case study? *Strategic Management Journal*, 29(13): 1465–1474.

Hardy, C., Phillips, N. and Clegg, S. 2001. Reflexivity in organization and management theory: a study of the production of the research 'subject'. *Human Relations*, 54(5): 531–560.

Hinds, P. J., Neeley, T. B. and Cramton, C. D. 2014. Language as a lightning rod: power contests, emotion regulations, and subgroup dynamics in global teams. *Journal of International Business Studies*, 45(5): 536–561.

Holm, U., Johanson, J. and Thilenius, P. 1995. Headquarters' knowledge of subsidiary network contexts in the multinational corporation. *International Studies of Management and Organization*, 25(1–2): 97–119.

Jack, G. and Westwood, R. 2006. Postcolonialism and the politics of qualitative research in international business. *Management International Review*, 46(4): 481–501.

Janssens, M. and Steyaert, C. 2014. Re-considering language within a cosmopolitan understanding: towards a multilingual franca approach in international business studies. *Journal of International Business Studies*, 45(5): 623–639.

Janssens, M., Lambert, J. and Steyaert, C. 2004. Developing language strategies for international companies: the contribution of translation studies. *Journal of World Business*, 39(4): 414–430.

Johnson, P. and Duberley, J. 2003. Reflexivity in management research. *Journal of Management Studies*, 40(5): 1279–1303.

Johnson, P., Buehring, A., Cassell, C. and Symon, G. 2006. Evaluating qualitative research: towards a contingent criteriology. *International Journal of Management Reviews*, 8(3): 131–156.

Kacmar, K. M. and Ferris, G. R. 1991. Perceptions of organizational politics scale (POPS): development and construct validation. *Educational and Psychological Measurement*, 51(1): 193–205.

Karnieli-Miller, O., Strier, R. and Pessach, L. 2009. Power relations in qualitative research. *Qualitative Health Research*, 19(2): 279–289.

Kirk, J. and Miller, M. L. 1986. *Reliability and Validity in Qualitative Research*. Beverly Hills: Sage.

Klitmøller, A. 2013. (Re)contextualizing cultural and linguistic boundaries in multinational corporations: a global ethnographic approach. PhD Dissertation, Aarhus University.

Kostova, T., Roth, K. and Dacin, M. T. 2008. Institutional theory in the study of multinational corporations: a critique and new directions. *Academy of Management Review*, 33(4): 994–1006.

Kristensen, P. H. and Zeitling, J. 2001. The making of a global firm. Local pathways to multinational enterprise. In G. Morgan, P. H. Kristensen and R. Whitley (eds.), *The Multinational Firm: Organizing Across Institutional and National Divides*. Oxford University Press, 172–195.

Lincoln, Y. S. and Guba, E. G. (1985). *Naturalistic Inquiry*. Beverly Hills: Sage.

Logemann, M. and Piekkari, R. 2015. Localize or local lies? The power of language and translation in the multinational corporation. *Critical Perspectives on International Business*, 11(1): 30–53.

Luo, Y. and Shenkar, O. 2006. The multinational corporation as a multilingual community: language and organization in a global context. *Journal of International Business Studies*, 37(3): 321–339.

Macdonald, S. and Hellgren, B. 2004. The interview in international business research. Problems we would rather not talk about. In R. Marschan-Piekkari and C. Welch (eds.), *Handbook of Qualitative Research Methods in International Business*. Cheltenham, UK: Edward Elgar, 264–282.

Maclean, M. and Hollinshead, G. 2011. Contesting social space in the Balkan region: the social dimensions of a 'red' joint venture. In C. Dörrenbächer and M. Geppert (eds.), *Politics and Power in the Multinational Corporation: the Role of Institutions, Interests and Identities*. Cambridge University Press, 380–414.

Marschan-Piekkari, R. and Reis, C. 2004. Language and languages in cross-cultural interviewing. In R. Marschan-Piekkari and C. Welch (eds.), *Handbook of Qualitative Research Methods in International Business*. Cheltenham, UK: Edward Elgar, 224–243.

Marschan-Piekkari, R. and Welch, C. (eds.) 2004. *Handbook of Qualitative Research Methods for International Business*. Cheltenham, UK: Edward Elgar.

Marschan-Piekkari, R., Welch, C., Penttinen, H. and Tahvanainen, M. 2006. Interviewing in the multinational corporation: challenges of the organisational context. In R. Marschan-Piekkari and C. Welch (eds.), *Handbook of Qualitative Research Methods in International Business*, Cheltenham, UK: Edward Elgar, 244–265.

Meriläinen, S., Tienari, J., Thomas, R. and Davies, A. 2008. Hegemonic academic practices: experiences of publishing from the periphery. *Organization*, 15(4): 584–597.

Michailova, S. 2004. Contextualising fieldwork: reflections on conducting research in Eastern Europe. In R. Marschan-Piekkari and C. Welch (eds.), *Handbook of Qualitative Research Methods in International Business*. Cheltenham, UK: Edward Elgar, 365–383.

Michailova, S., Piekkari, R., Plakoyiannaki, E., Ritvala, T., Mihailova, I. and Salmi, A. 2014. Breaking the silence about exiting from fieldwork: a relational approach and its implications for theorizing. *Academy of Management Review*, 39(2): 138–161.

Miller, S. 1952. The participant-observer and 'over-rapport'. *American Sociological Review*, 17(1): 97–99.

Neeley, T. 2013. Language matters: status loss and achieved status distinction in global organizations. *Organization Science*, 24(2): 476–497.

O'Connor, E. S. 1995. Paradoxes of participation: textual analysis and organizational change. *Organization Studies*, 16(5): 769–803.

O'Leary, Z. 2004. *The Essential Guide to Doing Research*. London: Sage.

Paul, B. D. 1953. Interview techniques and field relations. In A. L. Kroeber (ed.), *Anthropology Today*, University of Chicago Press, 430–451.

Pfeffer, J. 1992. Understanding power in organizations. *California Management Review*, 34(2): 29–50.

Piekkari, R. and Welch, C. (eds.) 2011. *Rethinking the Case Study in International Business and Management Research*. Cheltenham, UK: Edward Elgar.

Piekkari, R., Oxelheim, L. and Randøy, T. 2015. The silent board: how language diversity may affect work processes of the corporate board. *Corporate Governance: an International Review*, 23(1): 25–41.

Piekkari, R., Vaara, E., Tienari, J. and Säntti, R. 2005. Integration or disintegration? Human resource implications of a common corporate language decision in a cross-border merger. *International Journal of Human Resource Management*, 16(3): 333–347.

Piekkari, R., Welch, C. and Paavilainen, E. 2009. The case study as disciplinary convention: evidence from international business journals. *Organizational Research Methods*, 12(3): 567–589.

Prasad, P. 2005. *Crafting Qualitative Research: Working in the Postpositivist Traditions*. New York: M. E. Sharpe, Inc.

Ragin, C. C. 1992. 'Casing' and the process of social inquiry. In C. C. Ragin and H. S. Becker (eds.), *What is a Case? Exploring the Foundations of Social Inquiry*. Cambridge University Press, 217–226.

Reeves, C. L. 2010. A difficult negotiation: fieldwork relations with gatekeepers. *Qualitative Research*, 10(3): 315–331.

Roth, K. and Kostova, T. 2003. The use of multinational corporation as a research context. *Journal of Management*, 29(6): 883–902.

Ryen, A. 2002. Cross-cultural interviewing. In J. F. Gubriem and J. A. Holstein (eds.), *Handbook of Interview Research: Context and Method*. Thousand Oaks, CA: Sage, 335–354.

Steyaert, C. and Janssens, M. 2013. Multilingual scholarship and the paradox of translation and language in management and organization studies. *Organization*, 20(1): 131–142.

Steyaert, C., Ostendorp, A. and Gaibrois, C. 2011. Multilingual organizations as 'linguascapes': negotiating the position of English through discursive practices. *Journal of World Business*, 46(3): 270–278.

Strauss, A. 1978. *Negotiations: Varieties, Processes, Contexts and Social Order*. San Francisco: Jossey-Bass.

Symon, G. and Cassell, C. 2012. Assessing qualitative research. In G. Symon and C. Cassell (eds.), *Qualitative Organizational Research: Core Methods and Current Challenges*. London: Sage, 204–223.

Tenzer, H., Pudelko, M. and Harzing, A.-W. 2014. The impact of language barriers on trust formation in multinational teams. *Journal of International Business Studies*, 45(5): 508–535.

Tietze, S. 2004. Spreading the management gospel – in English. *Language and Intercultural Communication*, 4(3): 175–189.

Tietze, S. and Dick, P. 2013. The victorious English language: hegemonic practices in the management academy. *Journal of Management Inquiry*, 22(1): 570–582.

Vaara, E. 2003. Post-acquisition integration as sensemaking: glimpses of ambiguity, confusion, hypocrisy, and politicization. *Journal of Management Studies*, 40(4): 859–894.

Vaara, E. and Tienari, J. 2008. A discursive perspective on legitimisation strategies in multinational corporations. *Academy of Management Review*, 33(4): 985–993.

Vaara, E., Tienari, J., Piekkari, R. and Säntti, R. 2005. Language and the circuits of power in a merging multinational corporation. *Journal of Management Studies*, 42(3): 595–623.

Venuti, L. 1998. Strategies of translation. In M. Baker (ed.), *Routledge Encyclopaedia of Translation Studies*. London: Routledge, 240–244.

Watson, T. J. 2000. Ethnographic fiction science: making sense of managerial work and organizational research processes with Caroline and Terry. *Organization*, 7(3): 489–510.

Welch, C. and Piekkari, R. 2006. Crossing language boundaries: qualitative interviewing in international business. *Management International Review*, 46(4): 417–437.

Welch, C., Marschan-Piekkari, R., Penttinen, H. and Tahvanainen, M. 2002. Corporate elites as informants in qualitative international business research. *International Business Review* 11(5): 611–628.

Welch, C., Piekkari, R., Plakoyiannaki, E. and Paavilainen-Mäntymäki, E. 2011. Theorising from case studies: towards a pluralist future for international business research. *Journal of International Business Studies*, 42(5): 740–762.

Westney, D. E. and Van Maanen, J. 2011. The casual ethnography of the executive suite. *Journal of International Business Studies*, 42(5): 602–607.

Westwood, R. 2004. Towards a postcolonial research paradigm in international business and comparative management. In R. Marschan-Piekkari and C. Welch (eds.), *Handbook of Qualitative Research Methods in International Business*. Cheltenham, UK: Edward Elgar, 56–83.

Williams, C. 2011. Subsidiary manager socio-political interaction: the impact of host country culture. In C. Dörrenbächer and M. Geppert (eds.), *Power and Politics in the Multinational Corporation.* Cambridge University Press, 283–314.

Ybema, S. and Byun, H. 2011. Unequal power relations, identity discourse, and cultural distinction drawing in MNCs. In C. Dörrenbächer and M. Geppert (eds.), *Power and Politics in the Multinational Corporation.* Cambridge University Press, 315–345.

Reflections and new directions for research

Introduction

In the final chapters of Part IV we will reflect on some novel developments in the field and related new research directions, bringing together ideas of scholars from various academic disciplines, including economic sociology, international business and management, organization studies, political science and economics. Time and space constraints make it impossible for us to cover all the 'hot topics' in the field. Rather, our ambition here is to give a sense of some of the key new research questions in which the authors of the twelve chapters and other leading scholars in the field are currently interested and what new research directions are emerging out of these novel developments.

You will certainly notice that most of the contributions presented in this final part do not always neatly fit into the frames outlined in the two core chapters of our book: Chapter 2 on theoretical foundations and conceptual definitions, and Chapter 3 on past developments and current applications in the field. Ambiguity is part of stepping into and seeking novel ground for the study of power and politics in multinational corporations (MNCs). Many of the ideas presented in Part IV draw on various academic disciplines and also facets of actor-centred and critical systemic aspects of power and politics in MNCs. In short, our multidisciplinary and multifaceted approach makes describing new directions in the field a challenging task.

Still, we would like to invite you to reflect together with the authors of each of the chapters of Part IV on what the novel ideas presented here might mean for future research in the field. In Part IV we will consider studies on discursive sensemaking in MNCs (Chapter 9 by Geppert and Dörrenbächer), politicking and issue selling in MNCs (Chapter 10 by Dörrenbächer and Gammelgaard), global élites in MNCs (Chapter 11 by Dörrenbächer and Geppert) and micropolitics in emerging market MNCs (Chapter 12 by Lange and

242   *Reflections and new directions for research*

Becker-Ritterspach). You will notice that the new directions presented here start with developments and questions related to the micro- and meso-levels of analysis (Chapters 9 and 10), and then move towards macro-level related analytical challenges and questions (Chapter 11). Research on discursive sensemaking, discussed in Chapter 9, deals with new research on forms of political sensemaking, such as 'sensehiding' in sensegiving processes or 'self-censoring' and 'inaction' in sensemaking processes of local subsidiary managers. This work points to new directions for research on individual and collective identity-building in MNCs and the underpinning role of political sensemaking processes in all its facets.

Studies on global élites show that new research also needs to go beyond micro- and macro-levels of analysis by pointing to macro-level challenges triggered by the growing influence of global élites on the micropolitical underpinnings of contemporary MNCs. Crucial questions raised in Chapter 11 are: do global élites form a homogenous powerful group of actors in the international arena? Do they actually dominate identity construction and political interests of other important stakeholders such as local managers, employees, employee representatives or transnational civic movement actors?

Another new macro-level phenomenon is the rise of emerging market MNCs as new political actors within the transnational social space that turns them into new subjects of academic study. As Chapter 12 shows, new research is crucial, because we do not know much yet about the socio-political constitution and micropolitical underpinnings of MNCs originating from emerging economies. We, therefore, take a closer look at emerging market MNCs and explore in what way sets of actors, strutures of interests, resources and conflict dynamics might be peculiar to these types of MNCs.

We hope that the readers of Part IV will find some useful information and inspiring ideas for their on-going and future research. In short, we hope that these final chapters will stimulate new thought-provoking, practical and relevant studies on the vital topic of power, politics and conflict in MNCs.

9 Advancing research on political issues in and around multinational corporations (MNCs): the role of discursive sensemaking

MIKE GEPPERT AND CHRISTOPH
DÖRRENBÄCHER

Critical management studies on discourse put the 'central use language' on centre stage (Balogun *et al.* 2011: 768). A key interest has been to shed some light on discursive 'enactment of politics and power' in MNCs (Whittle *et al.* forthcoming). In Chapter 3 we have already stressed that, besides micropolitical approaches, discursive approaches have become quite prominent in studies of power and politics in MNCs. Here we have especially referred to critical discursive perspectives (CDP) which analyse the discursive and narrative construction of power relations within and around MNCs and stress that MNCs are full of discursive political struggles and 'language games' (Clegg *et al.* 2006).

In this section, we will concentrate on new developments in a central field of discursive studies of MNCs – the role of discursive sensemaking – in which politics and power are constitutive elements. In the centre of analysis is the question of how and why powerful actors engage in discourse and dialogue when making and giving sense about critical events – like mergers and acquisitions (M&As), corporate restructurings or closures – by providing justifications about the purpose of such events in order to gain internal and external legitimacy and by developing discursive strategies which justify and resist certain measures proposed by headquarters. Studies of sensemaking are focused on the ex-post-analysis of stories, narratives, vocabularies and texts which are used in dialogues by internal and external political key players (Geppert 2003; Riad 2005; Vaara and Tienari 2011).

Weick (1995: 18) stressed that sensemaking in organizations is 'grounded in identity construction', accordingly Clark and Geppert (2011) have proposed to concentrate the study of political sensemaking on 'politics of identity construction' and the on-going cycles of sense-making and sensegiving between the key political players within head-quarters and the subsidiaries, by emphasizing that:

In a *sensemaking* process social actors perceive, interpret, and evaluate each other's conduct as it impacts on their understanding[s]...in a *sensegiving* process, actors use power and other resources to enact their [headquarters and] subsidiary identity, to respond meaningfully to and thereby influence the behaviour of others. One actor's sensegiving prompts the other's sense-making responses, in turn leading to the latter's sensegiving acts and the emerging political process of [further] integration [or disintegration of the MNC]. (Clark and Geppert 2011: 399)

Political stances and interests of key players within the headquarters and within the subsidiaries are seen as central for the analysis of the dynamics of sensemaking and sensegiving. The political dynamics of political sensemaking is studied in reference to the perceptions of the key actors involved, and how they interpret and respond to each other when making and giving sense about critical events. Sensemaking and sensegiving cycles are analysed over a certain period of time along two trajectories: (i) in accordance with the question of whether the key players based at headquarters treat the subsidiary as a 'dependant' and try to impose centrally developed ideas and business practices, or whether they are interested in the creative potential and further devel-opment of the subsidiary, e.g. in enhancing its mandate; and (ii) in accordance with the question of whether key players within the local subsidiary are interested in getting actively involved in negotiations about the firm's future mandate and an enhanced subsidiary role, or whether they see themselves as 'local patriots' who – based on tradi-tional local networks – are more interested in passively and actively resisting any major (e.g. mandate or subsidiary role) changes (Clark and Geppert 2011).

Political stances and interests are, however, not always visible up front and often change over time related to the situational dynamics of political sensemaking and sensegiving cycles. Crucial questions which are directly related to political identity construction are: (i) whether the dynamics of the increased politicization of discursive sense-making and sensegiving cycles turns the MNC over time into a political 'battlefield' in cases of severe interest and identity conflicts (Kristensen and Zeitlin 2001), which would lead to instability and disorder (i) and (ii) whether the political identity construction processes are based on identifying joint interests and promoting negotiation, which would lead to stability and institution-building (Clark and Geppert 2011).

In the following sections we will firstly address some new studies, pointing to the strategic role of sensebreaking, i.e. 'breaking the previously established sense' (Monin *et al.* 2013: 257), and also to the tactical role of sensehiding, i.e. 'deliberately avoiding certain senses' (ibid.), based on hypocrisy and hidden agendas (see also Vaara 2003). Next we will discuss new research pointing to non-innovative and passive forms of political sensemaking at the subsidiary level, based on self-censoring and inaction, by addressing the crucial question of why local managers in a power position deliberately decided 'to hide, dilute or restrict their "local sense" from the headquarters' (Whittle *et al.* forthcoming). This will be followed by some suggestions of directions for future research.

Strategic and tactical political aspects of discursive sensemaking

Strategic and tactical political elements of sensegiving are the focus of current studies on M&As, which raise questions about how actors made and gave sense about the purpose and internal and external legitimacy of mergers. A key finding is that dialogue and discursive sensemaking can become highly politicized over time in post-merger integration situations. The latter problem has been related to key actors' perceptions of the equality, synergies and justice of the merger.

Vaara and Monin (2010), for instance, analyse the case of a failed merger in the pharmaceutical industry in France. A key focus of the study is the 'political nature' of legitimation and 'the risk associated with politicization' of the merger sites. Sensegiving is seen as a central element of the discursive legitimation of the merger which promotes a specific way of thinking and taking action. The authors especially show how manipulative acts of sensegiving by the top management team (TMT), which is responsible for managing the merger site, led to an increased politicization over time. They refer to these kinds of tactics as sensehiding in the paper and concentrate their analysis on the question of how and why particular ideas and the true motives behind the merger remain hidden (ibid.: 6). The authors provide dense empirical evidence for the tactics of sensehiding, e.g. by showing that the three strategic goals, which were provided in the initial press release to justify the merger to internal and external stakeholders, were successively reduced to only one motive in later press releases (ibid.: 13).

This kind of intentional manipulative tactic blocked any serious dialogue about the potential synergies between the two merged sites and about effective solutions when the merger faced a 'legitimacy crisis'. The study concludes that 'hiding' the true motives of the merger not only explains the increased politicization of discursive sensemaking but also why the merger faced a serious 'legitimacy crisis' which led to its failure in the end.

Another study by Monin *et al.* (2013) provides an even more comprehensive view of discursive sensemaking by pointing to both the political elements of sensegiving within TMT and sensemaking by lower-level managers and employees. The authors distinguish altogether three forms of sensegiving – in reference to the changing perceptions of the members of TMT with regard to the 'distributive justice' of the post-merger – and three forms of sensemaking – in reference to the changing perceptions of lower-level managers and employees with regard to the 'distributive justice' of the post-merger:

- sensegiving as 'sensebreaking', i.e. 'breaking previously established senses of justice';
- sensegiving as 'sensehiding', i.e. 'deliberately avoiding particular senses of justice';
- sensegiving as 'sense specification', i.e. 'providing specific meanings of justice';
- sensemaking as 'acceptance of specific senses of justice';
- sensemaking as 'resistance to senses of justice';
- sensemaking as taking 'distance from senses of justice' (ibid.: 257).

The research shows two important political aspects of sensegiving: on the one hand, as in the former study by Vaara and Monin (2010), the importance of sensehiding as manipulative sensegiving tactics is emphasized. It is shown how alternative senses and voices with regard to 'distributive justice' in the process of post-merger integration were 'silenced' and 'marginalised' (ibid.: 262). On the other hand, the strategic role of powerful key actors, like TMT, is stressed by showing how it played the role of a dominant force in the early stages of post-merger integration when sensegiving activities were undertaken, which were intended to 'break' the established 'ways of thinking' with regard to the equality and justice of the merger. Sensebreaking has been seen as a 'concrete rule-breaking' act (ibid.: 261).

Complementary attention is also paid to the political sensemaking tactics of lower-level managers and employees in response to the sensegiving acts of TMT. This is associated with active forms of resistance, where, e.g. a manager openly opposed the 'sensehiding' approach of TMT by referring to the merger not as a 'merger of equals' but as a 'take-over', a phrase which was not supposed to be officially used and thus was 'taboo'. On the other hand, the study also points to passive forms sensemaking like the 'distancing' of lower-level managers by their 'expressing distrust and negativity' with regard to the official interpretations of post-merger equality and justice expressed in the sensegiving acts of TMT (ibid.: 263).

In short, the study shows not just the socio-political importance of tactical sensehiding approaches but also the crucial strategic role of sensebreaking, which was deliberately used to systematically change the norms of justice in the post-merger site from 'equality to equity' (ibid.). The study especially points to the critical role of sensegiving acts in comparison to sensemaking acts, where the resistance and distancing tactics of lower-level managers and employees led to some dialogue but remained confined to the operational level and had little impact on the strategic direction of the overall sensegiving approach by senior management.

A central question for future research is, however, in how far concepts and findings related to specific post-merger situations can be applied to other critical events involving political sensemaking in MNCs such as mandate changes, corporate restructuring and closures. Moreover, different societal contexts of sensebreaking and sensehiding acts, such as the country of origin of the MNC and host country institutional features like labour law and industrial relations, have not been taken into consideration. We will come back to these questions at the end of this chapter, when we more systematically look into possible directions for future research.

Self-censoring and inaction in discursive sensemaking at subsidiary level

The stream of research on discursive sensemaking discussed above concentrates largely on the power of top management who intends both to deliberately change the 'rules of game' through sensebreaking activities and, based on more indirect and manipulative sensehiding tactics, to impose certain 'rules of the game' and dominate dialogues in the MNC. In contrast to these studies, but also highlighting the crucial role of 'authority-imposed' forms of sensegiving, is another way of studying the political dimensions of discursive sensemaking by taking a bottom-up view. This was the focus of Whittle *et al.* (forthcoming) which sheds some light on the dark side of MNC power relations and forms of dominance in MNCs by analysing 'why particular senses, ideas and voices are never actually "heard" or "shared" due to anticipatory, self-imposed censoring' at subsidiary level (ibid.). It is stressed that political sensemaking might not necessarily always lead to open conflicts and power struggles by pointing to situations where subsidiary managers develop strong interests to 'hide, dilute or restrict their "local sense" from the headquarters, including their knowledge of the local market and their preferred strategic direction for the firm' (ibid.). Whittle *et al.* call these tactical elements of political sensemaking 'sense-censoring'. A main contribution of the study is to show how and why 'sense-censoring' transforms strategic action into inaction. A key reason provided for this inaction are managers' past experiences of political struggles with headquarters. In stories told by them these struggles are mainly framed as lost battles, in which headquarters is referred to as an 'elephant' and the local subsidiary as an 'ant'.

When addressing these questions the researchers point to an important conceptual problem of mainstream international business studies on power and politics which are based on resource dependency theory. Here it is assumed that subsidiaries that show strong economic performance and have a solid local knowledge base will be in a strong bargaining position in negotiations with the headquarters (see e.g. Birkinshaw 2000). The case studied by Whittle *et al.*, a UK subsidiary of a large US MNC, ticked all the boxes for the structural features of a powerful subsidiary in terms of resource dependency theory. The firm behaved, however, very differently from expected. It was found that the self-perceptions of UK subsidiary managers did not match the subsidiary's structural position within the MNC but featured instead the position of a 'strategic dependant' (Clark and Geppert 2011). These perceptions of being in a weak bargaining position were treated by local managers as 'social facts' and therefore they did not materialize in recursive cycles of political sensemaking and sensegiving as emphasized in other studies (Clark and Geppert 2011; Monin *et al.* 2013).

What Whittle *et al.* (forthcoming) point to is the role of self-imposed passivity in discursive sensemaking at subsidiary level, where managers in their case study increasingly relied on sense-censoring which led to their inaction in terms of 'issue selling' (Gammelgaard 2009) and political bargaining (Birkinshaw *et al.* 2001). Perceptions of headquarters' domination and self-perceptions of a weak subsidiary position led to submissive behaviour, where subsidiary key actors were 'fearful of putting their "heads above the parapet"' (Whittle *et al.* forthcoming). The specific forms of political sensemaking discussed here cannot be captured by mainstream functionalist power concepts which remain on the episodic surface of the 'language games' played in organizations (see also Clegg *et al.* 2006). Discursive acts of sense-censoring and inaction point to the deeper and darker sides of MNC power relations in which actors accept the established 'rules of the game'; dominant power structures are taken for granted and turned into social facts in discursive sensemaking acts, which lead to the perception that 'there is no alternative' (the TINA effect). In short, in certain situational contexts, political sensemaking tends to manifest the established authority of the headquarters, based on strong beliefs at subsidiary level that 'resistance is useless' (Royle 2002), 'dangerous or counterproductive' (Whittle *et al.* forthcoming). This kind of political dynamics of discursive sensemaking leads to self-censoring and inaction at subsidiary level.

A vital question, however, is whether there are situational contexts in which the emergence of self-censoring and inaction of subsidiary management is more likely. From this point of view we need, for example, to ask how far the findings of this specific case study – of an MNC originating from a liberal market economy context, the US, which also operates in a liberal market economy host context, the UK – are relevant for MNCs originating from and operating in non-liberal market economies. Moreover, there might be differences between industrial sectors (Geppert and Hollinshead 2014) in terms of power relations and the dominance of MNC headquarters, which make self-censoring-related inaction more likely in some sectors than in others.

Challenges and new directions for future research

We have shown that there is a growing body of discursive sense-making studies which deal with novel aspects of power and politics in the MNC. We have especially concentrated on research pointing to the vital role of sensegiving strategies and tactics and also on political sensemaking processes that lead to passivity and the silencing of subsidiary voices. With reference to these arguments and empirical findings, we see at least two challenges and directions for future research on discursive sensemaking.

Conceptional and methodological challenges

At the beginning of this section, we stressed that research on discursive sensemaking raises questions about the political construction of individual and collective identities. Sensebreaking has been identified as a powerful way of sensegiving, which intends to delegitimize the old identities of the two merging parties in order to clear the ground for a new identity and institution-building. However, research has also shown that both sensebreaking and related tactics of sensegiving of powerful actors, focused on hiding the true motives and interests, might be contra-productive for a sustainable construction of new identities. We learned especially that TMTs, who try to sell a merger at any price and by hiding true senses, might cause legitimacy and identity crisis situations, which makes the failure of the merger highly likely. This raises the interesting question about how far sensegiving strategies and tactics developed by powerful actors in TMT or headquarters can be decoupled from the identities of the parties involved, i.e. the two post-merger sites or the local subsidiaries. The next and related question is how far sensehiding and hypocrisy, which are linked with an increased politicization of international ventures like M&As, can generally be seen as clear signs that political sensemaking cycles might be on a downward spiral leading to break-up, failure and battlefield scenarios in MNCs.

Other conceptual challenges for future research emerge when we consider the issue of self-censoring. This approach raises, first of all, important questions about the value of functionalist resource dependency theories for the interpretation of political 'episodes' of mandate development, innovation or issue selling. We have seen that such approaches have limited theoretical value for an in-depth case study analysis as to why subsidiaries with strong power positions show little interest in selling issues and influencing headquarters' decision-making acts.

Thus, there is a need to critically reassess and enrich functionalist ideas on power and politics in MNCs in mainstream international business, e.g. by applying social constructivist and discursive ideas. First attempts have been made by looking in the other direction in the study of subsidiaries which have limited structural power resources, but nevertheless feature strong forms of 'politicking' based on perceptions of them having a voice and the ability to influence decisions at headquarters level (see e.g. Bouquet and Birkinshaw 2008); this is the opposite of what Whittle *et al.* found in their study. However, political sensemaking approaches might help to fine-tune the research further, e.g. by showing when and how active politicking behaviour, self-censoring and inaction dynamics might kick in, regardless of whether subsidiaries are 'rich' or 'poor' in terms of their power resources. One reason given by Whittle *et al.* is that former political battles between headquarters and subsidiaries might create a strong sense and perception of powerlessness and the acceptance of headquarters dominance. However, further studies are needed which look into other reasons why subsidiaries which have the potential of using power to influence MNC decision-making remain silent in discursive sensemaking cycles.

From a comparative institutionalist point of view it should also be asked how far the lack of resources provided by societal institutions, as in the case of the UK subsidiary, can explain the local management's self-censoring approach, and how far ideas about systemic power and 'dominance effects' of US MNCs (see e.g. Smith and Meiksins 1995) can be applied to explain the dominance of the US headquarters and the submissive behaviour of local management. These questions need to be raised because the analysis of political sensemaking also makes us aware of deeper power structures like the rules of the game and domination (Clegg *et al.* 2006) in language and micropolitical games played in the MNC when there is the lack of initiative-taking and the inaction of supposed powerful subsidiaries. The question emerging here is: what kind of rules of the game and forms of dominance in contemporary capitalism trigger perceptions of TINA and the idea that 'resistance is useless' within local subsidiaries of MNCs?

Finally, we need to have in mind that there are some methodological challenges in an analysis of politicized sensemaking, especially when it involves sensehiding. Researchers might face difficulties in obtaining company access as well as access to critical materials and interview partners.

The role of the situational context

Research on sensebreaking and especially sensehiding has so far been primarily developed in the specific situational context of post-merger integration and has not been tested in other critical events which are seen as triggers for political sensemaking like e.g. mandate change (Dörrenbächer and Geppert 2009), MNC restructuring (Taplin 2006), shutdowns (Contu *et al.* 2013) or knowledge transfer from headquarters to subsidiaries (Kostova 1999). The questions emerging here are whether sensebreaking, which has been seen as especially relevant in the initial stages of post-merger integration (Monin *et al.* 2013), will be as prominent and carry the same strategic importance in other situational contexts and if so, why and how? It needs also to be asked whether sensegiving in post-merger cases always involves sense-breaking. If so, the latter might trigger battlefield scenarios à la Kristensen and Zeitlin (2001) which would undermine any serious post-merger integration approaches from the start.

The most interesting construct which needs to be examined much more systematically in other situational contexts is sensehiding. This might be an important tactical approach of headquarters when making sense and giving sense in reference to various political approaches of subsidiary managers, such as politicking and issue selling which we will also discuss further in Chapter 10. We might find very different political sensemaking dynamics in the various influence tactics listed in Table 10.1, when the headquarters sensegiving approach is more based on sensehiding by not revealing the underlying interests and goals in situations of mandate change negotiations when e.g. compared to corporate restructuring. Emerging questions for future research are: in which other situational contexts of discursive sensemaking does sensehiding play a similar important role as in post-merger integration situations, and are there host country contexts which make the use of sensehiding approaches more difficult, because of national institutional influences such as legal obligations and trade union and workers' representatives' rights, which require more open dialogue and negotiation?

The latter questions would also apply in the case of sense-censoring and inaction in subsidiary–headquarters relationships. The case-study analysed by Whittle *et al.* is a subsidiary situated in the liberal UK host market, where an expected strong strategic bargaining position of a subsidiary is more likely to be perceived as weak because wider societal resources for robust tool-building by local managers and representatives are missing (Williams and Geppert 2011). Situational contexts which provide weak incentives for tool- and coalition-building of local management with labour, are more likely to trigger a downward sense-censoring cycle in discursive sensemaking. Accordingly, we need to ask whether there are national and regional institutional contexts which make the appearance of self-censoring approaches less likely. More international comparisons of sense-hiding and sense-censoring approaches across diverse societal contexts are missing in the academic research so far and therefore provide interesting new routes for future studies of the political dimensions of discursive sensegiving and sensemaking.

References

Balogun, J., Jarzabkowski, P. and Vaara, E. 2011. Selling, resistance and reconciliation: a critical discursive approach to subsidiary role evolution in MNCs. *Journal of International Business Studies*, 42(6): 765–786.

Birkinshaw, J. 2000. *Entrepreneurship in the Global Firm*. London: Sage.

Bouquet, C. and Birkinshaw, J. 2008. Managing power in the multinational corporation: how low-power actors gain influence. *Journal of Management*, 34(3): 477–508.

Clark, E. and Geppert, M. 2011. Subsidiary integration as identity construction and institution building: a political sensemaking approach. *Journal of Management Studies*, 48(2): 395–415.

Clegg. S. R., Courpasson, D. and Phillips, N. 2006. *Power and Organizations*. London: Sage.

Contu, A, Palpacuer, F., Balas, N. 2013. Multinational corporations' politics and resistance to plant shutdowns: a comparative case study in the south of France. *Human Relations* 66(3): 363–384.

Dörrenbächer, C. and Geppert, M. 2009. Micro-political games in the multinational corporation: the case of mandate change. *Management Revue*, 20(4): 373–391.

Gammelgaard, J. 2009. Issue selling and bargaining power in intrafirm competition: the differentiating impact of the subsidiary management composition. *Competition and Change*, 13(3): 214–228.

Geppert, M. 2003. Sensemaking and politics in MNCs: a comparative analysis of vocabularies within in the global manufacturing discourse in one industrial sector. *Journal of Management Inquiry*, 12(4): 312–329.

Geppert, M. and Hollinshead, G. 2014. Multinationals, social agency and institutional change; variation by sector. *Competition and Change*, 18(2): 195–199.

Kostova, T. 1999. Transnational transfer of strategic organizational practices: a contextual perspective. *Academy of Management Review*, 24(2): 308–324.

Kristensen, P. H. and Zeitlin, J. 2001. The making of a global firm: local pathways to multinational enterprise. In G. Morgan, P. H. Kristensen and R. Whitley (eds.), *The Multinational Firm. Organizing Across Institutional and National Divides*. Oxford University Press, 172–195.

Monin, P., Noorderhaven, N., Vaara, E. and Kroon, D. 2013. Giving sense to and making sense of justice in postmerger integration. *Academy of Management Journal*, 56(1): 256–284.

Riad, S. 2005. The power of 'organization culture' as a discursive formation in merger integration. *Organization Studies*, 26(10): 1529–1554.

Royle, T. 2002. Resistance is useless! The problems of trade union organization in the European fast-food industry: the case of MacDonald's. In M. Geppert, D. Matten and K. Williams (eds.), *Challenges for European Management in a Global Context: Experiences from Britain and Germany*. Basingstoke: Palgrave Macmillan: 189–214.

Smith, C. and Meiksins, P. 1995. System, society and dominance effects in cross-national organizational analysis. *Work, Employment and Society*, 9(12): 241–267.

Taplin, I. M. 2006. Strategic change and organizational restructuring: how managers negotiate change initiatives. *Journal of International Management*, 12(3): 284–301.

Vaara, E. 2003. Post-acquisition integration as sensemaking: glimpses of ambiguity, confusion, hypocrisy, and politicization. *Journal of Management Studies*, 40(4): 859–894.

Vaara, E. and Monin, P. 2010. A recursive perspective on discursive legitimation and organizational action in mergers and acquisitions. *Organization Science*, 21(1): 3–22.

Vaara, E. and Tienari, J. 2011. On the narrative construction of multinational corporations: an antenarrative analysis of legitimation and resistance in a cross-border merger. *Organization Science*, 22(2): 370–390.

Weick, K. E. 1995. Sensemaking in organizations. Thousand Oaks: Sage.

Whittle, A., Mueller, F., Gilchrist, A. and Lenney, P. forthcoming. Sensemaking, sense-censoring and strategic inaction: the discursive enactment of power and politics in a multinational corporation. *Organization Studies*.

Williams, K. and Geppert, M. 2011. Bargained globalization: employment relations providing robuts 'tool kits' for socio-political strategizing in MNCs in Germany. In C. Dörrenbächer and M. Geppert (eds.), *Politics and Power in the International Corporation: the Role of Institutions, Interests and Identities*. Cambridge University Press, 72–100.

10 Zooming in on politicking and issue selling tactics as new research directions for the study of micropolitics in multinational corporations (MNCs)

CHRISTOPH DÖRRENBÄCHER AND
JENS GAMMELGAARD

'Politicking' refers to politics as an activity. It describes performative operations political actors undertake in their struggle for power. Hence, politicking is about the means and tactics of interest representation. Following an overview by Palonen 'politicking has received a minimal amount of attention in literature on the concept of politics, although it refers to a key aspect in the understanding of politics-as-activity' (2003: 177). An exception, however, is the literature on organizational politics. Here a number of authors – mostly from organizational behaviour and organizational psychology backgrounds – have studied politicking as influence tactics organizational actors apply in their struggle for power and interest representation.

In the remainder of this short section we will first take a look at the literature on influence tactics that has emerged through studying how supervisors, subordinates and peer/team members within collocated organizations interact politically. We will then shift attention to the few papers that up until now have addressed the issue of politicking in multinational (i.e. dislocated) corporations, mostly under the label of 'issue selling tactics'. Matching the insights the influence tactics literature has brought about for collocated organizations with the piecemeal literature on issue selling in multinational corporations, we will advance a set of new directions for researching 'politicking' in multinational corporations.

Influence tactics

Research on influence tactics goes back to the 1970s with Allen *et al.* (1979) breaking ground by specifying a list of 'organizational politics tactics'. The term 'influence tactics' then first appeared in an exploratory study of Kipnis *et al.* (1980) that aimed to measure categories of influence behaviour and reasons for making influence attempts in organizations. Following Pfeffer (1981: 137) influence tactics can be defined as a means to acquire power through the exercise of power in organizations. Over the next two decades a number of studies (e.g. Ansari 1990; Yukl and Falbe 1990; Ferris *et al.* 2002) used, refined and extended the list of influence tactics. Summarizing these works, an impressive reservoir of influence tactics, shortly described in Table 10.1 becomes visible.

This early research on influence tactics was also looking into the direction in which influence tactics are used, revealing strong differences among tactics, with for instance 'rational persuasion' widely used in all directions, 'pressure' mostly used downward and 'coalition building' mostly used laterally in the organization. On a more general account Yukl and Tracey (1992) proposed that the particular use of influence tactics is defined by five interrelated factors: '(1) consistency with prevailing social norms and role expectations; (2) agent possession of an appropriate power base for the use of the tactic in that context; (3) appropriateness for the objective of the influence attempt; (4) level of target resistance encountered or anticipated; and (5) costs of using the tactic in relation to likely benefits' (Yukl and Tracey 1992: 526). Early research on influence tactics also grouped them into hard and soft tactics. Hard tactics such as 'legitimating', 'assertiveness' or 'blocking' leave individuals less freedom to react and threaten or induce targets to comply, whereas soft tactics such as 'consultation', 'inspirational appeals' or 'rational persuasion' try to attract and co-opt targets. Although each tactic was found to be effective in an appropriate situation, Falbe and Yukl (1992) empirically showed that soft tactics were generally more effective than hard tactics. More recent research on influence tactics can be grouped into four streams.

A first stream of research looked at the relationship between *individual actor characteristics* and the use of influence tactics. Vredenburgh and Shea-VanFossen (2010), for instance, proposed that selected individual attributes such as aggressiveness, need for status or narcisism combined with particular organizational conditions (uncertainty, resource scarity, conflict) suggest specific political behaviours (e.g. forming informal coalitions, hoarding resources or installing dependency). Later, Barbuto *et al.* (2007) looked at the relationship between gender, age, and educational background of leaders and their use of influence tactics, with gender and education catering for significant differences in the use of influence tactics.

A second stream of more recent research on influence tactics looked at *particular situations in organizations*. For instance Bennenbroek, Gravenhorst and Boonstra (1998) studying the use of influence tactics in constructive change processes (i.e. far reaching organizational change with discernible consequences for the organizations' individuals, strategy, structure and culture) found that 'rational persuasion', 'consultation' and 'inspirational appeals' are most often used. Another example is the study by Lines (2007) who looked at situations of strategy implementation and the role of influence tactics.

A third stream of research analysed the use of influence tactics in *different types of organizations*. Wadsworth and Blanchard (2015), for instance, studied influence tactics in virtual organizations where interaction is computer-mediated instead of face to face. A main finding of their study is that there is a tendency to use harder, i.e. more assertive, tactics in virtual organizations than in face-to-face environments. Janneck and Staar (2010) studied influence tactics in virtual interorganizational networks, where work does not only span over time and space but also over legal organizational boundaries. Going beyond seminal intraorganizational tactics they identified three additional influence tactics for interorganizational networks: (i) 'mediating' (gaining influence from taking a neutral position in a conflict); (ii) 'being visible' (frequent tactical use of the virtual networks' communication channels and tools to demonstrate activity); and (iii) 'claiming vacancies' (voluntarily taking over tasks and roles such as moderating meetings or administrating IT platforms to gain influence).

Finally, more recent research was also concerned *with national differences* in the use of influence tactics. An example is Fu and Yukl's (2000) comparative study on the use of influence tactics in US and Chinese firms. This study found that American managers perceived 'rational persuasion' and 'exchange' as being more effective than Chinese managers did, whereas Chinese managers found 'coalition tactics' and 'upward appeals' more effective than American managers did. Despite the fact that respondents were sampled from an American and a Chinese subsidiary of the same multinational corporation (plus a replication sample made up by managers of a number of genuine American and Chinese companies) the study exclusively focused on the use of upward, downward and lateral influence tactics within the respective national subsidiary. Thus the specifics of the cross-border use of influence tactics were not addressed. In addition the incidences American and Chinese managers were asked to rate influence tactics for were of personal career matters as well as of minor operational issues within the subsidiary. Strategic issues that refer to the subsidiary as a whole and that involve headquarters' consent were not asked for. These limitations, that also apply to a later study of Fu *et al.* (2004) involving twelve countries, however, are a least partially dealt with in the literature on issue selling in multinational corporations, which we present next.

Issue selling in multinational corporations

Influence tactics that refer to broader strategic issues have been discussed under the label of 'issue selling'. Dutton and Ashford (1993) define issue selling as the 'individual's behaviours that are directed towards affecting others' attention to and understanding of issues' (ibid., p. 398), with issues seen as strategic events or developments that have implications for organizational performance.

Following Dutton and Ashford (1993), issue selling involves two distinct activities: issue packaging and the process of selling the issue.

(i) Issue packaging involves, first, the way the content of the issue is framed and bundled. Second, issue packaging also involves decisions about the way the issue is presented (e.g. as something dramatically new) and what persuasion tactic is used (making one- or two-sided arguments).

(ii) The issue selling process then is about lobbying for an issue. It involves decisions about the breath of involvement (going solo or building coalitions) as well as about the channels (e.g. regular strategy meetings) and the formality of how upper levels of the organizational hierarchy are approached regarding the issue.

While Dutton and Ashford (1993) develop a generic model of how middle managers sell strategic issues to top managers in organizations

Table 10.1 *An inventory of influence tactics in organizations*

Tactic	Description
Attacking or blaming others	Scapegoating, i.e. blaming others as a reaction for a situation that is negatively evaluated up in the hierarchy; actively blaming a rival (making others look bad in the eyes of influential organizational members)
Use of information	Using information as a political tool: hoarding and withholding information, selective disclosure, distorting information, avoiding situations in which explanations might be asked for; inundating others with information
Creating and maintaining a favourable image/ self-promotion	Proactive tactic: being sensitive to and fulfilling organizational norms, drawing attention to success, creating the image of being on the inside of important activities or being linked to important people; presenting oneself as competent, smart, successful, proficient
Developing a base of support	Making decision makers and supporters understand one's ideas, getting others to contribute to the idea, getting support before official decision
Coalition building	Developing allies and forming power coalitions in order to achieve a desired goal or to get support of further third actors
Ingratiation	Praising others, flattering, showing subservient/ helpful behaviour, making others feel important
Creating obligations	Securing compliance of others by performing services or favours
Offering exchange	Promising rewards or tangible benefits for support or compliance
Rational persuasion	Using logical arguments and factual evidence to persuade others that an initiative proposal meets jointly accepted objectives
Consultation	Voluntarily letting others participate in decision making by asking for their opinion and showing willingness to cater for others' concerns or suggestions
Personal appeals	Appealing to others' loyalty, friendship or good work relationship

(cont.)

Table 10.1 (cont.)

Tactic	Description
Inspirational appeals	Arousing enthusiasm by appealing to universal values, common beliefs and aspirations
Upward appeals	Seeking support through referring to (existing or alleged) compliance by higher levels in the organization
Legitimating	Showing compliance with accepted frames of reference: e.g. organizational goals, practices, traditions, legal provisions, etc.
Blocking	Ignoring others or spreading wrong information to thwart others
Sanctions	Threatening to withhold rewards or to impose sanctions
Assertiveness/pressure tactics	Seeking compliance through demands, coercion, threads, intimidation, tight control, persistent reminders

Source: own compilation based on Allen *et al.* 1979; Kipnis *et al.* 1980; Ansari 1990; Yukl and Falbe 1990; Ferris *et al.* 2002; Lines 2007.

touching upon a broad number of influence tactics set out by the influence tactics literature (see Table 10.1), they – similar to the influence tactics literature – do not emphasize such activities in multinational corporations, where attempts to sell issues or take influence occur across borders and involve headquarters and subsidiaries. There are only a very few studies so far that have taken on this perspective. Bouquet and Birkinshaw (2008a) maintain that in order to be successful in issue selling 'a subsidiary not only needs to maintain a basic track record of success, but also needs to reaffirm its commitment to the parent's objectives; and then, finally, it needs to take deliberate steps to manage impressions with power brokers at the head office' (594). In another paper, Bouquet and Birkinshaw (2008b) substantially enlarge their list of means and tactics subsidiaries low power actors have at hand in order to gain influence in an MNC. Some of them challenge the status quo of the MNC. This includes 'taking initiatives', 'breaking the rules' and 'building profiles'. Others relate to political games played in MNCs. Here one can distinguish between individual means of influence such as 'deference' or 'co-opetition' and collective modes of action such as 'representation', 'building coalitions' and 'seeking feedback'. Focusing on reactive tactics subsidiaries apply when resisting unwanted headquarters initiatives, Schotter and Beamish (2011) identified the following tactics: 'ignoring', 'shifting emphasis', 'ceremonial adoption', 'obstructing and attacking'.

Going beyond a phenomenology of subsidiary means and tactics in issue selling, Ling *et al.* (2005) propose that subsidiary managers socialized in different cultures (collectivistic vs. individualistic, high vs. low status identity and ambiguity tolerance cultures) vary according to their choice of issue selling tactics with e.g. managers from collectivistic countries more likely to use 'coalition tactics' than managers from individualistic countries. Drawing on the subsidiary staffing literature, Gammelgaard (2009) shows that subsidiaries managed by expatriates more effectively apply issue selling tactics vis-à-vis headquarters than local managers in order to enlarge the strategic mandates of their subsidiary. Finally, Dörrenbächer and Gammelgaard (forthcoming) look into the impact the MNC size as well as headquarters–subsidiary power relations have on the use of issue selling tactics.

New directions for research

Summing up previous research on influence tactics and issue selling, it turns out that there is a substantial body of literature on politicking in organizations. However this literature hardly applies to multinational corporations, and where it does, it is based on concepts that do not cater for the specifics of multinational corporations. Both the influence tactics literature as well as the original works on issue selling assume that actors seek influence in nationally uniform co-located organizations. Therefore, there is first and foremost a strong need for a thorough conceptual foundation of research on politicking in multinational corporations. Such a concept would need to systematically incorporate features that distinguish multinational corporations from national corporations, including country-of-origin and host country effects, differences in multinationality, the headquarters–subsidiary divide, geographic, psychic and cultural distance, corporate language and the fact that an MNC is a hierarchy, and therefore power is asymmetrically distributed among different legal units of the organization. What could be expected is that such conceptual groundwork might reveal more systematically new, more refined and more suitable categories of influence or issue selling tactics in multinational corporations. Here conceptual research can also draw on some more recent case-based research that has tentatively described some MNC-specific tactics such as capitalizing on headquarters' insecurity zones (Dörrenbächer and Gammelgaard 2011) or shifting emphasis through translation (Logemann and Piekkari 2015).

A second new direction for further research calls for a more systematic evaluation of the use of influence tactics in multinational corporations. Given the rather piecemeal state-of-the-art on politicking in MNCs it is not surprising that the literature so far is mostly explorative in nature. Two aims have been followed here so far and need to be complemented by further research:

(i) Many efforts went into detecting, describing and building up a phenomenology of influence tactics. Given the fact that so far most research has taken a subsidiary perspective with a considerable number of papers addressing active political manoeuvring in the case of subsidiary initiative taking, there is room for more explorative case-based research both on defensive tactics of subsidiary managers as well as in general on headquarters managers' use of tactics (e.g. regarding subsidiary suboptimizing behaviour). Also some more recently described offensive subsidiary tactics such as discourse building (Koveshnikov *et al.* forthcoming) need further attention through qualitative research. Going beyond individual tactics, more research is also needed to theoretically categorize influence tactics in order to make them more accessible for empirical research. Categorizations might follow traditional lines such as hard vs. soft tactics, offensive vs. defensive tactics and more cautious vs. daring tactics. However, tactics might also be grouped according to MNC characteristics (e.g. tactics mostly used by subsidiary managers vs. tactics used by headquarters' managers, tactics used within vs. tactics used across borders). Also Dutton and Ashford's (1993) original framework of tactics for packing an issue and tactics for the selling process could be considered.

(ii) Only a few papers have made an attempt to generate hypotheses on the use of influence tactics in MNCs (e.g. Ling *et al.* 2005). While this is helpful, empirical investigations based on these hypotheses are still missing. In addition, given the many features MNCs harbour, there is ample room to develop hypotheses beyond the impact of cultural differences, as put forward by the research of Ling *et al.* (2005). For instance the link between a subsidiary manager's use of tactics and various subsidiary properties such as subsidiary role, subsidiary size and subsidiary power and autonomy could be theorized. Another idea is to explore the impact national laws and regulations have on the use of influence tactics. For instance, while gift-giving ingratiation and exchange strategies might be a viable option in some countries they are an illegal no-go tactic in other countries.

A third new direction for research on politicking in MNCs zooms in on performative aspects of politicking that are hardly studied so far. Following Gammelgaard (2009), expatriate subsidiary managers are more effective in selling issues to headquarters, but are there downsides to it in terms of seeking influence within the subsidiary, and how important are these downsides? Next, what are the personal characteristics of effective political actors in the international environment of an MNC? In particular, what role does language command, a binational or a bicultural personal background and different types of national and international experience (in- or outside the MNC, in the MNCs' headquarters, in foreign subsidiaries) play? Linked to that, another interesting aspect to study would be the relationship between (different types of) MNC managers' career aspirations and their use of influence tactics. Do strongly career-minded managers use more daring or more cautious influence tactics or a specific combination of both? Are the tactics these managers use directed more towards the headquarters or to subsidiaries, etc? Finally, future research could address what are considered as functional or dysfunctional and legitimate or illegitimate tactics in MNCs, and to what extent these perceptions depend on the organizational positioning, the cultural as well as the individual background of the beholder.

References

Allen, R. W., Madison, D. L., Porter, L., Renwick, P. A. and Mayes, B. 1979. Organizational politics. *California Management Review*, 22(1): 77–83.
Ansari, M. A. 1990. *Managing People at Work: Leadership Styles and Influence Strategies*. London/Thousand Oaks/New Delhi: Sage Publications, Inc.

Barbuto Jr, J. E., Fritz, S. M., Matkin, G. S. and Marx, D. B. 2007. Effects of gender, education, and age upon leaders' use of influence tactics and full range leadership behaviors. *Sex Roles*, 56(1–2): 71–83.

Bennebroek Gravenhorst, M. and Boonstra, J. K. 1998. The use of influence tactics in constructive change processes. *European Journal of Work and Organizational Psychology*, 7(2): 179–196.

Bouquet, C. and Birkinshaw, J. 2008a. Weight versus voice: how foreign subsidiaries gain attention from corporate headquarters. *Academy of Management Journal*, 51(3): 577–601.

2008b. Managing power in the multinational corporation: how low-power actors gain influence. *Journal of Management*, 34(3): 477–508.

Dörrenbächer, C. and Gammelgaard, J. 2011. Subsidiary power in multinational corporations: the subtle role of micro-political bargaining power. *Critical Perspectives on International Business*, 7(1): 30–47.

forthcoming. Subsidiary initiative taking in multinational corporations: the relationship between power and issue selling. *Organization Studies*.

Dutton, J. E. and Ashford, S. J. 1993. Selling issues to top management. *Academy of Management Review*, 18(3): 397–428.

Falbe, C. M. and Yukl, G. 1992. Consequences for managers of using single influence tactics and combinations of tactics. *Academy of Management Journal*, 35(3): 638–652.

Ferris, G. R., Hochwarter, W. A., Douglas, C., Blass, F. R., Kolodinsky, R. W. and Treadway, D. C. 2002. Social influence processes in organizations and human resources systems. *Research in Personnel and Human Resources Management*, 21: 65–128.

Fu, P. P. and Yukl, G. 2000. Perceived effectiveness of influence tactics in the United States and China. *The Leadership Quarterly*, 11(2): 251–266.

Fu, P. P., Kennedy, J., Tata, J., Yukl, G., Bond, M. H., Peng, T.-K. and Cheosakul, A. 2004. The impact of societal cultural values and individual social beliefs on the perceived effectiveness of managerial influence strategies: a meso approach. *Journal of International Business Studies*, 35(4): 284–305.

Gammelgaard, J. 2009. Issue selling and bargaining power in intrafirm competition: the differentiating impact of the subsidiary management composition. *Competition and Change*, 13(3): 214–228.

Janneck, M. and Staar, H. 2010. Virtual micro-politics: informal tactics of influence and power in inter-organizational networks. 43rd Hawaii International Conference on System Sciences (HICSS), IEEE, 1–10.

Kipnis, D., Schmidt, S. M. and Wilkinson, I. 1980. Intra-organizational influence tactics: exploration in getting one's way. *Journal of Applied Psychology*, 65(4): 440–452.

Koveshnikov, A., Ehrnrooth, M. and Vaara, E. forthcoming. Discursive sensemaking around subsidiary initiatives and HQ–subsidiary relations in the multinational. In C. Dörrenbächer and M. Geppert (eds.), *Multinational Corporations and Organization Theory: Post Millennium Perspectives*. Bingley: Emerald.

Lines, R. 2007. Using power to install strategy: the relationships between expert power, position power, influence tactics and implementation success. *Journal of Change Management*, 7(2): 143–170.

Ling, Y., Floyd, S. W. and Baldridge, D. C. 2005. Toward a model of issue-selling by subsidiary managers in multinational organizations. *Journal of International Business Studies*, 36(6): 637–654.

Logemann, M. and Piekkari, R. 2015. Localize or local lies? The power of language and translation in the multinational corporation. *Critical Perspectives on International Business*, 11(1): 30–53.

Palonen, K. 2003. Four times of politics: policy, polity, politicking, and politicization. *Alternatives*, 171–186.

Pfeffer, J. 1981. *Power in Organizations*. Marshfield and London: Pitman Publishing.

Schotter, A. and Beamish, P. W. 2011. Intra-organizational turbulences in multinational corporations. In C. Dörrenbächer and M. Geppert (eds.), *Politics and Power in the Multinational Corporation: the Role of Institutions, Interests and Identities*. Cambridge University Press.

Vredenburgh, D. and Shea-VanFossen, R. 2010. Human nature, organizational politics, and human resource development. *Human Resource Development Review*, 9(1): 26–47.

Wadsworth, M. B. and Blanchard, A. L. 2015. Influence tactics in virtual teams. *Computers in Human Behavior*, 44: 386–393.

Yukl, G. and Falbe, C. M. 1990. Influence tactics in upward, downward, and lateral influence attempts. *Journal of Applied Psychology*, 75(2): 132–140.

Yukl, G. and Tracey, J. B. 1992. Consequences of influence tactics used with subordinates, peers, and the boss. *Journal of Applied Psychology*, 77(4): 525–535.

11 | *Advancing research on micropolitics in multinational corporations (MNCs): an élite perspective*

CHRISTOPH DÖRRENBÄCHER AND
MIKE GEPPERT

As a promising new direction on micropolitics in MNCs we propose to investigate MNC managers and their behaviour from an élite
perspective. Linking macro-, meso- and micro-level factors, such an
approach calls for investigating the impact the MNC actors' socio-
nomic background and class membership has on his or her organizational identity and behaviour. While the study of managerial élites is
far from being new (cf. Useem 1984; Pettigrew 1992; Maclean *et al.*
2006), hardly any work has been done with particular reference to
MNCs (Morgan 2011). In the remainder of this section we first take
a broader look at the literature on corporate élites, not covered in the
book so far. Starting with the more general literature on managerial
élites we first touch upon the literature on top management teams and
global élites, that both operate with a rather narrow élite definition.
Then we move on to discuss the literature on international teamwork
and managerial élite interaction in foreign subsidiaries that operate
with a broader élite definition. Based on the findings of these literature
streams we finally elaborate on a set of new research directions for an
élite-based understanding of power, politics and conflict in MNCs.

Managerial élites

Élites, in very general terms, are small groups of people who control
a disproportionate amount of access to resources and decision-making
rights (Mills 1956). Even though there have been élites throughout
history, the term 'élite', which is of French origin (*élire*, meaning 'to
elect'), is only about 200 years old. It originally described the group of

people who, in the aftermath of the French revolution, were appointed to rule by selection instead of royal succession. With the subsequent rise of democracy in the Western world and its inherent claim of equality, the term 'élite' further developed into an antonym for the term 'masses', singling out a small group of (still today) mostly men, who, driven by unique values, feel called upon to rule a country, a party or a firm (Schäfers 2004).

According to Pettigrew, the managerial élite is composed of all those 'who occupy formally defined positions of authority, those at the head of, or who could be said to be in strategic positions in private and public organizations of various sizes' (Pettigrew 1992: 163). Managerial élites are ascribed great power and influence, both within and across their organizations. However, managerial discretion, power stemming from interlocking directorates and concerted political action are nevertheless constrained by the countervailing influences of other inside and outside actors, as well as by legal provisions, institutional arrangements, industry sector contingencies and traditions (Pettigrew 1992). A central theme of this on-going debate is the power distribution between capital owners (sometimes named the 'financial élite') and the managerial élite. While in the early days of this debate a hegemony of the managerial élite was assumed (Friedman 1970; Kosnik 1987), managerial control in large corporations came under increasing attack by owners through the shareholder value discourse of the 1980s (Useem 1989). Currently the major shareholders and their fund managers are seen as the ruling class in contemporary capitalism, with the managerial élite ranked second as less powerful agents (e.g. Murray and Scott 2012; van der Zwan 2014).

Similarly to other élites, members of the managerial élite show common characteristics in terms of their social origin and their educational backgrounds as well as in their career progression. Hartmann (2006, 2010), for instance, showed that members of the German upper class are much more likely to become part of the managerial élite (in a narrow sense) than equally qualified peers from the working or the middle class. As an explanation for the rather homogenous recruiting of the managerial élite, Hartmann refers to Bourdieu's concept of a class-specific habitus. According to Bourdieu, it is the habitus of a person, i.e. a socially constituted system of dispositions that orient 'thoughts, perceptions, expressions, and actions' (Bourdieu 1990: 55), which makes up for distinction and informs the selection process to the inner circle of top managers.

Despite similarities in demography, the behaviour of the managerial élite is not entirely homogeneous, and élite factions are considered to show systematically different attitudes and behaviours. For example, Fligstein (1987) showed that the professional background of individuals that make it to the top of large US firms has changed over the duration of the nineteenth century, with entrepreneurs and personnel who came up through manufacturing increasingly being replaced first by sales and marketing personnel, and then later by finance personnel. According to Fligstein, such changes represent intraorganizational power struggles about 'how to view the world' that have significant repercussions on (top) management decision making.

Research on top management teams

The heterogeneity of the managerial élite is also the starting point for a large number of studies on top management teams (TMT). According to upper echelons theory (Hambrick and Masen 1984; Hambrick 2007), it is the top management team members' functional and educational backgrounds, age, industry and firm tenures, socio-economic roots and financial position that inform their decision making. In the same vein, it is the particular composition of managers in a top management team that is responsible for organizational outcomes as diverse as financial performance, environmental fit, intraorganizational conflict and competitive moves, as well as innovation, diversification and internationalization (for an extended overview of this literature see Pettigrew 1992 and more recently Carpenter *et al.* 2004).

A considerable number of studies has also discussed the impact of the international experience of TMT members and the national diversity of the TMT composition. Unsurprisingly, firm performance was one major concern of such studies (e.g. Carpenter *et al.* 2001; Carpenter 2002; Gong 2006). A second area of interest centred around the link between TMT internationalization and the level of corporate internationalization, with a larger number of the earlier studies focusing on the impact of the international experience of TMT members (Reuber and Fischer 1997; Tihanyi *et al.* 2000; Carpenter and Fredrickson 2001; Carpenter 2002; Carpenter *et al.* 2003; Jaw and Lin 2009; Oxelheim *et al.* 2013). More recent work has looked at the impact that national diversity in TMTs has on particular features of inter-nationalization, such as market entry strategies (Nielsen and Nielsen 2011). Recently, Kaczmarek and Ruigrok (2013) provided an integration of the two main streams of research, finding that good performance only materializes from national diversity in TMTs when companies have a high degree of internationalization. In a slightly different vein, a few authors viewed the issue from the opposite angle and explored the reasons underlying different levels of TMT internationalization. In this instance, van Veen and Marsman (2008) showed that the level of corporate internationalization is particularly significant, as is the governance regime of the MNC's country of origin. Overall, however, the international demography of TMTs produces rather structural accounts of the various impacts national diversity in TMTs or international experience of TMT members bring forth. This is also the case for the few studies that deal with conflicts in TMTs (e.g. Amason and Sapienza 1997). An exception to this is the work of Eisenhardt *et al.* (1997), which looked at how conflicts can be infused in TMTs in order to force their members to more carefully recognize a broader diversity of perspectives. What is more, the proposition made by Hambrick (2007), that the socio-economic and financial position of a TMT member impacts his or her behaviour in TMTs, has not found an inroad in empirical investigations so far. Finally, it is still appropriate to conclude that Pettigrew's (1992) evaluation largely holds true today: i.e. that no-one has studied a TMT in an organizational setting directly observing the team in action; nor have they interviewed members about the links between their individual socio-demographics and their behaviour in organizational decision making.

Research on global élites

This evaluation also holds true for a completely different approach studying international top managers, i.e. the global élite approach. Going beyond the rather empiricist explorations of the TMT literature, a broader and more political debate about the emergence of a trans-national élite (also referred to as a cosmopolitan or global élite) has taken off since the new millennium (Kobrin 1998; Sklair 2002; Robinson 2004). Here it is assumed that a notable and growing fraction of the national corporate élites (i.e. top managers and owners of large firms) is detaching from national interests and power sources and moving towards a deterritorialized profit maximization orientation that is supported by liberal transnational institutions (Caroll 2010). These and some other studies in the global élite tradition (Van der Pijl 1984; Overbeek *et al.* 2007) are mainly interested in the political ramifications of an increasing transnational concentration of power made up by cross-border mergers and acquisitions (M&As) and alliances, interlocking corporate directorates and transnational policy boards (such as the European Roundtable of Industrialists). While recent empirical studies e.g. on interlocking directorates hardly find empirical evidence that the transnational level is outpacing the national level (Murray and Scott 2012) and some authors in this debate (see the contributions in Morgan *et al.* 2015) keep emphasizing the social embeddedness of national élites in their particular variety of capitalism, the global élites literature is nevertheless assuming an 'ideological solidarity' of national élites across borders and a common interest in class hegemony (Caroll 2010: 228). However, how this ideological solidarity and class hegemony looks in detail, how it plays out in MNCs and how it influences the interaction of members of different national élites (in a narrower sense) in MNCs has not been studied so far.

As we will see over the next two sections, élite interaction has only been addressed when assuming a broader élite definition. Such a broad definition is given by, e.g., Micklethwait and Wooldridge (2000: 225–245). According to their phenomenology, the global élite (also referred to as cosmocrats) is made up of internationally minded, well-educated, high-income, job- and performance-oriented people who travel frequently and follow mainly Western values. This includes not only transnationally active professionals (such as lawyers and consultants) but also the large group of upper-middle managers in MNCs who work in international teams and/or manage foreign subsidiaries.

Research on international teamwork

Research on international teamwork (also known as global or cross-border teamwork) has significantly increased over the last two decades. As discussed, it concentrates on cross-border teams formed by upper-middle managers. Nurtured by different academic disciplines such as international management, organizational behaviour, social-psychology, innovation studies, etc. research on international teamwork has been predominately driven by the practical needs of multinational corporations that increasingly organize work across borders. According to a survey by Maznevski and Athanassiou (2006: 631), 85 per cent of a group of 250 senior managers from 53 countries indicated that they conduct more than half of their work in global teams, which they defined as 'a group of people with a common purpose, working on interdependent tasks, that functions across boundaries of space time and organization'.

Previous research efforts have concentrated on the question of what makes international teams effective, initially using linear approaches to map the impact of, for example, individual factors such as the configuration of teams, leadership issues, task interdependence and degree of virtuality. Recently, efforts have been complemented by a more integrated treatment of the many complex interrelated factors that make up particular configurations (Maznevski and Athanassiou 2006; Zimmermann 2011).

A great deal of research on team effectiveness focuses on interpersonal relationships in cross-border teams (Zimmermann 2011; Menz 2012; Mäkelä *et al.* 2012), addressing issues such as team identity (Shapiro *et al.* 2005) or trust (Jarvenpaa and Leidner 1999). According to the basic premises of social identity theory (Tajfel 1982) – that individuals identify with a group based on their perceived similarity to others in the team – team heterogeneity is seen as an obstacle to achieving team effectiveness. Even though this view has been challenged (e.g. Stahl *et al.* 2010a; 2010b) many authors elaborate on the impact of team heterogeneity.

Team heterogeneity is often conceptualized as cultural diversity (e.g. Bartel-Radic 2006; Stahl *et al.* 2010b; Lewis 2012). Other accounts of diversity extend to include the nationality of the team members (Athanassiou and Roth 2006), their professional backgrounds (e.g. Menz 2012), their (sub)-organizational affiliation (e.g. Maznevski and Athanassiou 2006) and their gender (Harrison and Klein 2007), with some authors addressing several of these aspects simultaneously (e.g. Athanassiou and Roth 2006; Zoogah *et al.* 2011). Managing these heterogeneities is seen as vital for team effectiveness. According to Davis and Bryant (2003), strong organizational cultures might be able to tame the negative effects of team heterogeneity, with team members in such cases 'leaving their cultural identity at the door'. Drawing on the notions of social capital and social networks, Maznevski and Athanassiou (2006) propose that international teams are social networks in which social capital can yield positive results on team effectiveness. However, the social capital effects of a common socio-economic background or class membership have not been investigated so far.

Research on managerial élite interaction in foreign subsidiaries

A final stream of literature that promises to address the cross-border interaction of managerial élites is stemming from the more recent literature on subsidiary staffing. While it might be exaggerated to assume élite interaction in the case of every foreign subsidiary, a considerable number of subsidiaries are rather large entities with strategic importance both for the MNC and the career of the subsidiary manager.

Historically, most of the literature on staffing foreign subsidiaries deals with expatriate managers, their selection, adjustment and return (for an overview see Scullion and Collings 2006). The literature on expatriate selection, for instance, has dealt with national origin, race/ethnicity, gender and age as demographic characteristics that inform the selection of expatriates (Olsen and Martins 2009). Moreover, in addition to assignment characteristics (such as position filling, developing managers and developing organizations, cf. the classical taxonomy of Edström and Galbraight 1977), individual factors such as personality traits, relational skills, language skills and international experience have been studied (Caliguri *et al.* 2009; Cheng and Lin 2009; Blazejewski 2012). However, the socio-economic or class background of expatriates that impacts both their personality and behaviour has so far been neglected.

This is also true for the increasing number of publications that focus on the interpersonal relations of expatriates (also named parent country nationals, or PCNs) with host country national (HCN) managers. However, it has to be mentioned that a few studies at least partly touched upon issues that link up to a study of subsidiary managers' socio-economic and class backgrounds. Already Hailey (1996), who conducted one of the first studies to look at the dynamics between expatriates and local managers, maintained that the traditional respect accorded to expatriate managers appears to be waning as a result of the privileges they enjoy. Similarly, Toh and DeNisi (2007) hypothesized that status and pay differences, among other factors, might have a negative impact on the support expatriate managers can expect from local managers. However, this literature is still far from thoroughly recognizing the potential effects that subsidiary managers' élite status or class membership might have. This is, for instance, demonstrated by a recent paper of Mahajan and Toh (2014) that argued that expatriate adjustment also depends on the level of credibility and trustworthiness local managers have in the eyes of expatriates. Credibility and trustworthiness were narrowly defined here as the local managers' technical knowledge. Alternative impacts that might equally trigger credibility and trustworthiness, such as a common socio-economic background or élite membership, are not considered.

New directions

While a number of older conceptual studies have argued that the élite concept has the power to explain managerial identity and behaviour in MNCs (e.g. Sklair 2001; Mazlish and Mross 2005), the way this has found an inroad into empirical studies is disappointing. Overall, the preceding literature review has demonstrated that despite an increasing interest in the demographics and interactions of decision makers in boardrooms, international teams and subsidiary management, hardly any study so far is interested in investigating to what extent the organizational behaviour of managerial actors in MNCs is influenced by their socio-economic background or their class membership. While these topics – despite some isolated referencing (e.g. Hambrick 2007) – seem to be an anathema in the mainstream international business (IB) literature, the global élite literature, that explicitly looks at the impact of class membership, is rather interested in the political ramifications of an increased power concentration in the hands of a global managerial élite. This situation opens two broad directions for further research:

(i) Mainstream IB studies in the realm of top management teams, international teamwork and managerial interaction at the subsidiary level would certainly benefit from considering the socio-economic background or class membership of the actors they study. It can be assumed that class membership or adherence to the same or a similar socio-economic stratum has a strong impact as it works against heterogeneity and problems of trust and credibility that are seen as a particular burden for the inner workings of an MNC. The crucial question here is to what extent do same or similar actor socio-demographics offset differences that stem from different nationalities, cultures and religions prevalent in top management teams, international work teams or subsidiary management teams? While this at first sight just looks like an extension of mainstream IB studies, the study of MNC actors' class membership also has potential from a power and politics perspective. First, going beyond a rather narrow perspective on performance, a re-evaluation of decision making in MNCs in light of actors' socio-demographics might provide ideas and insights about long-term political strategies of MNC actors to gain or maintain power. Second, studying managerial decision making in MNCs from the perspective of the actors' class membership allows for an integrated understanding of how societal inequalities trickle down from the macro-level, over different meso-level indicators such as the MNC actors' educational and professional backgrounds to the actors' individual behaviour and decision making in the MNC. Again what seems to be most interesting here are frictions that stem from the fact that MNCs are organizations that cut across many divides but at the same time harbour a particular organizational culture that might be spurred by its country of origin or international best practices.

(ii) Using the global élite approach to empirically study intra-organizational processes in MNCs is another interesting new research direction. However, in order to take this direction, first and foremost, research is needed to systematically identify and map the different factions of MNC élites. As discussed above the general debate assumes that there are narrower and broader definitions of who is part of the global élite. In MNCs, top managers and middle managers seem to represent different factions of the managerial élite. However, adherence to these different factions might be to some extent influenced by the particular organizational anchoring of actors in headquarters, in central or peripheral subsidiaries or in particular host countries. Given the strong differences societies show in terms of (in)equality, the country of origin of the MNCs is also supposed to have a considerable impact. Next to identifying and assessing the blending of such impacts in order to come to an understanding of the different factions of the managerial élite in MNCs, future research should then try to gather what is the mindset, or in other words, the dominant ideology, of such managerial élites. Research so far has only provided a sober picture, just claiming that there is an interest in class hegemony as the lowest common denominator. Taking a Bourdieusian perspective, this leaves ample room to empirically explore common thoughts, beliefs, perceptions, expressions and actions of élite members in MNCs through in-depth case-studies. Such research should not only provide full descriptions of the mindset and the way it is propagated and diffused throughout the MNC, but it should also analyse the core beliefs that extend to all élite factions in MNCs and any variations across the different national, cultural and hierarchical élite factions. Moreover, it would be interesting to study these mindsets: (i) from a constructivist perspective, i.e. to what extent are they the result of purposeful action and whose interests went into it?: and (ii) from a conflict perspective that not only involves the different factions of the managerial élite but also other actors in and around the MNC and its constituent parts. Studying the impact of the financial market élite – where power by and large resides nowadays after three decades of financialization (Morgan 2015) – seems to be very relevant here. Moreover, from a power and politics perspective, the study of conflict and resistance to the growing extent of inequality that results from the rapidly growing income of the managerial top élite, seems promising. Finally, linking up the global élite approach to the strongly growing literature on global mangers and global careers, opens up a last set of new research directions. Interestingly, this literature so far offers surprisingly little insights into the processes of social mobility in relation to the MNC élite and its factions. While principles of élite production have been discussed in general (e.g. Clegg *et al.* 2006: 341–357) the question of what makes up for promotion in MNCs of different countries of origin and industries is still widely unanswered. Is the promotion to the global MNC élite based on merit, on class membership in general or on the membership of a particular national élite? What role does gender play? Are there glass ceilings between the different élite fractions in MNCs? And what in general are processes of in- and exclusion as well as signs of distinction? Moreover, is it unclear what role international education and foreign work experience play in moving up to the top of an MNC? While 'going global' is still a mantra of many business schools, there is scattered evidence that careers going to the top are made in the home country and the headquarters of an MNC (e.g. Goxe and Belhoste 2015; Pohlmann 2009). More research is also needed to uncover the dark sides and the personal and psychological costs that often lurk behind a global career (McKenna *et al.* 2015) that often is portrayed as a glamorous opportunity for young ambitious aspirants.

To sum up, the élite concept holds strong potentials for the study of MNCs as politial organizations. Next to fertilizing a number of mainstream IB debates by infusing a power and politics perspective, it also offers the opportunity to work against Zald and Lounsbury's (2010) conlusion that organizational theorists for a number of decades have distanced themselves 'from the study of core societal power centers' (963).

References

Amason, A. C. and Sapienza, H. J. 1997. The effects of top management team size and interaction norms on cognitive and affective conflict. *Journal of Management*, 23(4): 495–516.

Athanassiou, N. and Roth, K. 2006. International heterogeneity effects on the top-management-team advice network. *Management International Review*, 6(46): 749–769.

Bartel-Radic, A. 2006. Intercultural learning in global teams. *Management International Review*, 46(6): 647–677.

Blazejewski, S. 2012. Betwixt or beyond the lines of conflict? Biculturalism as situated identity in multinational corporation. *Critical Perspective on International Business*, 8(2): 111–135.

Bourdieu, P. 1990[1980]. *The Logic of Practice*. Translated by Richard Nice. Stanford, CA: Stanford University Press.

Caliguri, P., Ibraiz T. and Jacobs, R. 2009. Selection for international assignments. *Human Resource Management Review*, 19(8): 251–262.

Caroll, W. K. 2010. *The Making of a Transnational Capitalist Class. Corporate Power in the 21st Century*. London and New York: Zed Books.

Carpenter, M. A. 2002. The implications of strategy and social context for the relationship between top management team heterogeneity and firm performance. *Strategic Management Journal*, 23(3): 275–284.

Carpenter, M. A. and Fredrickson, J. W. 2001. Top management teams, global strategic posture, and the moderating role of uncertainty. *Academy of Management Journal*, 44(3): 533–546.

Carpenter, M. A., Geletkanycz, M. A. and Sanders, Wm. G. 2004. Upper echelons research revisited: antecedents, elements, and consequences of top management team composition. *Journal of Management*, 30(6): 749–778.

Carpenter, M. A., Pollock, T. G. and Leary, M. 2003. Governance, the experience of principals and agents, and global strategic intent: testing a model of reasoned risk-taking. *Strategic Management Journal*, 24(9): 803–820.

Carpenter, M. A., Sanders, W. G. and Gregersen, H. B. 2001. Bundling human capital with organizational context: the impact of international assignment experience on multinational firm performance and CEO pay. *Academy of Management Journal*, 44(3): 493–511.

Cheng, H. L. and Lin, C. Y. Y. 2009. Do as the large enterprises do? Expatriate selection and overseas performance in emerging markets: the case of Taiwan SMEs. *International Business Review*, 18(1): 60–75.

Clegg, S. R., Courpasson, D. and Phillips, N. 2006. *Power and Organizations*. Newbury Park: Pine Forge Press.

Davis, D. D. and Bryant, J. L. 2003. Influence at a distance: leadership in global virtual teams. *Advances in Global Leadership*, 3: 303–340.

Edström, A. and Galbraith, J. R. 1977. Transfer of managers as a coordination and control strategy in multinational organizations. *Administrative Science Quarterly*, 22(2): 248–263.

Eisenhardt, K. M., Kahwajy, J. L. and Bourgeois, L. J. 1997. Conflict and strategic choice: how top management teams disagree. *California Management Review*, 39(2), 42–62.

Fligstein, N. 1987. The intraorganizational power struggle: rise of finance personnel to top leadership in large corporations, 1919–1979. *American Sociological Review*, 52(1): 44–58.

Friedman, M. 1970. The social responsibility of business is to increase its profits. *The New York Times Magazine*, 13 September.

Gong, Y. 2006. The impact of subsidiary top management team national diversity on subsidiary performance: knowledge and legitimacy perspectives. *Management International Review*, 46(6): 771–790.

Goxe, F. and Belhoste, N. 2015. Showing them the door (nicely): rejection discourses and practices of a global élite. *Critical Perspectives on International Business*, 11(2): 189–206.

Hailey, J. 1996. The expatriate myth: cross cultural perspections of expatriatre managers. *The International Executive*, 38(2): 255–271.

Hambrick, D. C. 2007. Upper echelons theory – an update. *Academy of Management Review*, 32(2): 334–343.

Hambrick, D. C. and Mason, P. A. 1984. Upper echelons: the organization as a reflection of its top managers. *Academy of Management Review*, 9(2): 193–206.

Harrison, D. A. and Klein, K. J. 2007. What's the difference? Diversity constructs as separation, variety, or disparity in organizations. *Academy of Management Review*, 32(4): 1199–1228.

Hartmann, M. 2006. *Sociology of Élites*, London: Routledge.

2010. Achievement or origin: social background and ascent to top management. *Talent Development and Excellence*, 2(1): 105–117.

Jarvenpaa, S. L. and Leidner, D. E. 1999. Communication and trust in global virtual teams. *Organization Science*, 10: 791–815.

Jaw, Y. and Lin, W. 2009. Corporate characteristics and firm's internationalization: CEO-level and TMT-level roles. *The International Journal of Human Resource Management*, 20(1): 220–233.

Kaczmarek, S. and Ruigrok, W. 2013. In at the deep end of firm internationalization: nationality diversity on top management teams matters. *Management International Review*, 53(4): 513–534.

Kobrin, Stephen J. 1998. Back to the future: neomedievalism and the postmodern digital world economy. *Journal of International Affairs*, 361–386.

Kosnik, R. D. 1987. Greenmail: a study of board performance in corporate governance. *Administrative Science Quarterly*, 32(2): 163–185.

Lewis, R. D. 2012. *When Teams Collide. Managing the International Team Successfully*. London: Nicholas Brealey Publishing.

Maclean, M., Charles, H. and Press, J. 2006. *Business Elites and Corporate Governance in France and the UK*. Basingstoke: Palgrave Macmillan.

Mahajan, A. and Toh, S. M. 2014. Facilitating expatriate adjustment: the role of advice-seeking from host country nationals. *Journal of World Business*, 49(4): 476–487.

Mäkelä, K., Andersson, U. and Seppälä, T. 2012. Interpersonal similarity and knowledge sharing within multinational organizations. *International Business Review*, 21(3): 439–451.

Mazlish, B. and Mross, E. R. 2005. A global elite? In A. D. Chandler and B. Mazlish (eds.), *Leviathans. Multinational Corporations and the New Global History*. Cambridge University Press, 167–186.

Maznevski, M. L. and Athanassiou, N. A. 2006. Guest editors' introduction to the focused issue: a new direction for global teams research. *Management International Review*, 46(6): 631–646.

McKenna, S., Ravishankar, M. N. and Weir, D. 2015. Critical perspectives on the globally mobile professional and managerial class. *Critical Perspectives on International Business*, 11(2): 118–121.

Menz, M. 2012. Functional top management team members. A review, synthesis, and research agenda. *Journal of Management*, 38(1): 45–80.

Micklethwait, J. and Wooldridge, A. 2000. *A Future Perfect. The Essentials of Globalization*. Crown Business: New York.

Mills, C. W. 1956. *The Power Elite*. Oxford University Press.

Morgan, G. 2011. Reflections on the macro-politics of micro-politics. In C. Dörrenbächer and M. Geppert (eds.), *Power and Politics in the Multinational Corporation. The role of Institutions, Interests and Identities*. Cambridge University Press, 415–436.

2015. Elites, varieties of capitalism and the crisis of neo-liberalism. In G. Morgan, P. Hirsch and S. Quack (eds.), *Elites on Trial, Research in the Sociology of Organizations*, Vol. 34. Bingley: Emerald Group Publishing, 55–80.

Morgan, G., Hirsch, P. and Quack, S. (eds.). 2015. *Elites on Trial, Research in the Sociology of Organizations*, Vol. 34. Bingley: Emerald Group Publishing.

Murray, G. and Scott, J. (eds.). 2012. *Financial Elites and Transnational Business: Who Rules the World?* Cheltenham: Edward Elgar Publishing.

Nielsen, B. B. and Nielsen, S. 2011, The role of top management team international orientation in strategic decision-making: the choice of foreign entry mode. *Journal of World Business*, 46(2): 185–193.

Olsen, J. E. and Martins, L. L. 2009. The effects of expatriate demographic characteristics on adjustment: a social identity approach. *Human Resource Management*, 48(2): 311–328.

Overbeek, H., van Apeldoorn, B. and Nölke, A. (eds.). 2007. *The Transnational Politics of Corporate Governance Regulation*. London: Routledge.

Oxelheim, L., Gregorič, A., Randøy, T. and Thomsen, S. 2013. On the internationalization of corporate boards: the case of Nordic firms. *Journal of International Business Studies*, 44(3): 173–194.

Pettigrew, A. 1992. On studying managerial elites. *Strategic Management Journal*, 13(2): 163–182.

Pohlmann, M. 2009. Globale ökonomische Eliten – eine Globalisierungsthese auf dem Prüfstand der Empirie. *Kölner Zeitschrift für Soziologie und Sozialpsychologie*, 61(4): 513–534.

Reuber, R. and Fischer, E. 1997. The influence of the management team's international experience on the internationalization behaviors of SMEs. *Journal of International Business Studies*, 28: 807–825.

Robinson, W. I. 2004. *A Theory of Global Capitalism: Production, Class, and State in a Transnational World*. Baltimore: Johns Hopkins University Press.

Schäfers, B. 2004. Elite. *Aus Politik und Zeitgeschichte*, B 10: 3–6.

Scullion, H. and Collings, D. G. 2006. *Global Staffing*. New York and London: Routledge.

Shapiro, D. L., Von Glinow, M. A. and Cheng, J. L. 2005. *Managing Multinational Teams: Global Perspectives*. Oxford: Elsevier/JAI Press.

Sklair, L. 2001. *The Transnational Capitalist Class*. Oxford: Blackwell. 2002. *Globalization: Capitalism and its Alternatives*. New York: Oxford University Press.

Stahl, G. K., Mäkelä, K., Zander, L. and Maznevski, M. L. 2010a. A look at the bright side of multicultural team diversity. *Scandinavian Journal of Management*, 26(4): 439–447.

Stahl, G. K., Maznevski, M. L., Voigt, A. and Jonsen, K. 2010b. Unraveling the effects of cultural diversity in teams: a meta-analysis of research on multicultural work groups. *Journal of International Business Studies*, 41(4): 690–709.

Tajfel, H. (ed.). 1982. *Social Identity and Intergroup Relations*. Cambridge University Press.

Tihanyi, L., Ellstrand, A. E., Daily, C. M. and Dalton, D. R. 2000. Composition of the top management team and firm international diversification. *Journal of Management*, 26(6): 1157–1177.

Toh, S. M. and DeNisi, A. S. 2007. Host country nationals as socializing agents: a social identity theory perspective. *Journal of Organizational Behavior*, 28(3): 281–301.

Useem, M. 1984. *The Inner Circle: Large Corporations and the Rise of Business Political Activity in the US and UK*. Oxford University Press.
1989. The revolt of the corporate owners and the demobilization of business political action. *Critical Sociology*, 16(May): 7–25.

Van der Pijl, K. 1984. *The Making of an Atlantic Ruling Class*. London/New York: Verso Books.

van der Zwan, N. 2014. Making sense of financialization. *Socio-economic Review*, 12(1): 99–129.

van Veen, K. and Marsman, I. 2008. How international are executive boards of MNCs? Nationality diversity in 15 European countries. *European Management Journal*, 26(3): 188–198.

Zald, M. N. and Lounsbury, M. 2010. The wizards of Oz: towards an institutional approach to elites, expertise and command posts. *Organization Studies*, 31(7): 963–996.

Zimmermann, A. 2011. Interpersonal relationships in transnational, virtual teams: towards a configurational perspective. *International Journal of Management Reviews*, 13(1): 59–78.

Zoogah, D., Vora, D., Richard, O., Peng, M. 2011. Strategic alliance team diversity, coordination, and effectiveness. *International Journal of Human Resource Management*, 22(3): 510–529.

12 Micropolitics in emerging market multinational corporations (EMNCs) as a field of new research

KNUT S. G. LANGE AND FLORIAN A. A.
BECKER-RITTERSPACH

In recent years, foreign direct investment from and to emerging markets has seen an unprecedented rise. In 2013, 61 per cent of worldwide foreign direct investment (FDI) was targeted at developing countries and emerging markets (UNCTAD 2014). At the same time, the share of emerging market FDI in total FDI has been growing rapidly over the last decade. In 2013, 39 per cent of worldwide FDI (outflow) was undertaken by MNCs from developing countries and emerging markets (UNCTAD 2014).

The growing importance of FDI to and, more importantly, from emerging markets has triggered a debate in international business and management (IB&M) as to what extent Western models of internationalization appropriately capture the internationalization motivations and internationalization advantages of EMNCs.

Paralleling the general discussion in IB&M on the adequacy of arrived theories within the context of EMNCs, we would like to raise the question to what extent our current perspective on politics, power and conflict in MNCs adequately captures such processes in EMNCs. As we will outline below, there is reason to believe that the different competitive advantages, motives and patterns of internationalization that have been associated with EMNCs may also play out in different dynamics of micropolitics within these firms.

Taking a closer look at the politics and power literature on MNCs, it is fair to say that this strand of literature has so far failed to ask how and why politics, power and conflict may play out differently in emerging market multinationals (see Chapter 3, or recent reviews by Geppert and Dörrenbächer 2014; Blazejewski and Becker-Ritterspach

2011). Looking at the nascent literature on EMNCs there is also little concern with politics, power and conflict. Notable exceptions are here some contributions in an edited volume from Hadjikhani *et al.* (2012) entitled *Business, Society and Politics: Multinationals in Emerging Markets* and a special issue edited by Yeung *et al.* (2008) entitled 'Growth and globalisation: evolution of human resource management practices in Asia'. The edited volume by Hadjikhani *et al.* (2012) explores, for instance, how MNCs interact with socio-political actors in emerging markets. While this work offers interesting insights into the relevant socio-political actors in the business environments of MNCs in and from emerging markets, it does not provide a genuine perspective on politics and power within EMNCs. In a similar vein, the literature on international human resource management in EMNCs has hardly discussed the issue of power and politics. In the *Human Resource Management* special issue on 'Growth and globalisation: evolution of human resource management practices in Asia' (Yeung *et al.* 2008), only Tung's contribution touches upon power and politics by analysing the effect of race and gender on the selection of executives (Tung 2008). While there is no space in this chapter to review the literature on EMNCs in detail, we discuss the micropolitical relevance of a few seminal contributions on EMNCs in this contribution. We hope to demonstrate that the issue of power, politics and conflict in EMNCs is a very promising area of future research.

In the following two sections, we will briefly discuss what is generally meant by emerging markets, and how they can be distinguished from developing economies. We then proceed with discussing different types of emerging market multinationals and differences in relation to their counterparts from developed economies. Building on this discussion, we ask in what way the potentially different nature of EMNCs might also go along with different political dynamics in EMNCs. Specifically, we call for studies that explore if and how EMNCs differ with regard to the sets of relevant and key actors, their interests and resources and, relatedly, with regard to conflict dynamics. We conclude by formulating these reflections into new directions for research.

What are emerging economies?

Many different 'emerging market' definitions and conceptualizations have been suggested. Basically, there are two types of emerging market definitions: broader and narrower ones. Ciravegna *et al.* define the term broadly. They distinguish between rich countries – the US, Canada, Western Europe, Japan, Australia, New Zealand, South Korea, Taiwan, Hong Kong and Israel – and emerging markets; the latter term 'refers to all other countries' (2013: 15). Other international business (IB) scholars distinguish between emerging markets and developing economies. According to Cavusgil *et al.*:

Emerging markets are countries which are in a transition phase from developing to developed markets due to rapid growth and industrialization. Hence, markets which have (a) started an economic reform process aimed at alleviating problems, for example poverty, poor infrastructure and over-population, (b) achieved a steady growth in gross national product (GNP) per capita, and (c) increased integration in the global economy, may truly be called EMs. (Cavusgil *et al.* 2013: 5)

Thus, they make a difference between economies that have already made a significant progress in catching up to fully developed economies – emerging economies in the true sense – and other relatively poor economies that, despite having the potential to emerge, have not significantly progressed in their development in recent years. The latter type of countries are considered developing economies.

More recently, efforts have been made to distinguish emerging markets in a more systematic way (e.g. Hadjikhani *et al.* 2012; Hoskisson *et al.* 2013; Zhang and Whitley 2013). For instance, exploring the diversity in Asian business systems, Zhang and Whitley (2013) find substantial differences in terms of varying state direction of the economy and in terms of the nature and degree of business coordination of economic activities (i.e. co-governed, state-led, networked and personalized). Notwithstanding major differences in these approaches, they share the insight that dominant institutions of economic governance, the nature of socio-political actors and the diverse modes of government–business relations are key to understanding both substantial differences across emerging markets and emerging market multinationals.

Emerging market multinationals

The IB&M literature has discussed a range of traits that EMNCs tend to have in common and that distinguish them from Western MNCs. For instance, there is some agreement that a major prerequisite for EMNC

Table 12.1 *The new multinational enterprises compared to traditional multinationals*

Dimension	New MNEs	Traditional MNEs
Speed of internationalization	Accelerated	Gradual
Competitive advantages	Weak: upgrading of resources required	Strong: required resources available in-house
Political capabilities	Strong: firms used to unstable political environments	Weak: firms used to stable political environments
Organizational adaptability	High, because of their meagre international presence	Low, because of their ingrained structure and culture

Source: Adapted from Guillen and Garcia-Canal 2009: 27.

internationalization are both advantageous and disadvantageous conditions in their home countries (Cuervo-Cazurra and Genc 2008; Deng 2012; Lessard und Lucea 2009; Luo and Tung 2007; Ramamurti 2009; Rugman 2009). With regard to internationalization motives, a range of scholars suggest that EMNCs often internationalize to acquire rather than to exploit firm assets (Luo and Tung 2007; Mathews 2006).

Guillen and Garcia-Canal (2009) suggest that new MNCs from emerging markets differ systematically from traditional MNCs in their speed of internationalization, their competitive advantages, their political capabilities and their organizational adaptability (see Table 12.1 above).

In a similar vein, Kale *et al.* (2009) contrast the different approaches to international mergers and acquisitions between traditional MNCs and EMNCs. Kale *et al.* (2009) argue that EMNCs tend to follow a partnering approach. The partnering approach involves that EMNCs keep the acquired companies separate and only coordinate a few selected activities. As part of their approach they also retain top executives and allow for a high autonomy of the acquired unit. Hence, integration is rather slow and piecemeal. This contrasts with the fast integration approach by traditional MNCs. The latter are seen to absorb the acquired company. This entails integrating core and supporting activities very fast. In this approach top executives tend to be replaced and there is no or very little remaining autonomy for the acquired company.

Other scholars have made efforts to map differences among EMNCs. In their seminal contribution, Luo and Tung (2007) discuss major differences among EMNCs. They 'define EM MNEs as international companies that originated from emerging markets and are engaged in outward FDI, where they exercise effective control and undertake value-adding activities in one or more foreign countries' (2007: 482). This definition excludes companies from emerging markets that have not engaged in FDI or engaged in FDI only for the purpose of 'round-tripping' of investment. The latter involves companies setting up and investing in a foreign subsidiary, usually in tax haven countries such as the Cayman Islands, and then reinvesting their money back into their home countries to obtain preferential treatment which is offered to foreign investors by their home country (see also Dunning and Lundan 2008). The above definition also excludes state-owned companies that solely pursue political objectives and do not aim for the optimization of corporate returns.

Luo and Tung (2007) categorize EMNCs into four groups based on the dimensions: ownership (non-state owned versus state-owned) and international diversification (breadth of geographical coverage of international markets). State-owned EMNCs that have invested aggressively to seize market opportunities abroad are categorized as transnational agents, and as commissioned specialists if their international diversification is more limited. Both transnational agents and commissioned specialists pursue business objectives and, due to their ownership by the state, political objectives. Non-state-owned EMNCs are categorized as niche entrepreneurs when they operate in a narrow band of international markets, and as world-stage aspirants when their geographical coverage is more diversified.

Luo and Tung's elaborate categorization of EMNCs can be further complemented by the insights of the vast business group literature (e.g. Khanna and Palepu 2000). This literature suggests that the ownership and the international diversification dimensions are not sufficient to differentiate EMNCs. The business group literature suggests that EMNCs also vary substantially along the industry diversification dimension (focused versus diversified) and the type of private ownership. While some EMNCs are focused on a particular industry, a large number of EMNCs are business groups that operate businesses, which

are interconnected through cross-shareholdings, in a variety of industries (often they are also termed diversified conglomerates). The other
distinguishing feature among EMNCs is the type of private ownership.
In emerging markets a large percentage of businesses is owned and controlled by families. Often, these family firms are organized in the form
of business groups (Amsden 2009; Khavul *et al.* 2009). Hence, given
the fact that there is an extensive literature on the differences between
family and non-family firms (Classen *et al.* 2014; Miller *et al.* 2009),
not least in terms of internationalization (Strike *et al.* 2015), this distinction seems to be also relevant.

Based on the brief review of key features of EMNCs, we will exemplarily ask in the next section how common traits and differences in
EMNCs translate into new research directions for the research on politics, power and conflict in MNCs.

New research directions

New sets of actors: A crucial element in understanding micropolitics
and conflict in MNCs involves a sound understanding of who the key
and relevant actors are. While not systematically researched so far, different ownership modes of EMNCs suggest different sets of key and
relevant actors in the political arena of EMNCs. For instance, state-
owned enterprises may involve either the presence of powerful government actors within the MNC or at least a high relevance of government
actors in the EMNCs' environment (cf. Hadjikhani *et al.* 2012).

The fact that many emerging markets are rich in resources has also
led to the emergence of sovereign wealth funds in countries such as
Russia (e.g. Russian National Wealth Fund), or Qatar (e.g. Qatar
Investment Authority). The individual mandates of sovereign wealth
funds, which are state actors, differ. The sovereign wealth funds of Abu
Dhabi, for instance, are required to invest in the economy of the United
Arab Emirates to support the development of economic clusters (Hurst
2014). Hence, sovereign wealth funds and their specific representatives
might also be a group of actors which deserves more attention when
analysing sets of actors in the political arena of EMNCs. As EMNCs
are seeking to become truly global companies, these funds might play
a more prominent role as influencial actors in the future.

In a similar vein, the business group literature suggests that next to
professional management, members of the owning family may play a

crucial role in influencing business decisions in family-owned business groups. The interplay of family and non-family actors deserves a closer examination in these types of EMNCs.

Overall, we have little systematic knowledge about how sets of key and relevant actors differ between developed country MNCs and EMNCs, but also between different types of EMNCs.

New types of actor interests and resources: Different types or sets of key and relevant actors also introduce a range of different interests and resources into the micropolitical dynamics of EMNCs. In state-owned or partly state-owned EMNCs we can imagine that managers feel the need to serve two masters or that different actors within the same firm serve different masters. This may lead to a situation where some actors pursue business objectives and others seek to promote the political agenda. With respect to sources of power, these different actors may also have access to different kinds of networks or social capital and thereby to different kinds and scales of resources. In China, for instance, the internationalization of state-owned EMNCs is strongly supported by government funds (e.g. Gökgür 2011), which potentially provides those actors who represent the government interests with abundant resources within the firm.

Family-owned companies may also witness specific constellations of actor interests and diversity wherein family interests may systematically differ from those of professional/non-family managers. For instance, while family interest may involve long-term growth and sustainability or simply providing employment and senior positions for family members, professional managers may be inclined to promote more short-term business success. Relatedly, based on the family ownership and governance, family members might find it much easier to mobilize resources through the internal family network and to influence micropolitical processes and organizational outcomes in their interests.

Overall, we still have rather limited knowledge about how the corporate governance varies in different types of EMNCs and how this, in turn, informs structures of interests and resource distribution.

However, it is not only the ownership and governance modes of EMNCs that have a bearing on micropolitics. The condition that many EMNCs are seen to internationalize with the goal to acquire assets rather than to exploit extant assets and the fact that these firms are prone to adopting a partnering approach with international acquisitions may translate into different interests of EMNC managers. In such a scenario, expatriate subsidiary managers' main interests may be reflected in long-term learning objectives rather than in quick integration, synergies or efficiency gains.

Similarly, an accelerated speed of internationalization combined with a partnering approach in post-merger integration and a higher autonomy for the acquired firm may also give more room and opportunity for local interest articulation.

Relatedly, if an acquisition is driven by the EMNCs' motivation to learn, actors in the acquired subsidiary may find it much easier to leverage their capabilities and competences as political resources compared to a situation in which the acquisition is driven by fast integration, efficiency seeking and synergy realization.

At the same time, the asset-seeking motive of EMNCs, especially when it is in a south–north direction, may trigger interest structures in subsidiaries of withholding knowledge and competences. Such interest could be based on the actors' fear of losing key knowledge, not receiving crucial assets in return and weakening the subsidiaries' role in the long run.

Lastly, a deeper concern with the different kinds of emerging markets and their socio-political actors also opens new perspectives for understanding different kinds of dominant coalitions (cf. Zhang and Whitley 2013), related interest structures and resource mobilization opportunities within and outside EMNCs (cf. Hadjikhani et al. 2012). The strong relevance of access to local personal networks (i.e. Guanxi in China), limitations on foreign ownership (e.g. oil and gas sector in Egypt), and the weak market supporting institutions in some emerging economies put pressure on foreign MNCs to form joint ventures with local players (Peng and Meyer 2011). These local companies can be expected to have a set of interests (such as access to proprietary technology) and resources (such as state support) that MNCs investing in emerging markets may find difficult to accommodate (especially if enforcement of intellectual property rights is absent or ineffective).

In sum, diverse ownership patterns, internationalization motives and paths of EMNCs as well as different institutional settings in emerging markets not only bring new actor constellations into the picture, but also corresponding interests and sources of power. A key challenge of future research on micropolitics in emerging markets will involve relating typical EMNC features and EMNC diversity, as well as emerging market diversity to specific interest structures and resource mobilization opportunities of key actors or actor coalitions. Understanding such different actor sets, interests and resource structures may, in turn, play a crucial role in understanding both the organizational behaviour and strategic choices of internationalizing EMNCs as well as of those MNCs successfully operating in emerging markets.

New lines of conflicts: The potentially different nature and behaviour of EMNCs may also imply different kinds of conflict when comparing traditional and new MNCs or different types of EMNCs. A crucial element will again be different types of ownership and corporate governance of EMNCs. For instance, as mentioned earlier, state-owned EMNCs might witness lines of conflict that are related to the condition that they need to respond to business and political objectives at the same time. In the host context, in turn, such political objectives might be greeted with suspicion leading to conflict within both the foreign affiliate and the host context (see Sauvant and Strauss (2012) on regulatory responses by the USA to state-owned and controlled multinational enterprises).

Similarly, family-controlled EMNCs hold the potential for conflict for various reasons. Conflicts can arise from interference of family members in the management of these companies (Cavusgil *et al.* 2013: 75). There are indications that Southeast Asian societies have particular problems to trust outsiders (Fukuyama 1995; Santiago 2000). This might lead to conflicts within companies based in emerging markets when they internationalize and are increasingly reliant on professional non-family managers to succeed in foreign markets. An additional source of conflict, which might become more pressing in the future, is the succession in family-controlled EMNCs. Most EMNCs are relatively young compared to their counterparts from developed countries, they are usually only a few decades old, and the founders of these companies are often still involved in strategic decision making (Ciravegna *et al.* 2013). In the coming years and decades, however, a change at the head of the company will become inevitable. Power struggles may arise between members of the family and non-family managers over the future leadership as well as between different members, or even branches, of the family. This problem might be particularly pronounced in EMNcs in which foreign subsidiaries account for the majority of the revenues. Examples that fit into these categories are the Indian MNC Tata Group (controlled by the Tata family; *c.* 75 per cent of revenues from foreign markets), and Reliance Industries (controlled by the Ambani family, *c.* 68 per cent of revenues from foreign markets) (Karnik 2014).

In such EMNCs, the top managers of foreign subsidiaries are usually not members of the family. They can be expected to be influential and opposed to, the selection of successors based on family relationships instead of performance. This may lead to conflicts because owners of family-controlled EMNCs might prefer family members as successors. In fact, a comparative study on succession in family firms found out that family relationships are more important successor attributes for Indian owners than for Canadian owners; conversely, interpersonal skills, past performance and experience are more important for Canadian owners of family businesses (Sharma and Rao 2000; see also Ward 2000).

Business groups may also see conflicts that are related to their conglomerate structure. A large percentage of companies in emerging markets can be considered business groups or diversified conglomerates (e.g. Cavusgil *et al.* 2013; Ciravegna *et al.* 2013). When these companies internationalize, the need to get access to increasingly large amounts of capital to finance the internationalization might put these EMNCs under pressure to sell off assets (in the form of non-core businesses) in their home country. The Mexican EMNC Cemex, for instance, sold non-core business activities to become a world leader in the cement business (Cavusgil *et al.* 2013). Such attempts to finance the internationalization can be expected to meet heavy resistance from management in the domestic market, since vested interests are bound to be affected. The internationalization of TATA motors is a similar case, where the costly internationalization of the business division required cross-subsidizations and resource concentrations that potentially drained the resource endowment of other business divisions in the conglomerate (Becker-Ritterspach and Bruche 2012). Such cross-subsidizations and resources diversions are likely to produce hefty internal battles around the internationalization efforts of different business divisions. Hence, this organizational form, which is widespread in emerging markets, might be a key source of micropolitical conflicts. Combining this insight with previous insights into family-controlled EMNCs suggests family-owned business groups to be particularly interesting for further research, due to the wide range of sources of conflict they may host.

Apart from different ownership modes, corporate governance mechanisms in EMNCs have been argued to be often weak (Luo and Tung 2007). This is attributed to different factors such as underdeveloped stock markets in home countries, poor accountability and a lack of transparency stemming from close ties between some EMNCs and governments (Luo and Tung 2007). Weak governance mechanisms, in turn, may give rise to conflicts between subsidiary and headquarters actors, especially when subsidiaries are embedded in institutional contexts that demand high transparency and accountability from subsidiary management (Brennan 2015). Referring to Chinese MNCs, Brennan states for instance:

Some European states have been reluctant to accept Chinese enterprises as legitimate since they are perceived as opaque in their governance, as being unfairly subsidized by the government and as serving the interests of the Chinese state rather than being commercially driven. This reluctance has been reinforced by a perception that China has failed to adhere to, and enforce, adequate minimum standards related to employment law, health and safety and the environment. Coming from a home country environment in which there is little history or necessity to engage in public relations, Chinese enterprises have not been adept at managing their image and reputational issues and have struggled to adjust to the exigencies of the host region. (Brennan 2015: 1)

Yet, there are potentially other sources of conflict that spring from the speed and motivation of EMNC internationalization. A high speed of internationalization of EMNCs might lead to conflicts between different factions of management in the headquarters. Such factions and related conflicts may develop around the challenges of post-merger or post-acquisition integration or absorption of newly acquired assets (see also Lou and Tung 2007 on challenges of rapid internationalization and post-acquisition difficulties). For instance, there may be conflicts around the speed at which the knowledge of a large number of newly acquired units shall be or can be leveraged and diffused throughout the multinational.

Relatedly, the fact that EMNCs are seen to internationalize to acquire (e.g. natural resources or proprietary knowledge) rather than to exploit organizational advantages might trigger suspicion, political tension and resistance in both foreign affiliates and host contexts (cf. Sauvant and Chen 2014). Such resistance can be based on the fear that once knowledge is acquired, sites get downsized or shut down. It can also be based on concerns about a lack of contribution to the development of or knowledge transfer to local subsidiaries or more broadly lacking developmental effects on the local context. A case in point are the concerns that have been voiced with respect to Chinese resource-seeking FDI in Africa (Sauvant and Chen 2014). However, resistance can also be based on national pride and prejudice when supposedly 'backward' EMNCs take over companies that are considered national 'crown jewels'.

In addition to internationalization motivation and speed, there may also be diverse conflicts that spring from the condition that EMNCs are only at the beginning of building global experience. In this context Luo and Tung argue:

Since many EM MNEs do not have sufficient experience in structuring, organizing, and managing large-scale and sophisticated world-wide operations, they are more likely to encounter friction with external business stakeholders. They may also face conflicts in managerial philosophies, corporate culture, incentive schemes, leadership styles, and formalized managerial procedures with local executives at foreign subunits. (Luo and Tung 2007: 16)

However, there are also features of EMNCs that suggest reduced conflict in their path of internationalization. We base this on contributions emphasizing their organizational adaptability (Guillen and Garcıa-Canal 2009) and partnering approach in international mergers and acquisitions (Kale *et al.* 2009), which may mitigate conflicts with local subsidiary management. Specifically, keeping an acquired company separate and selectively coordinating only a few activities or granting autonomy and retaining local top management or implementing integration in a gradual way with a long-term outlook may all serve to avoid hefty clashes with local management and employees (see Hutton 2013 on TATA's careful approach in its Jaguar Land Rover acquisition).

Moreover, the political capability attributed to EMNCs (Guillen and Garcıa-Canal 2009) may also have some repercussions for their conflict propensity. On the one hand, the EMNCs' familiarity with emerging markets and their related political capability to navigate unstable institutional environments and to deal with high levels of government involvement or intervening host context governments may serve to reduce conflict within their subsidiaries and also with key actors in the host environment. On the other hand, these very political capabilities, that are often based on 'relationship-based governance mechanisms' (Luo and Tung 2007: 15), may create tension and conflict if they are applied in non-emerging market contexts. We may see, for instance, conflict between headquarters and subsidiary actors or between expatriates and local employees, if headquarters or expatriates find it difficult to understand that certain types of political strategies and governance mechanisms that work well in emerging market contexts may not work in developed economies.

Finally, while cultural differences (e.g. Hofstede 1980) in work-related values and culture-specific leadership styles (House *et al.* 2004) have been widely researched, there is so far little systematic knowledge on how such differences translate into different types of conflict within EMNCs but also within developed market MNCs entering emerging markets. In this context, Brennan (2015) provides us with a glimpse of the manifold intercultural challenges Chinese MNCs face in Europe:

Perhaps the greatest challenge facing Chinese enterprises in Europe is adjusting their style of organizing and of managing their operations from their traditional hierarchical mode of organization, as well as the command-and-control-based approach to management, to one that is more compatible with the more autonomous work culture prevalent in Europe. Chinese acquirers that tend to be more successful in Europe have largely adopted a hands-off approach to the acquired entity; those that have not adjusted their style of management tend to face challenges, such as the loss of key human capital as well as related reputational capital. Navigating the very different cultural and institutional environment in Europe and operating according to local norms and practices requires preparation and training for Chinese managers. (Brennan 2015: 2)

In a same vein, we are also still at the beginning with regard to the question of how colonial pasts, geopolitical hierarchies and related notions of superiority and inferiority (Frenkel 2008) translate into micropolitical battles in EMNCs or traditional MNCs that operate across the developing-developed world divide.

Conclusion

In this chapter, we showed that there is still only little knowledge about how traditional or developed economy MNCs differ from emerging market MNCs in their micropolitical constitution. At the same time, there is hardly any knowledge about how EMNCs differ from one another in their micropolitical constitution. We suggested that this gap can be addressed in a first step by a cross-fertilization of the literature on EMNCs and micropolitical perspectives within the field of IB&M. Specifically, we tried to show that common and diverse features of EMNCs might go along with specific sets of key actors, structures of interests and resources as well as related lines of conflict. Our brief discussion also suggested that we need a more systematic exploration of how the embeddedness of MNCs across diverse cultural and institutional environments influences actor constellations, actor interests and resources and thereby the organizational politics and conflicts that ultimately help to explain the organizational behaviour of MNCs in and from emerging markets. Overall, we see here the opening of a vast field of research that would systematically compare the antecedents, patterns and consequences of micropolitics between both developed market MNCs and emerging market MNCs as well as between different types of MNCs from emerging markets. We acknowledge that while offering a vast field of research such a research agenda comes with substantial challenges. Apart from the logistical and methodological challenges of working in intercultural research teams, the nature of micropolitics research itself makes company access generally difficult and particularly to companies and contexts where outsiders need to engage in long-term trust-building efforts before being allowed into the company.

References

Amsden, A. H. 2009. Does firm ownership matter? POE vs. FOEs in the developing world. In R. Ramamurti and J. V. Singh (eds.), *Emerging Multinationals in Emerging Markets*. Cambridge University Press: 64–77.

Becker-Ritterspach, F. and Bruche, G. 2012. Capability creation and internationalization with business group embeddedness – the case of TATA motors in passenger cars. *European Management Journal*, 30(3): 232–247.

Blazejewski, S. and Becker-Ritterspach, F. (2011). Conflict in headquarters–subsidiary relations: a critical literature review and new directions. In C. Dörrenbächer and M. Geppert (eds.), *Politics and Power in the Multinational Corporation*. Cambridge University Press, 139–190.

Brennan, L. 2015. The challenges for Chinese FDI in Europe. *Columbia FDI Perspectives*, 142: 1–3.

Cavusgil, S. T., Ghauri, P. N. and Akcal, A. A. 2013. *Doing Business in Emerging Markets* (2nd edn). London: Sage.

Ciravegna, L., Fitzgerald, R. and Kundu, S. K. 2013. *Operating in Emerging Markets. A Guide to Management and Strategy in the New International Economy*. Upper Saddle River: FT Press.

Classen, N., Carree, M., Gils, A. and Peters, B. 2014. Innovation in family and non-family SMEs: an exploratory analysis. *Small Business Economics*, 42(3): 595–609.

Cuervo-Cazurra, A. and Genc, M. 2008. Transforming disadvantages into advantages: developing-country MNEs in the least developed countries. *Journal of International Business Studies*, 39(6): 957–979.

Deng, P. 2012. Accelerated internationalization by MNCs from emerging economies: determinants and implications. *Organizational Dynamics*, 41(4): 318–326.

Dunning, J. H. and Lundan, S. M. 2008. *Multinational Enterprises and the Global Economy*. Cheltenham: Edward Elgar.

Frenkel, M. 2008. The multinational corporation as a third space: rethinking international management discourse on knowledge transfer through Homi Bhabha. *Academy of Management Review*, 33(4): 924–942.

Fukuyama, F. 1995. *Trust: the Social Virtues and the Creation of Prosperity*. New York: The Free Press.

Geppert, M. and Dörrenbächer, C. 2014. Politics and power within multinational corporations: mainstream studies, emerging critical approaches and suggestions for future research. *International Journal of Management Reviews*, 16(2): 226–244.

Gökgür, D. 2011. Are resurging state-owned enterprises impeding competition overseas? *Columbia FDI Perspectives*, 36: 1–3.

Guillen, M. and Garcia-Canal, E. 2009. The American model of the multinational firm and the 'new' multinationals from emerging economies. *Academy of Management Perspectives*, 23(2): 23–35.

Hadjikhani, A., Elg, U., Ghauri, P. and Ghauri, P. M. 2012. *Business, Society and Politics: Multinationals in Emerging Markets. International Business and Management*. Bingley, UK: Emerald Group Publishers.

Hofstede, G. 1980. *Culture's Consequences*. Beverly Hills, CA: Sage.

Hoskisson, R., Wright, M., Filatotchev, I. and Peng, M. 2013. Emerging multinationals from mid-range economies: the influence of institutions and factor markets. *Journal of Management Studies*, 50(7): 1295–1321.

House, R. J., Hanges, P. J., Javidan, M., Dorfman, P. and Gupta, V. 2004. *Culture, Leadership and Organizations: the GLOBE Study of 62 Societies*. Thousand Oaks, CA: Sage.

Hurst, G. 2014. The world's largest sovereign wealth funds go private. *Institutional Investor*. Available at: www.institutionalinvestor.com/article/3382248/investors-sovereign-wealth-funds/the-worlds-largest-sovereign-wealth-funds-go-private.html#.VV3KsqBwaUk (accessed 22 May 2015).

Hutton, R. 2013. *Jewels in the Crown: How Tata of India Transformed Britain's Jaguar and Land Rover*. New York: Elliott and Thompson.

Kale, P., Singh, H. and Raman, A. P. 2009. Don't integrate your acquisitions, partner with them. *Harvard Business Review*, 87(12): 109–115.

Karnik, M. 2014. India's large firms look abroad to raise revenues. *Livemint.com*. Available at: www.livemint.com/Companies/r8g888Ks2ZoXvtLTyu0cYP/Indias-large-firms-look-abroad-to-raise-revenues.html (accessed 22 May 2015).

Khanna, T. and Palepu, K. 2000. The future of business groups in emerging markets: long-run evidence from Chile. *Academy of Management Journal*, 43(3): 268–285.

Khavul, S., Bruton, G. D. and Wood, E. 2009. Informal family business in Africa. *Entrepreneurship: Theory and Practice*, 33(6): 1219–1238.

Lessard, D. and Lucea, R. 2009. Mexican multinationals: insights from CEMEX. In R. Ramamurti and J. Singh (eds.), *Emerging Multinationals in Emerging Markets*. Cambridge University Press, 280–311.

Luo, Y. and Tung, R. L. 2007. International expansion of emerging market enterprises: a springboard perspective. *Journal of International Business Studies*, 38(4): 481–498.

Mathews, J. 2006. Dragon multinationals: new players in 21st century globalization. *Asia-Pacific Journal of Management*, 23(1): 5–27.

Miller, D., Lee, J., Chang, S. and Le Breton-Miller, I. 2009. Filling the institutional void: the social behavior and performance of family vs. non-family technology firms in emerging markets. *Journal of International Business Studies*, 40(5): 802–817.

Peng, M. W. and Meyer, K. 2011. *International Business*. London: South-Western Higher Publication.

Ramamurti, R. 2009. What have we learned about emerging market MNEs? In R. Ramamurti and J. V. Singh (eds.), *Emerging Multinationals in Emerging Markets*. Cambridge University Press: 399–426.

Rugman, A. 2009. Theoretical aspects of MNEs from emerging countries. In R. Ramamurti and J. V. Singh (eds.), *Emerging Multinationals in Emerging Markets*. Cambridge University Press: 42–63.

Santiago, A. L. 2000. Succession experience in Philippine family businesses. *Family Business Review*, 13(1): 15–40.

Sauvant, K. and Chen, V. Z. 2014. China needs to complement its 'going-out' policy with a 'going-in' strategy. *Columbia FDI Perspectives*, 121: 1–3.

Sauvant, K. and Strauss, J. 2012. State-controlled entities control nearly US$2 trillion in foreign assets. *Columbia FDI Perspectives*, 64: 1–8.

Sharma, P. and Rao, A. S. 2000. Successor attributes in Indian and Canadian family firms: a comparative study. *Family Business Review*, 13(4): 313–330.

Strike, V. M., Berrone, P., Sapp, S. G. and Congiu, L. 2015. A socioemotional wealth approach to CEO career horizons in family firms. *Journal of Management Studies*, 52(4): 555–583.

Tung, R. L. 2008. Do race and gender matter in international assignments to/from Asia Pacific? An exploratory study of attitudes among Chinese. *Human Resource Management*, 47(1): 91–110.

UNCTAD 2014. *World Investment Report*. Available at: http://unctad.org/en/pages/PublicationWebflyer.aspx?publicationid=937 (last accessed 1 May 2015).

Ward, J. L. (2000). Reflections on Indian family groups. *Family Business Review*, 8(4): 271–278.

Yeung, A., Warner, M. and Rowley, C. 2008. Guest editors' introduction. Growth and globalisation: evolution of human resource management practices in Asia. *Human Resource Management*, 47(1): 1–13.

Zhang, X. and Whitley, R. 2013. Changing macro-structural varieties of East Asian capitalism. *Socio-Economic Review*, 11(2): 301–336.

Index

Abu Dhabi, 286
actor-centred institutionalism, 92
actor-context relations, 54, 57, 65, 70, 75, 80, 85, 88, 93, 98
actors
  behavioural orientation, 53, 131, 132, 134, 135, 138, 188, 198, 199, 200
  constellations, 288, 294
  economic, 75, 76, 83
  individual, 23, 55, 63, 78, 79, 82, 88, 91, 94, 97, 100, 122, 126, 135, 149, 150, 151, 186, 194, 199
  individual actor characteristics, 256
  interest, 29, 82, 93, 120, 130, 147, 154, 160, 162, 189, 193, 195, 287, 294
  key, 71, 94, 141, 142, 143, 145, 149, 150, 152, 154, 158, 160, 161, 162, 163, 188, 189, 191, 195, 197, 199, 201, 202, 226, 244, 245, 246, 249, 282, 289, 293, 294
  low-power, 79, 130, 131, 132, 133, 134, 135, 136, 260
  micro-level, 76, 85, 86, 88, 147
  nature of, 53
  organizational level, 55, 71, 128, 135, 185, 196, 200
  positioning, 193
  relevant, 188, 189, 191, 192, 198, 286, 287
  sets, 189, 289
  strategic, 19, 20, 22
advantage
  competitive, 64, 81, 123, 292
agency
  perspective, 79
  theory, 77, 126
alliance, 217, 229
  strategic, 217

allocation, 25, 33, 35, 38, 146, 161, 163
Ambos, T. C., 72, 77, 78, 81
American, 32, 197, 257
analytical grid, 120, 121
analytical level, 56
analytical levels, 6, 91, 194, 197
Andersson, U., 5, 73, 74, 75, 76, 127, 128, 129, 130, 131, 135, 136, 137, 138
Antwerp, 186, 196
apolitical, 60
Asia, 282
asset-seeking, 64, 123, 288
authority, 21, 30, 40, 73, 74, 79, 88, 98, 130, 190, 194, 248, 249, 267
  formal, 79
authorization, 98

back translation, 223
bargaining
  power, 76, 77, 78, 81, 123, 124, 125, 126, 127, 136, 174, 175
  processes, 73, 128, 129
Bartlett, C. A., 4, 69, 70, 71, 90
Becker-Ritterspach, F., 1, 6, 7, 8, 17, 51, 87, 88, 91, 92, 94, 123, 149, 150, 151, 160, 162, 163, 185, 186, 188, 193, 201, 242, 281, 290
behavioral orientations, 63, 70, 71, 80, 82
Bélanger, J., 6, 91, 188
Belgium, 186, 196
benchmarking, 143, 145
benchmarks, 144, 229
best practices, 274
biography, 201
Birkinshaw, J., 33, 77, 78, 79, 80, 81, 82, 130, 248, 249
Björkman, I., 29

Printed in the United States
By Bookmasters